# Unmasking LATINX Ministry for Episcopalians

## An Anglican Approach

Carla E. Roland Guzmán

CHURCH
PUBLISHING
INCORPORATED

For

Mami—an expert in resilience.

Rosalind, Caroline, Dad, Abuela, Tio, Normita, Carlitos, Natja, Evan,

Andrew, Hermancito, Sofía, and all of my extended family—

thank you for the laughter.

Friends that are always there—Suyin, Jennifer, Susan, Liz,

Kathy, Ellen, and Amanda.

SMST—a faithful worshipping community.

Latinx colleagues—Pedro, George, Gladys, Altagracia, Yamily, Juan, and Anthony

Colleagues in the dioceses of New York and Puerto Rico, and classmates from CDSP.

Joanne y la familia de HTI—experts in theologizing *en conjunto*.

Bernie and the CLGS family.

Current students, staff, and faculty at GTS.

———

Unless otherwise noted, the Scripture quotations are from New Revised Standard Version Bible, copyright © 1989 National Council of the Churches of Christ in the United States of America. Used by permission. All rights reserved worldwide.

Church Publishing
19 East 34th Street
New York, NY 10016
www.churchpublishing.org

Cover design by Jennifer Kopec, 2Pug Design
Typeset by Rose Design

A record of this book is available from the Library of Congress.

ISBN-13: 978-1-64065-150-0 (paperback)
ISBN-13: 978-1-64065-151-7 (ebook)

# Contents

# Foreword

One of the great pleasures of my fifteen years of priestly service in New York City was my friendship and shared ministry with the Rev. Carla Roland Guzmán, PhD.

In her new book, *Unmasking LATINX Ministry for Episcopalians: An Anglican Approach*, Dr. Roland invites us into reflection and learning about the Episcopal Church's "ministry to, with, and among Latinx people and communities." Most of all, Dr. Roland challenges the church to stop hyphenating our ministry for groups that are not of European descent, and to see ministry to, with, and among people of different cultures as the normative practice of following the gospel. She calls the whole church into putting their baptismal promises to work in fulfilling the mission of the Gospel.

Dr. Roland also reminds our churches that there is no single, monolithic "LATINX MINISTRY." A shared heritage of coming from Spanish (or Portuguese) speaking countries does not result in the same spiritual expectations and needs between a first generation, Roman Catholic immigrant from Guatemala; a third generation Mexican descendent who grew up Pentecostal and does not speak Spanish; or a cradle Episcopalian from Puerto Rico.

As the Episcopal bishop of Arizona, I oversee congregations and clergy from a remarkable number of backgrounds, who bring diverse needs for Spanish, bilingual, and English liturgy and leadership. And many of them are experiencing generational transition between those needs in their congregations.

I invite you into *Unmasking LATINX Ministry for Episcopalians* to learn our history and participate in envisioning a future church that is distinctly Anglican *and* open to change in which we dismantle structures that are racist, exclusionary, and regard "whiteness" as normative. This is urgent work: the decisions we make today will shape the church in the 22nd Century and beyond.

—The Rt. Rev. Jennifer A. Reddall
Sixth Episcopal Bishop of Arizona

# Introduction

n 2008, I attended my first CREDO clergy conference offered by the Church Pension Group (CPG). This wellness conference allows clergy to set aside a time of reflection in four areas: vocation, spirituality, health, and finances. At that time, one of the assignments was to establish a series of long- and short-term goals, including a "Big Hairy Audacious Goal" or BHAG. Underlying some of my goals and my BHAG was my desire to contribute to the Episcopal Church in a manner that would make us stand firm in our tradition while doing the prophetic work that needed to be done to push us toward better inclusion of all who are currently marginalized in the Church, and by extension build a glimpse of the reign of God and a better society. Over a decade later, I am now trying to do this through writing a book that grounds MINISTRY to, with, and among LATINX people and communities in our Anglican/Episcopal tradition.

This book is a combination of research, analysis, and reflection. The research is based on archival sources and a review of secondary literature. The analysis is putting the research into a framework for understanding how we got to where we are. The reflections are based on my more than twenty-five years of MINISTRY experiences, including participating in various Episcopal churches and serving the Church of Saint Matthew and Saint Timothy for over fifteen years, a close to 225-year-old congregation—bilingual, multiracial, multicultural, multigenerational, and mostly of people of lower socioeconomic means—located in a now mostly white and more affluent neighborhood in New York City's Upper West Side.[1]

As I embarked on the journey of writing this volume, I became even more aware of the need for this book. Although there is a great deal of archival material, little is known about the content, and there are few monographs that deal with, or allude to, the history of LATINX MINISTRIES in the Episcopal Church. Therefore, the need arose to dedicate more space to a more expansive contextualization of MINISTRY to, with, and among LATINX people and communities than I expected. As a result, this book has more historical information than I initially anticipated, where I set forth a framework from which to understand where we are, how we got to this place, and make suggestions on how to move forward. There is so much more that I have learned during my research, but as my doctoral thesis advisor emphatically told me about two-thirds into my time writing my dissertation, "STOP READING."[2] Great advice; sometimes, you just must stop reading.

As should be apparent, I am making some specific language choices. First, I use the term LATINX (pronounced "la-teen-ex"). This is a specific choice to use a nonbinary gender term instead of Latino, which also goes beyond Latino/a or Latin@, which remain within a binary of gender. This is also a conscious choice not to use Latine, a term gaining traction in 2019. Although HISPANIC is inclusive gender-wise (in English), it is not a pan-category that I prefer, as it is used more predominantly in Texas and the Southwest. I am aware that there are LATINX people and segments of LATINX communities that prefer Latino, and others Hispanic, and, even more specifically, many LATINX people prefer to identify by national background.[3] Thus none of these terms should be used loosely.

As with any made-up term, there is yet to be consensus around the use of LATINX in the United States, and it is deemed problematic in Latin America— as an imposition from the United States imperial context. Furthermore, there are even others that disagree with its use in Spanish from a grammatical point of view. The reader does not need to agree with me on the use of LATINX, but I hope folks agree with writing in a more inclusive manner that goes beyond gender binaries, in both English and Spanish. With some effort and intentionality this is something that is attainable. Second, and I will expound on this later, I prefer to use the phrase "MINISTRY to, with, and among LATINX people and communities" rather than "LATINX MINISTRIES." These choices, as well as many others in the book, are intentional and, I hope, disruptive. To the extent that current publishing conventions allow me, whenever I use SMALL CAPS, **bold**, *italics*, or quotation marks, a mix of singular and plural, I intentionally want the reader to be interrupted and made to slow down.

This book is in English, as so many books on MINISTRY to, with, and among LATINX people and communities in the United States context are, and as such it is not accessible to a minority of monolingual (Spanish-speaking) LATINX people. The fact is that in the United States the majority of LATINX people are either bilingual (Spanish-English or other combinations) or English-dominant, and the vast majority of those in power and in decision-making positions are also English speaking. It is my hope that I can take this book and interpret the volume into Spanish. This will require an adaptation to the contexts of Episcopalians in majority LATINX locations (such as churches in Province IX), while at the same time speaking to Spanish-reading LATINX people living in the United States. It cannot be solely a translation given the different majority/minority dynamics in Spanish-speaking regions/countries from those of the United States. Yet some of the principles and challenges faced by Episcopal/Anglican churches in these places are the same, especially since some of the very challenges have to do with their relationships to the Episcopal Church in the United States. For example, individual congregations or dioceses geographically located in the United States may approach LATINX MINISTRIES from a "deficiency" point of view, thus ministry "to." Using a wider lens, the same is done by dioceses and the denomination when looking at dioceses in Province IX, also from a deficiency/dependency perspective.

One of the most difficult tasks that confronts the Episcopal Church is how to dismantle structures/systems of oppression that are in fact generally being perpetuated by people of good will. One of the challenges is how to have the hard conversations,[4] as Martin Luther King Jr. noted, without creating bitterness, but by building up the beloved community.

I am a lifelong Episcopalian. I love the Episcopal Church and feel that it can be a place where LATINX people and communities can have a deep sense of belonging. It is my hope that the Church realizes its role in perpetuating systems that prevent this from being realized, and prophetically move forward to fulfill its mission (#BCP855). I do not want the result of the institutional work done over the last five decades to be measured as useless, yet it is certainly lacking, or as W. E. B. Du Bois said over a century ago about the Episcopal Church's work among African American communities:

> Although the Episcopal Church was the first American church to receive negro members, the growth of that membership has been small. This was the one great church that did not split on the slavery question, and the result is that its Negro membership before and since the war has been a delicate subject, and the church has probably done less for black people than any other aggregation of Christians.[5]

The same result is in danger of occurring if the work among LATINX people and communities continues to be considered and resourced as a project of the church, at best a hyphenated-type of MINISTRY.

It is my hope that this book is useful to LATINX and non-LATINX people, lay and ordained, from seminaries and congregations, from within and outside the Episcopal Church. I hope it has a broad appeal and a broad impact.

The aims of this book include:

1. To (re)focus the Episcopal Church toward and remind about the basic understanding of MINISTRY and what this means with and among LATINX people and communities. This means understanding that we need to acknowledge and move beyond what I call "hyphenated-ministry," the "demographic panic," and "marketing/social media" approaches.

2. To remind the Episcopal Church of the strengths of our theology and tradition as the Episcopal branch of the Jesus Movement. In fact, people and communities that embody and understand intersectionality and have

polycentric identities are in a unique position to understand the idea of "both/and" in an intuitive and essential manner. Put differently, I believe that the experience of many LATINX people and communities in the United States is inherently Anglican. Furthermore, rather than thinking of LATINX people and communities as homogenous, we must understand that they as a group bring a multicultural perspective to the Church.

3. To propose a direction for the Episcopal Church that is inclusive of LAT-INX people and communities, authentic, and autochthonous. This will require the intentional recovery and work on a vision of liberative LAT-INX theologies from the Anglican/Episcopal perspectives, and Anglican/Episcopal liberative theologies from LATINX perspectives.

I brought rigor to my research for this book; yet I do not pretend to be objective nor comprehensive. This book reflects who I am as a child of God, a gender nonconforming queer Puerto Rican woman living in the diaspora who is also a priest. This book contains my experiences, observations, research, and analysis. There will be aspects with which some may agree, others will disagree, and which will seem oppositional to some of the current individual successful approaches to MINISTRY to, with, and among LATINX people and communities in the Episcopal Church. This overview is institutional. My intention is to promote hard conversations that in the end will strengthen our Church and the foundations of our Church's witness and mission. All too often when we agree, we reinforce our opinions with each other, and when we disagree, we alienate ourselves and continue in our own silos of influence. The Episcopal and Anglican traditions have never required agreement or consensus or uniformity of thought—our traditions have always valued our ability to pray together and gather around God's table despite our disagreements or differences. Increasingly I have come to believe that as a Church we may, in fact, be more anti-intellectual and moralistic than we are able to admit or even notice.

The hard conversations required are by/from people on all sides of the topic. LATINX people must be more involved in understanding and dismantling racism in our Church and stand by other minoritized Episcopalians. We all have far to go when it comes to issues of gender, gender identity, and sexuality. Other Episcopalians need to understand the issues surrounding immigration and xenophobia that affect some LATINX people and communities in a myriad of ways. No one gets a pass; everyone needs to step up. As a Church we need a common language to talk about these issues.

A recent example, at Nuevo Amanecer 2018,[6] Rev. Stephanie Spellers gave the last key-note address. Spellers, a black leader and teacher in the church, spoke about standing in solidarity with LATINX people and communities. This was rooted in an understanding of intersectional and polycentric identities and how we all need to stand together cohesively.[7] I was moved by Spellers's sensitivity and empathy in presenting this address. I also sensed that many in the room had no idea what Spellers was talking about. For LATINX and Black people to come together in solidarity with a deep understanding of intersectionality, we also need to come up with a shared language and do mutual work. Through this common language may come a common commitment, which then will require the Church and society to change.[8]

Dispersed throughout this book will be autobiographical stories and anecdotes. My trajectory to this day informs what will be found in these pages and will at times serve as additional context to the history and insights being presented. I stand confident that what I present is accurate to my experience, and I do not pretend to speak for others. I provide a minority experience that should neither be minoritized nor reified. Since this is "living" church history and church history that has been neglected, I expect to get feedback from some readers who may have experienced firsthand or have insight into the events presented here; I look forward to receiving information that corrects, adds, and corroborates the narrative.

## My Puerto Rican, Anglican, and Episcopalian Roots

Anglicanism arrived in Puerto Rico from the Diocese of Antigua of the Province of the West Indies in the last third of the nineteenth century.[9] The first non–Roman Catholic Church in a Spanish colony was Santísima Trinidad in Ponce, Puerto Rico.[10] After the Spanish-Cuban-American War, the ecclesiastical jurisdiction of Puerto Rico was ceded to the United States as approved at the General Convention of 1901 and became a missionary district.[11] My great-grandfather Erasmo Figueroa's family came to know the Episcopal Church in Quebrada Limón, a community across a narrow interior valley from their home. Imagine my surprise in finding parishioners at the church I serve in New York City from this community.

The Episcopal Church in Quebrada Limón finds its roots in the extraordinary ministry called Iglesia de Jesús, a ministry begun around 1898 by the ex–Roman Catholic Spanish priest Manuel Ferrando. The Iglesia de Jesús and its approximate 1,500 members began the process to join the Episcopal Church in 1921.[12] As part of this merger, Ferrando, who was already a bishop, was consecrated "subconditione" at the Cathedral of St. John the Divine on March 15, 1923. Ferrando was the first native Spanish-speaking bishop in the Episcopal

Church, elected in February 1924 at the House of Bishops meeting in Dallas, suffragan for the Missionary District of Puerto Rico.[13]

From Quebrada Limón, you can see the communities where my grand-mother's family lived: Guaraguao and El Rusio. At times, they attended La Reconciliación by horseback. Not everyone in the family became an Epis-copalian, but my grandmother went to nursing school at (Old) St. Luke's Hospital.[14] As a matter of fact, Rev. Donald F. Gowe, the medical director of the hospital, married my grandparents and later even delivered my mom. My mother remained connected to the Episcopal Church through the decades because of my grandmother's first cousin Armando Figueroa's continued involvement in the Episcopal Church (La Encarnación) and attending Epis-copal Cathedral School in San Juan. My mom remembers Rt. Rev. A. Ervine Swift, diocesan bishop starting in 1951, standing at a portico every morning and greeting every student by name as they arrived at school. In 2016, my cousin Herman Valentín found and gave me a 1950 Spanish-language edition of the Book of Common Prayer. The book belonged to a Lucía González, cousin of my great-grandmother Leonor Ramos de Figueroa. The book was dedicated by Rev. Lorenzo Álvarez, father of the Rt. Rev. David A. Álvarez, the bishop who ordained me.[15] We have many connections to the Episcopal Church in Puerto Rico.

My father grew up in the Lutheran tradition, grandson of a Lutheran pastor, Rev. E. Victor Roland (1879–1970), with roots in western Penn-sylvania, later with a long-term ministry in Tulsa, Oklahoma. In 1936 my great-grandfather was elected president of the Synod of Kansas and Adjacent States; I wore his pectoral cross to my ordination. My parents met in Lubbock, Texas, and had the ultimate destination wedding at the Episcopal Cathedral of St. John the Baptist in Puerto Rico.[16] By the time I was born, they attended St. Peter's Episcopal Church in Amarillo, Texas. After my parents divorced and we returned to Puerto Rico, we attended St. Hilda's in Trujillo Alto, with Rev. David Álvarez and Rev. Julio Cintrón, and the Cathedral. This was the 1970s.

I attended Julio Sellés Solá grade school in a neighborhood called Villa Nevárez, in Rio Piedras, Puerto Rico. Villa Nevárez, a planned community, had been a dairy farm owned by Ramón Nevárez. This was a time of urban planning in Puerto Rico and many, including my grandparents and several of their siblings and first cousins, moved from more rural areas to the newly built planned neighborhoods. My grandparents and their relatives all moved in the early 1950s; all of them first owners of their respective homes. For many this was shortly after their service in the Korean War. My mom and uncle grew up in this neighborhood, and this is where my older sister and I also grew up.

My middle school was Sotero Figueroa and then I attended University Gardens High School. This was one of the best public school districts in all of Puerto Rico; the high school had a science and math program. I was very lucky and, in many ways, living in this neighborhood was a very good upbringing. Many of my classmates were also grandchildren of those that moved to the urbanization at the same time as my grandparents.

The 1970s and early 1980s were a visible time for the Episcopal Church in Puerto Rico and the Rt. Rev. Francisco Reus Froylán was known for being an outspoken voice in social justice issues, especially environmental ones.[17] Given my mother's work with the government, we distanced ourselves from the Episcopal Church and began attending a Roman Catholic church that included as founders my great-aunt (my grandmother's sister) Edith and great-uncle Herman Valentín. It is at St. Luke's that I did my "first communion." From 1983 to 1985, I lived in Texas and again attended St. Peter's Episcopal Church, led by Rev. Bruce Green. Back in Puerto Rico, during high school we occasionally attended the Episcopal Cathedral. I graduated University Gardens High School in San Juan, Puerto Rico, in 1989.

By the time I went to college, the Episcopal Church was my tradition. It is my sense that by that time I knew that the Episcopal Church was a place that accepted me fully and that the Roman Catholic Church did not. I'm not sure I could have articulated this that clearly then, but it never occurred to me to look for the Roman Catholic worship services on campus. All my experiences in the Episcopal Church (TX and PR) had been affirming, not so much in the Roman Catholic tradition. Wrapped up in this sense was the treatment of women in the Church and the terrible stance of the Roman Catholic Church in Puerto Rico with respect to HIV/AIDS, and relatedly gay men.[18]

I remember vividly during my first year at Cornell University looking up the time and place of Episcopal worship on campus. I got up of my own volition on a Sunday morning for 9:30 a.m. worship and attended, for the first time, the Episcopal Church at Cornell (ECC), and met Rev. Gurdon Brewster. ECC held services at Anabel Taylor Hall, just a short uphill walk from West Campus. During my coming out process at Cornell, I was proud to be an Episcopalian, and saw the Episcopal Church as a welcoming place. In addition to ECC, pivotal in my discernment were two spring-break mission trips with the Protestant Cooperative Ministry (PCM), another chaplaincy in Anabel Taylor Hall, with an office down the hall from ECC. The mission trips to St. Simon's Island in Georgia and Robbins, Tennessee, in the beautiful Cumberland Plateau were led by Rev. Barbara Heck.

My call to ordained ministry was first recognized and affirmed at Cornell. I am but one of dozens of people who discerned ordained ministry with Chaplain Brewster. To me, very important among them are the Rt. Rev. Jennifer Baskerville-Burrows, the bishop of Indianapolis, and the Rev. Eric H. Law, founder of the Kaleidoscope Institute. Rev. Ann Tillman, long before her own ordination, was on my discernment committee. Brewster's influence went beyond the campus community and the Diocese of Central New York. Brewster worked with Martin Luther King Sr. in 1961 and 1965; and, as priest and sculptor was one of the founders of Episcopal Church and the Visual Arts (ECVA).[19]

After a time of discernment, in 1994, Brewster drove me to Syracuse to meet with the Rt. Rev. David B. Joslin and explore whether I could begin the process toward ordination in the Diocese of Central New York. Joslin indicated at that time that "Hispanic ministry" was not foreseen in their diocese.

Brewster, probably understanding more clearly all that that rejection meant—text and subtext—was very disappointed; as we drove back to Ithaca, the chaplain's hands were white-knuckled. When I met with Joslin, I was in my very early twenties, finishing college, and eager to go to seminary. I was also out, an LGBT activist, and had a shaved head. I carry white skin and do not have an accent. I mention all of this because Joslin's response was overtly racist, and the subtext was clearly homophobic—attitudes that were not uncommon in the Church, then or now. There were seminaries at the time that required the signing of celibacy clauses; only twenty years had passed since women's ordination and the creation of a structure for ethnic ministries.

I need to add a few things to this story. First, I do not know how Joslin understood the statement, and I cannot recall whether this meeting occurred before the House of Bishops wrote their pastoral letter on the sin of racism (March 1994). Second, Joslin was gracious enough to sign an endorsement for seminary, not choosing to be a stumbling block. Third, I do not know where the broader diocese stood on issues of sexuality and LATINX ministries. Fourth, the canon to admit someone, regardless of sexual orientation, into the ordination process had not been changed—that happened at the General Convention of 1994.[20] Finally, by the time I was able to go to seminary in 1997, it was a better time. It was God's time. I say all of this, because this story is not so much about Joslin, but about the Church.

Let me explain. In my experience, in the Church it is more common to encounter overt racism than overt homophobia. In historical perspective, the issue of "homosexuality" has moved more swiftly and progressively in the Episcopal Church, and some could argue in society as well. This is because within the LGBTQ+ community there are white gay males, who have always been part of the institution of the Church, and thus the power structures. This is not the same for Latinx people and, in some ways, for women in the church. We can look at 1974 as a benchmark: the Philadelphia Eleven, the founding of Integrity, and the beginning of the work of the various ethnic ministries. It has been my experience that the Church has been more open to sexuality issues than those of gender, race, or ethnicity.

Let me explain my observation further. The crystalizing moment that the tension around Rt. Rev. Gene Robinson's election, consent, and consecration had more to do with gender than sexuality came with the announcement in December 2006 that the archbishop of the Anglican Church of Uganda, Most Rev. Henry Luke Orombi, would not sit with the new Presiding Bishop Katharine Jefferts-Schori at the upcoming Primates Meeting.[21] Although the archbishop specifically mentioned that it was not about the gender of the presiding bishop, the underlying unresolved issue is that of gender in the Church. Kate Bornstein puts it this way:

> And so, we have a good excuse for violence in the name of gender. The reason for exclusion by the dominant culture of both homosexuality and gender ambiguity has less to do, I think, with sexual orientation than it does with gender role. When a gay man is bashed on the street, it's unlikely that the bashers are thinking [or imagining] of the gay man [having sex with another man]. [Instead] it has a lot to do with seeing that man violate the rules of gender in this culture. The first commandment in this culture for men is "Thou shalt not be a woman." And the corresponding commandment for a woman in this culture "Thou shalt not be a man."[22]

Agreeing with Bornstein's thesis means understanding that the issue of Robinson is one of gender betrayal and that the issue of Jefferts-Schori is one of being the wrong gender. The fact that this has to do with gender was reaffirmed in 2016 with the delayed response by the Episcopal Church, as a denomination, regarding House Bill 2 in North Carolina.[23] The Church structures are racist, patriarchal, and heteronormative.

In the early 1990s, I believed that the Church was moving forward with respect to "homosexuality." Looking back from 2020, it doesn't seem that we have moved much farther.[24] And, notwithstanding how painful this is, it is farther back with respect to Latinx people and communities and in terms of race, than in sexuality. Another way of looking at this is as an analogy to Zora Neale Hurston's observation "I feel most colored when I am thrown against a sharp white background"; I feel most Latinx when I'm thrown against the sharp background of the Episcopal Church.[25] If I felt Christian or Episcopalian against this background it would not be problematic; being *othered* is.

## Getting on the Same Page

Over my years of ordained ministry, I have had the privilege of mentoring many seminarians. Inevitably, at some point, I convey to them that they need to understand and know our prayer book so thoroughly that all they would ever need to lead worship, in any setting, would be a Bible and a Book of Common Prayer. As we attest in ordination, scripture contains all things necessary for salvation; the prayer book contains many of the things idiosyncratic to our branch of the Jesus Movement.[26] These are not the only tools, but they are foundational. The answer to how we do things and what we believe as Episcopalians can often be found in the words of our liturgy, in the Outline of the Faith, and even in the rubrics and additional directions found in the prayer book. I hope that I can prove this mantra in this book. Our tradition is abundant, robust, and flexible.

As Episcopalians, we have a lot of jargon that we use to describe who we are as community and what we do together. The use of our specific language can give us a sense of tradition and belonging but should not be used to alienate others as exclusionary in-speak. It is my intention to get us on the same page with some common language, underlined by a specific understanding of the power of language. For example, when I teach about our vessels of communion—chalice and purificator, corporal and paten, pall, flagon, and ciborium—I not only use our "holy language" but also our quotidian language—plates and placemats, cups and napkins, pitchers, and bread boxes. I do this not only to demystify and make more accessible what happens at the altar, but to remind us that what Jesus accomplished for us is to be continually enacted even in the most ordinary moments. In LATINX theologies this is *lo cotidiano*: the quotidian.

One of the principal acts we do together as Episcopalians is worship. It is a meaningful and unifying act that we are called to do in the fulfillment of our mission. Although worship is a unifying factor, we may not always have the same definitions for some common vocabulary. Yet although I spend significant time and space defining terms and getting us on the same page, it does not mean that these terms are stable, but that for a brief time we will use the same definitions in this book. To accomplish this, a few definitions on nomenclature are needed.

Shortly after starting my work at the Church of Saint Matthew and Saint Timothy, I was bothered by the *us-them* dichotomy between those attending the 9 a.m. service and those attending the 11 a.m. This *us-them* extended to the vessels used for communion at each service, 9 a.m. (Spanish) and 11 a.m. (English), and even different sets of offering plates. Although not two congregations with separate vestries, the church functioned as such. Although the parish has its own specific history that informed this division, many working in MINISTRY to, with, and among LATINX people and communities know the challenges of achieving a polycentric congregation that functions as *one* when there are competing interests, unequal power structures, and differing views about resources.

As a result, I began to think of ways in which the community could increasingly function as one community. One way we began to change that culture was by changing how we spoke about our community. From this process came the slogan of St. Matthew and St. Timothy's as "*one* congregation that worships in *two* languages," which meant speaking about the 9 a.m. service rather than the 9 a.m. congregation. It also meant two other things: first, the willingness of a "mixed" congregation to put being together ahead of being comfortable— and enshrining this as a value; second, a willingness of people to accept that they didn't have their own priest/chaplain. Until I came to the congregation, the staff had usually been an English-speaking rector with LATINX or Spanish-speaking assistants. Changes also extended to the budget of the church. Language is important. Not only can language speak to the reality of people and communities, but language can be a starting point to change communities.

## MINISTRY and LATINX MINISTRY Are Co-Terminus

"MINISTRY," as defined in a dictionary, is the "the office, duties, or functions of a minister."[27] Ministers are all the faithful: lay and ordained. In the Outline of the Faith, MINISTRY is defined as the ways all laypeople, deacons, priests, and bishops help to carry out the mission of the Church "to restore all people to unity with God and each other in Christ."[28] Every Episcopalian should know what the mission of the Church is; one of our social-media campaigns should be #BCP855. For me, MINISTRY is about relationships and the Baptismal Covenant.

Each of the orders fulfills the mission of the church in different ways, and those are the ACTIONS OF MINISTRY, which are prayer and worship; the proclamation of the gospel; and the promotion of justice, peace, and love.[29] This definition of MINISTRY is obvious and is in the Outline, yet in practice we have taken MINISTRY out of LATINX MINISTRIES. This means that if we talk about MINISTRY alongside of LATINX MINISTRY, we normalize MINISTRY as white and in English and non-LATINX. Yet MINISTRY is MINISTRY regardless of who is sitting in the pew and the vernacular of the liturgy.

MINISTRY is about the way we live out the Baptismal Covenant, and the Baptismal Covenant is the same whether in Spanish or in English. Outreach, service, and evangelism are all ACTIONS OF MINISTRY. MINISTRY is all encompassing to how we do church, yet the directionality of MINISTRY is toward the fulfilling of the mission of the church, not toward a commodified group of people. For some this definition of MINISTRY may be too narrow; others will not agree with me at all, and both positions may be right. I want us to hold three things about MINISTRY while reading this book:

- MINISTRY is not social service, or outreach, or even evangelism. MINISTRY is the way we build reconciling relationships with God and one another. There are biblical and theological foundations to this work of reconciliation.
- MINISTRY is not social justice; MINISTRY is the ways we strengthen people and communities in the Church to proclaim and do justice in the world. This is the necessary and constant oscillation between discipleship and apostleship.
- All people can do MINISTRY and fulfill the promises of the Baptismal Covenant; all people have spiritual and pastoral needs. Or put differently, church is not where white people get their spiritual needs met and LATINX people get their material needs met.

These are all elements found in the formulation of liberation theologies and the foundational purpose of base ecclesial communities (*comunidades eclesiales de base*), something I will discuss later.

LATINX MINISTRY is MINISTRY. Although it is problematic, at times I will use LATINX ministry/ministries as a substitute to the Office of Latino/Hispanic Ministries of the Episcopal Church. In LATINX MINISTRIES who or what does the LATINX refer to? Does LATINX refer to the object or target of the MINISTRIES? Or is it the subject and agent of the MINISTRIES? Or does a LATINX person always do LATINX MINISTRY because they identify or are identified as LATINX, regardless of the communities they minister among? The pitfalls of such a nomenclature are, in part, the result of thinking of SPECIALIZED MINISTRIES in a reified way, or what I refer to as HYPHENATED-MINISTRIES. Or put differently, once a SPECIALIZED MINISTRY becomes reified, it is detached from the most basic understandings of MINISTRY.

What is it about LATINX MINISTRIES that I am trying to (un)mask? For starters, it is my sense that there are a plethora of convenient excuses for many in the Episcopal Church not to have a presence in LATINX communities and not reach out to LATINX people, in ways other than social services, programs, and outreach—meaning in liturgy, pastoral care, Christian formation, evangelism. These are excuses to hide behind, thus hiding behind masks. The first of these excuses is the Spanish language. I know Spanish (LATINX)-speaking priests that are not called to LATINX MINISTRY and know priests with limited Spanish language gifts that are incredibly gifted in and called to MINISTRY among

LATINX people and communities. These are two different kinds of pigeon-holing (external and internal, from within and from without).[30]

The type of mask that I see in my mind's eye looks like the mask of Zorro or Black Lightning, or Black Thunder, or glasses for Clark Kent or Kara Danvers.[31] These masks in actuality are a farce or reveal in their hiding the willingness of some to not want to see the reality of the person behind the mask. The Spanish-language barrier is a made-up (in)convenient barrier. Masks conceal and hide truths and can be a protective and soothing covering from reality and the hard work required to have unmasked truth laid bare.

These questions should give the reader some insight into the ideological "racialization/somatization" of certain ministries as a way of othering them from MINISTRY in general, and thus absolving those in normative ministry from engaging in HYPHENATED-MINISTRY. Non-hyphenated-ministry, in general, is assumed to be the normative white and affluent, English-speaking, heteronormative ministry. Or put differently, "If I'm not them, I don't have to minister to them"; thus, "I don't need to have a reconciling relationship with them." Because of these challenges I use the phrase "MINISTRY to, with, and among LATINX people and communities."

## MINISTRY to, with, and among LATINX People and Communities

The phrase "MINISTRY to, with, and among LATINX people and communities," albeit imperfect, is important in the conceptualization of this book. It works in chronological, ideological, and theological ways. As a conceptualization, it is just a "crutch" for conversation, rather than a soon to be "reified" phrase for LATINX MINISTRIES. "To" is the easiest to define since it is directional and less ambiguous: toward, directed to, in the direction of. This means that the actions of ministry are directed to a group of people or communities based on some "defining" characteristic. The object of the "to" in our case refers to LATINX people and communities. Yet something to consider, in this case MINISTRY to LATINX people and communities is not MINISTRY at all; it is at best an ACTION OF MINISTRY. The primary way "ministry to" has been enacted is as outreach or social services "to those people who need." In the best possible terms, it is Episcopalians (whites) living out the Baptismal Covenant.

It is my contention that "MINISTRY to" is still a significant portion of the Episcopal witness to LATINX people and communities and is emblematic of the Episcopal Church's most common dealings with them. Some of the problems with "MINISTRY to," even when it accomplishes evangelism and discipleship, are the pitfalls of "paternalism" and "dependence," problems that inherently limit liberation and the full realization of each person and community. This is inherently scary to those doing the ministering, because it requires them to surrender control and power.

Leonardo and Clodovis Boff, in writing about how to "do liberation theology" call out the limitations of "MINISTRY to":

> "Aid" is help offered by individuals moved by the spectacle of widespread destitution. They form agencies and organize projects: the "Band-Aid" or "corn-plaster" approach to social ills. But however perceptive they become and however well-intentioned—and successful aid remains a strategy for helping the poor, but treating them as (collective) objects of charity, not as subjects of their own liberation. The poor are seen simply as those who have nothing. There is a failure to see that the poor are oppressed and made poor by *others*; and what they do possess—strength to resist, capacity to understand their rights, to organize themselves and transform a subhuman situation—tends to be left out of account. Aid increases the dependence of the poor, tying them to help from others, to decisions made by others: again, not enabling them to become their own liberators.[32]

To be clear, all congregations should minister to the communities[33] around them, especially the poor, the marginalized, the hungry, the homeless, according to their means and gifts; all Episcopal churches should welcome all in the communities around them, regardless of language, race, sexuality, ethnicity, and gender identity. Our churches should not function as if certain groups come to church and other groups have material needs from church. Even the poor, marginalized, hungry, and homeless in our congregations have the ability to minister to others.

Although many may envision the existence of "Ethnic Ministries" as liberating, being a program or project of the Church limits its growth and potential and continues to keep these specific types of ministry as different than "mainstream" ministry. The Boff brothers name this "reformism":

> "Reformism" seeks to improve the situation of the poor, but always within existing social relationships and the basic structuring of society, which rules out greater participation by all and diminution in the privileges enjoyed by the ruling classes. Reformism can lead to great feats of development in the poorer nations, but this development is nearly always at the expense of the oppressed poor and very rarely in their favor.[34]

Another example that places LATINX people and communities as a program of the Church can we seen in the way the website of the Episcopal Church is organized. Under the ministries tab of the main page, listed in alphabetical order are: Armed Forces and Federal Ministries, Asiamerica Ministries, Black Ministries, Creation Care, Domestic Poverty, Ecumenical/Interreligious, Episcopal Migration Ministries, Episcopal Service Corps, Episcopal Volunteers in Mission, Evangelism Initiatives, Global Partnerships, Healthcare Chaplaincies, Indigenous Ministries, Latino Ministries, New Episcopal Communities, Office of Government Relations, Racial Reconciliation, Social Justice & Advocacy Engagement, Office of Transition Ministry, United Thank Offering, Young Adult & Campus Ministries, Young Adult Service Corps, and Youth Ministries.[35] In looking at this list, I hope that the reader can agree that the use of MINISTRY in the various ethnic ministries is inherently different than the use of MINISTRY in other programs of the Church; yet all are placed on the same level. It is a pull-down menu of interests, thus commodifying specific communities. LATINX persons in the Episcopal Church are part of a "drop-down menu."

As an institution, and seen generously, it took until the 1960s for the Episcopal Church to begin to see the possibility for MINISTRY with LATINX people and communities; unfortunately, this led to the institutionalization of this MINISTRY as a program of the Church. In many dictionaries, the terms "with" and "among" are synonymous. Perhaps it is in this similarity—like the confusion between mission, ministry, and outreach—that the nuanced difference between the two finds its importance. The term "with" is a bilateral term that requires an *us/them* binary. The idea of "with" can have two elements that are disconnected or dissociated from one another. This allows for different communities within a congregation to function independently, or as different congregations. On the other hand, the term "among" implies ideas of mingling and intermixing of distinct or separate objects and is multilateral. Whereas the term "with" can still allow for segregation, the term "among" can allow for integration, solidarity, and belonging. It is my estimation that we have made some inroads into ministry "with" and are awakening to ministry "among." "With" is about inclusion; "among" moves this inclusion toward solidarity—solidarity being the outward and visible sign of inclusion; solidarity as sacramental inclusion.

Perhaps the following statement will clarify the above explanations. A 1988 report "The Hispanic Challenge to the Diocese of New York" has a section titled "The 'Ecclesiological Challenge'—a Church of Hispanics, a Church of the Poor."

There is a distinct difference between a Church that ministers to and a Church that is of. We are of the conviction that only as Hispanics become fully participants in and subjects of the life and witness of the Church, will there be true and lasting development of Hispanic work in the Diocese. The Committee affirms that, because of the above mentioned factors and for sound missionary policies, one of the primary goals in response to the Hispanic challenge is to enable the Episcopal Church to become a Church that not only ministers to Hispanics, and for that matter the poor, but that is also of Hispanics and of the poor. The Committee believes that this goal has, in turn, consequences and implications for many aspects of the Church mission and ministry among and with Hispanics.[36]

I use the three terms "to," "with," and "among" in a progressive manner—again, as a model. None of them fits perfectly and should not be used as absolute terms or ones taken solely for their negative connotations. For example, although I see "among" as better than "with," "among" in its extreme can be used by the dominant culture as a dangerous means of acculturation and erasure of constitutive identities. In a way these three terms have a sense of directionality and can describe the various ways LATINX MINISTRIES have gone since the 1960s. Yet what are the desired positive effects of each of the stages in this model? For this I will use another model: welcome, inclusion, solidarity, and belonging.

## More Terminology

I use the term "Anglicanism" to refer to the tradition as it is expressed in various contexts throughout the world. There is no "one" Anglicanism, but Anglicanism as contextualized in various places, or "Anglicanisms." It is also my opinion and assessment that although all Anglicanisms are contextualized, they also all have elements in common. This characteristic unity and diversity are in fact a brilliant aspect of our traditions. Perhaps enshrined in the *both/and* ethos and ability to historically find synthesis.

"The Church of England" refers to Anglicanism as expressed in England and referent to the specific history of Anglicanism as an institution and established church, whether national or colonial. "The Episcopal Church" refers to the expression of Anglicanism as it relates to the United States, but it is not contiguous to the United States since it is present in many international jurisdictions, such as other countries included in Province IX. I use "Roman Catholic" as the Western tradition that is still in communion with Rome and the pope. Whenever I use "Anglican/Episcopal," I am alluding to broader expression that may have dual origins.

Whenever I use the binary English-Spanish, it should be understood as inclusive of a spectrum that includes monolingual people/communities on both extremes and various levels of bilingual experience throughout. It is important to remember that there are different levels of language knowledge: not everyone who speaks a language can read or write that language. As I describe later, "the EYE is not (always) bilingual." Or just because you can read or write in a language does not mean that you can speak it or understand it when spoken. I am aware that I make no reference to indigenous languages spoken by many Latinx people and communities.

Please note that I recognize that my "own" use of these terms is anachronistic, something that I do not promote especially in works of history or historiography. I am deeply aware that the terminology I have presented has not always been used at all times and in all places. A better historical approach would be to use the terms that were in use at the historical period being referred to, such as Hispanic, Latino, or PECUSA. Yet the terms I'm using are shorthand solely for the purpose of this book. Reader be aware of this and know how you are using the terminology! This epistemological awareness is the responsibility of the reader.

## Guiding Assumptions

It is my hope that all readers of this book can find something relevant for ministry, not just MINISTRY to, with, and among Latinx people and communities. Latinx ministry is MINISTRY. This means that there should be something in this book for any person involved in MINISTRY, which should be ALL the baptized. This requires that the reader ask themselves, "Why am I making this aspect of MINISTRY something specific to HYPHENATED-MINISTRY?" And, "What are the guiding assumptions behind the decisions we are making and approaches we are taking?" This book presents what I believe to be some hard and necessary truths; and I believe that the Episcopal Church is uniquely called to MINISTRY among Latinx people and communities.

The Episcopal branch of the Jesus Movement has a message and ethos that appeals to Latinx people and communities. Our Anglican and Episcopal heritage can speak powerfully to the Latinx experience in the United States. And the Latinx witness can speak powerfully to the prophetic nature and potential of Anglicanism. It is a lens intuitively understood by Latinx people in the United States, who know that in God they live, and move, and have their being, and that is in the *both/and*. An adaptation of Latin American liberation theologies to the United States context is a gift Latinx people and communities bring to the Episcopal Church.

Even as the Episcopal Church is a gift, I believe that there are structures that need to be dismantled. These structures are hindering the fulfillment of the mission of the Church, thus amounting to sin. This means that the Church must understand and dismantle the structures that continue to prevent LATINX and black people, women, and many other *others* from fully sharing in the power and resources of the Church. Sadly, we are a Church that has not fully grappled with racism and sexism, let alone with xenophobia, homophobia, and transphobia. What I call HYPHENATED-MINISTRY, as institutionalized in the Ethnic Ministries section of the Episcopal Church, is part of the problem. Even something as familiar as the phrase "The Episcopal Church welcomes you" is part of the problem; welcome is not enough because it does not dismantle structures. Innovation in the same deficient structure will not innovate; it will be stifled.

Language matters, and the way we speak about things can make the difference in how they are accomplished. Related to this, the vernacular matters. Since LATINX MINISTRY is MINISTRY is MINISTRY is MINISTRY, I am trying to break down the idea that there is an unbreachable *us/them* between LATINX people and communities and others already in the Episcopal Church, as a language barrier is made to be, including showing where some of the biases that lead to the *us/them* historically come from and suggest ways to dismantle them.

*Us/them* is outwardly directional. By no means am I saying that all that we are challenged by is related to those in the majority culture of the Church, or that all the gifts come from LATINX communities, as I argue against LATINX being the saviors of the Episcopal Church. Some issues are inter-group; other issues are intra-group. Within these there are also broader inter- and intra-contexts. So although there may not be complete balance showing all these dynamics and areas to work on or work with, that does not mean that any one person or group is absolved from doing the work. In this book, I invite Episcopalians that are part of the majority church into conversion with LATINX people and communities. I do so because those in majority culture have much to learn and to give. LATINX people also have much to give and learn, and bear some responsibility, just not the same kind of responsibility.

## Conversation Partners in This Book

Writing this book has been an awesome and fun adventure. I have thoroughly enjoyed all the learning that I've done over the year I spent reading, analyzing, and writing; I've loved the study of the data. As I've explored and researched the various aspects of this book, it has become even clearer that there was indeed a need for it. I've also come to realize that rather than completely learning new fields, beyond those of my competency, that I'd rather lift up the work of others who already have great insight and whose voices are important for the readers of this book to know and to hear. Those researchers and others I am calling my conversation partners. These conversation partners include the writings of mentors and friends such as Rev. Juan M. C. Oliver, Rev. John L. Kater Jr., and Rev. Justo L. González. I have come to know and greatly appreciate the work of Rev. Harold T. Lewis through reading about the history of race in the Episcopal Church and of the General Convention Special Program (GCSP). I have learned much about the Episcopal Church and I'm grateful for spending time with the history of the GCSP. In researching about the GCSP, I have concluded that it is a big piece in the institutionalization of ethnic ministries in the Episcopal Church, and its legacy continues to inform the treatment of "ethnic groups" as programs of the Church. To my knowledge, this is a connection that has not been done before.

In addition to a score of reports and some articles, in the Episcopal Church there are two books that deal with LATINX Ministries in this Church. The first is Rev. Juan M. C. Oliver's *Ripe Fields: The Promise and Challenge of Latino Ministry* (2009).[37] Ironically, in 2011, I wrote a review of the book where I identified the need for expanding the work begun by Oliver, not thinking that I would be the one to take up part of this task close to a decade later. In the review, I wrote:

> It is a book that I hope he will expand, or that others will take the challenge to expand; it would greatly lend itself to a series on Latino/a ministry. This book should be a wake-up call to the church, and has been written in a very even-handed and useful manner for the person who has already been involved in Latina/o ministry or for those who feel the need to become bicultural and bilingual in their ministry and approach. As the book title indicates, Oliver shows that although Latina/o ministry is full of challenges, it is above all full of promise.[38]

The second, and more recent book, is by Rev. Isaías A. Rodríguez, *Historia del Ministerio Hispano en la Iglesia Episcopal* (2015).[39] This book takes a chronological look at this ministry as presented in a variety of primary sources (reports, newsletters, etc.), which Rodríguez translates into Spanish, although all are reports that are available in English. It is through Rodríguez's book that I was able to begin to sketch and then expand an outline of the institutionalization of these MINISTRIES through its meetings and reports. It is important that Rodríguez's book is in Spanish and opens to Spanish speakers some of this history.

Histories of the Episcopal Church and other mainline Protestant histories have very little in them about LATINX people and communities. Analogously, many Protestant histories of LATINX ministries in the United States have very little, if anything, about the Episcopal Church. The work of Rev. Juan Francisco Martínez goes far in addressing the LATINX gap in Protestant histories, although it does not include much from the Episcopal Church. Nevertheless, Martínez's academic and ministerial insights have been important in helping me organize the content of sections of this book. Finally, a more recently published work by Lutheran scholars Rev. Alberto L. García and Rev. John A. Nunes, *Wittenberg Meets the World: Reimagining the Reformation at the Margins*, helps me imagine further the possibilities of LATINX theologizing in the Episcopal Church and the transformative expression this important work may have in the lives of all in the Church.[40]

## Part and Chapter Descriptions

The book before you is divided into two parts. Part I, "(Re)Framing the Historical Context," is our Episcopal/Anglican Church History as it relates to LATINX people and communities, and the institutionalization of "LATINX MINISTRIES." Part II, "Unmasking and (Re)Framing LATINX MINISTRIES," is an analysis of where we are in this ministry and how we can prophetically move forward to more truly have the mission of the church as our focus.

Part I includes three aspects: two chapters and a chronology. Chapter 1 provides an overview of this church history prior to institutionalization. Chapter 2 presents a history since the institutionalization, basically the past five decades. Part II has three chapters. I borrow from Oliver's book the ideas of "challenges" and "promises." Chapter 3, the challenges, is about "things done and left undone." Chapter 4 deals specifically with leadership development and theological education. Chapter 5 presents some avenues of promise as we are all invited into the potential and possibilities of MINISTRY among LATINX people and communities.

## Notes

1. The congregation I serve is majority-LATINX and minority-white, with several other racial and ethnic constituencies. New York City defines the Upper West Side as the area west of Central Park between 74th and 106th Streets. It has a population of over 130,000 people (65.8 percent White, 16.4 percent Latino/Hispanic, 7.2 percent Black, 7.9 percent Asian, 2.7 percent other). LATINX is distributed as 32 percent Dominican, 30.5 percent Puerto Rican, 12.3 percent South American, 7.6 percent Mexican, 5.1 percent Cuban, 4.3 percent Central American, 8.2 percent other. The median income is $99,320; 10 percent living below the poverty level; 14 percent receiving some sort of government assistance. The immediate census tract that includes the church is 169: W. 82nd–W. 86th between CPW and Amsterdam Avenues. It has a population of over 8,500 people (79.9 percent White, 9.6 percent Latino/Hispanic, 6.8 percent Asian, 3 percent Black, 0.7 percent other) and a median income of $102,030. All data from NYC Planning: Population Fact Finder, accessed January 11, 2019, *https://popfactfinder.planning.nyc.gov*. Includes data through the 2016 American Communities Survey (ACS). There are over a dozen languages spoken near the church.

2. Dr. Yahya Michot, emeritus professor of Islamic thought and Christian-Muslim relations at Hartford Seminary.

3. Juan Francisco Martínez, *Walking with the People: Latino Ministry in the United States* (Eugene, OR: Wipf & Stock, 2016), 1; *Los Protestantes: An Introduction to Latino Protestantism in the United States* (Santa Barbara, CA: Praeger, 2011), 16.

4. Rev. Dr. Michael Battle speaking at "Meet the Faculty" at General Theological Seminary's orientation in the fall of 2018.

5. W. E. B. Du Bois, *The Negro Church: A Social Study* (Atlanta, GA: Atlanta University Press, 1903), 139.

6. The biannual Episcopal Latino/Hispanic Ministries gathering.

7. One of my favorite words for 2018. I first came across the use of the term and idea "polycentric" identity in the various writings of Juan Francisco Martínez on LATINX Protestantism in the United States. Juan Francisco Martínez, *The Story of Latino Protestants in the United States* (Grand Rapids, MI: William B. Eerdmans, 2018), 214; *Walking*, xvi, 4, 17, 23, 51, 52, 110; *Los Protestantes*, 20, 113, 132.

8. Rev. Stephanie Spellers, canon to the presiding bishop for evangelism, reconciliation and stewardship of creation, Wednesday Morning Keynote Address at Nuevo Amanecer Conference, Kanuga Conference Center, Hendersonville, NC, Wednesday, August 29, 2018. Spellers has written *Radical Welcome: Embracing God, the Other, and the Spirit of Transformation* (New York: Church Publishing, 2006).

9. Jorge Juan Rivera Torres, *Documentos Históricos de la Iglesia Episcopal Puertorriqueña*, vol. I, 2nd ed. (Saint Just, PR: Taller Episcográfico, IEP, 2008), 5.

10. Organized in 1869, consecrated in 1874. This church was possible because of Article 21 of the 1869 Spanish constitution, which afforded freedom of religion. Rivera Torres, *Documentos Históricos*, 10. See also Samuel Silva Gotay, *Protestantismo y política en Puerto Rico, 1898–1930: hacia una historia del protestantismo evangélico en Puerto Rico*, 2nd rev. ed. (San Juan, PR: Editorial de la Universidad de Puerto Rico, 1998). According to Silva Gotay in FN2, the freedom of religion would be lost in 1874 with the restoration of the monarchy in favor of a limited "tolerance" of religion, 7–8.

11. Rivera Torres, *Documentos*, 25.

12. Rivera Torres, *Documentos*, 66.

13. "Subject to condition." Rivera Torres, *Documentos*, 66, 72–73. This does not surprise me given the Episcopal Church's at times obsessive distrust of "other" bishops, or difficulty in sharing the episcopate with outsiders. See footnote 84 (p. 36) for a proposal that changes this asertion.

14. Founded in 1907. Rivera Torres, *Documentos*, 7.

15. The dedication read: "May this holy book serve you in knowing, loving, and serving our Lord Jesus Christ every day more and more" (my translation). Rev. Álvarez was serving the congregation of St. Mary the Virgin in Ponce, Puerto Rico.

16. They were married on December 22, 1967. The wedding was officiated by Rev. J. Antonio Ramos Orench.

17. Rivera Torres, *Documentos*, chapter VIII; see also Episcopal News Service (ENS), "Grant Made to Assist Diocese of Puerto Rico in Mining Concerns," September 25, 1974 [74249]. Unless otherwise noted, all ENS articles are found in the digital Episcopal Archives (www.episcopalarchives.org). All articles were accessed between June 2018 and June 2019. The bracketed number is the index number used by the archives.

18. At the time Cardinal Luis Aponte Martínez was the archbishop of San Juan.

19. Gurdon Brewster, *No Turning Back: My Summer with Daddy King* (New York: Orbis, 2011).

20. Resolution D007: Amend Canon III.4.1 [Equal Access to Ordination Process]. Resolved, That Title III, Canon 4 be amended by adding a new sentence to Section 1 as follows: No one shall be denied access to the selection process for ordination in this Church because of race, color, ethnic origin, sex, national origin, marital status, sexual orientation, disabilities or age, except as otherwise specified by these Canons. No right to ordination is hereby established. General Convention, *Journal of the General Convention of . . . The Episcopal Church, Indianapolis, 1994* (New York: General Convention, 1995), 811–12.

21. ENS, "Uganda: Orombi Says He Will Not Sit with Jefferts Schori at Primates Meeting," The Episcopal Church, December 15, 2006, *https://www.episcopalchurch.org/library/article/uganda-orombi-*

*says-he-will-not-sit-jefferts-schori-primates-meeting*; see also "Global South Primates Meeting—Kigali Communique," Anglican Communion News Service, September 22, 2006, *https://www.anglicannews. org/news/2006/09/global-south-primates-meeting-kigali-communique.aspx*.

22. Kate Bornstein, *Gender Outlaw: On Men, Women, and the Rest of Us* (New York: Routledge, 1994), 104.

23. The Public Facilities Privacy & Security Act, commonly known as House Bill 2, became law on March 23, 2016. A statement from the presiding bishop and the president of the House of Deputies was issued on June 28, 2016, even with the tragedy at the Pulse Nightclub occurring on June 12 and Executive Council having spoken about the issue on June 10.

24. Mary Frances Schjonberg, ENS, "Same-Sex Spouses Not Invited to Next Year's Lambeth Conference of Bishops: Archbishop of Canterbury Bases Decision on 20-Year-Old Resolution from Previous Gathering," February 18, 2019; ENS, "Diocese of New York Bishops and Spouses Will Be at Lambeth 2020 Despite Same-Sex Spouse Exclusion," March 1, 2019; "Welby's Lambeth Invite Apology Smooths Way for Anglican Consultative Council to Talk Together: Weeklong Effort by Oklahoma Bishop to Have ACC Speak on LGBTQ People Ends in Negotiated Measure," March 4, 2019; David Paulsen, "House of Bishops Opens Fall Meeting with Discussions of Same-Sex Spouse Exclusion from Lambeth 2020," September 17, 2019. *https://www.episcopalnewsservice.org*.

25. Richard Nordquist, "How It Feels to Be Colored Me, by Zora Neale Hurston." ThoughtCo. *https://www.thoughtco.com/how-it-feels-to-be-colored-me-by-zora-neale-hurston-1688772* (accessed September 19, 2019). See also, Sharon Lynette Jones, *Critical Companion to Zora Neale Hurston: A Literary Reference to her Life and Work* (New York: Facts On File, c2009), 66.

26. Episcopal Church, *Book of Common Prayer and Administration of the Sacraments and Other Rites and Ceremonies of the Church: According to the Use of the Protestant Episcopal Church in the United States of America: Together with the Psalter, or, Psalms of David* (New York: Seabury Press, 1979), declaration on pages 513, 526, and 538 (hereafter BCP). "The Episcopal branch of the Jesus movement" is a phrase that, to my knowledge, comes into wide use under Presiding Bishop Michael Curry (elected 2015).

27. Merriam-Webster.com, s.v. "ministry," accessed August 1, 2018, *https://www.merriam-webster.com/ dictionary/ministry*.

28. BCP, 855.

29. BCP, 855.

30. Curiously enough, to me this is a type of "Donatism."

31. The "cover personas" of Superman and Supergirl.

32. Leonardo Boff and Clodovis Boff, *Introducing Liberation Theology*, trans. Paul Burns (Maryknoll, NY: Orbis Books, 1987), 4–5, originally published as *Como fazer teologia da libertação* (1986); *Como hacer teología de la liberación* (Bogotá, Colombia: Ediciones Paulinas, 1986), 13.

33. The congregation's "parish."

34. Boff and Boff, *Introducing Liberation*, 5; *Como hacer*, 13.

35. *https://www.episcopalchurch.org/ministries*, accessed July 12, 2019.

36. José Enrique Irizarry, "The Hispanic Challenge to the Diocese of New York," A Working Paper Prepared by The Committee on Mission and Strategy of the Hispanic Commission of the Diocese of New York, 5. Irizarry, "El Reto Hispano a la Diócesis de Nueva York," in *Reflexiones Teológicas: Modelos de Ministerios, Revista Teológica de la Comisión Hispana de la Diócesis de Nueva York: Publicación Cuatrimestral*, 2 no. 2 (Jan.–Jun. 1989), 2:11–23.

37. Juan M. C. Oliver, *Ripe Fields: The Promise and Challenge of Latino Ministry* (New York: Church Publishing, 2009).

38. Carla E. Roland Guzmán, review of *Ripe Fields: The Promise and Challenge of Latino Ministry* by Juan M. C. Oliver, *Anglican Theological Review* 93, no. 3 (Summer 2011): 732.

39. Isaías A. Rodríguez, *Historia del Ministerio Hispano en la Iglesia Episcopal: Logros, frustraciones y esperanzas* (Atlanta, GA: Sauters, Diocese of Atlanta, 2015).

40. Alberto L. García and John A. Nunes, *Wittenberg Meets the World: Reimagining the Reformation at the Margins* (Grand Rapids, MI: William B. Eerdmans Publishing, 2017).

# PART I

## (RE)FRAMING THE
## HISTORICAL CONTEXT*

n the spring of 1998, the Rev. Herbert Arrunátegui, after more than twenty
years as missioner for LATINX communities, issued a report, from the Office of
Hispanic Ministry of the Episcopal Church Center, titled *Hispanic Ministry:
Opportunity for Mission*.[1] I was in my second semester of my master of divinity
studies at the Church Divinity School of the Pacific in Berkeley, California. I did
not know Arrunátegui, and it would not be until 1999 that I became aware of
the Office of Hispanic Ministry, through Rev. Daniel Caballero's, the new missioner for LATINX communities, (re)gathering of LATINX seminarians. By that
time, I was deeply aware that I loved church history, that being queer was less of
an issue in the Church and in seminary than being Puerto Rican (Lambeth 1998
had not yet happened), that I was back on an ordination track after meeting with
the Rt. Rev. David Álvarez in Puerto Rico, and that I still had great optimism
about the Episcopal Church and our Anglican traditions. Over the subsequent
twenty years I have gained a different point of view of the Episcopal Church and
my place within it. My optimism has waned and my frustration increased at how
much farther away the Church seems from fulfilling its mission (#BCP855).

As a church historian, the question of how we got here is interesting and
important. I see the following aspects in this question: the actual chronological events that we can identify and describe, the analysis and interpretation
of those events, and the impact those events have now and how they are currently interpreted.

As I hope will become clear, some of the narratives presented are very contextual and limited, and others have permeated the whole history of these ministries. Sometimes that has to do with the epistemological privilege given to one type of narrative over another. Such privilege while intentionally suppressing voices creates gaps in the accepted records and narratives. As you can imagine, this history is not exhaustive given the space constraints and purpose of this book. A full-length monograph about this LATINX-specific church history has yet to be written; much remains to be done to "correct" our standard histories of the Episcopal Church, as they need to include this history and be challenged by it. No church history is exhaustive, and I am aware that the more information I include, the more gaps I create.

As a researcher, the challenge of finding one's creative voice while at the same time corroborating one's analysis and findings is fun. When I was writing my dissertation, I felt my stomach drop—more than once—when I would find something specific to my topic. I loved the validation of recognizing an argument that agreed with my analysis, while I also wondered if my findings were innovative enough. It came as a relief when I realized the corroborating material validated my particular contribution and approach as original. Nowadays, since I spend a lot of time researching, I find things that have to do with my narrow academic field, and my stomach still drops because now I realize that I failed to include it in my dissertation or was not aware of the study beforehand. In reading and researching for this book, my experience of finding writings that resonate has been much different. It is sad and frustrating that I'm not the first person reaching these conclusions, but that it has been said before and the Church has yet to wake up to the message.

I first came across the 1998 report in 2018, yet these words ring true today. I believe Arrunátegui's analysis is still relevant, although I would express the same points differently and adapt them to my own framework and experience and contemporary context. I wonder where we would be if we didn't find ourselves still trying to convince the institutional Church to change its approach to and treatment of LATINX people and communities twenty years later. For example, similar to what I will elaborate in this book, in 1998 Arrunátegui called for "Hispanic Ministry" to cease

> being an "appendix ministry," or merely a project or program, but rather a
> ministry of the whole church whether nationally, provincially or at a diocesan
> level. These factors are crucial for the future development of ministry among
> people of Hispanic heritage. Ministry with and among Hispanic people is in
> reality a part of the total/whole ministry of the Church and needs to be seen

and accepted as such. A food bank, a clothes chest, a clinic, tutoring children, or providing ESL classes, etc. are **"outreach projects or programs"** in which many congregations are involved; and because of the demographics of this country, the people often served may be Hispanic and therefore many times we believe ourselves to be involved in Hispanic ministry exclusively because of these **"projects."**

However, when we refer to Hispanic ministry in this paper we are referring to a group of people of Hispanic ancestry who gather together for worship, for teaching the faith as in Catechism classes or Bible study groups, and for celebration of the liturgy and music, as well as pastoral care and/or social outreach of those less fortunate. **Therefore, Hispanic Ministry is in essence the church in its mission and ministry conducting itself in another language and/or another culture—i.e., Spanish.**[2]

Notable here are the ideas of "appendix ministry," the understanding of "with and among" rather than "to," the differentiation between "ministry" and "outreach," and finally, Arrunátegui's insistence that this is not "other"—it is "mission and ministry."

Sadly, this was not the first time that Arrunátegui had tried to challenge the Church with these words and insight. Arrunátegui had been doing so for over twenty years. Rather than thinking of a twenty-year span of inaction by the Church (1998 to the present), we are really talking about more than forty years—more than my entire active adult involvement in the Episcopal Church. We know that the Church does not move swiftly, but doesn't it say something even more about the Church when it moves this slowly?

In this first half of the book I have divided the relevant chronological events and their respective analysis and interpretation into two time periods: prior to what I call the "Institutionalization of LATINX Ministries" in the Episcopal Church and after that institutionalization. There is an "in-between" excursus regarding the important changes with respect to Latin America that occurred at the 1958 and 1968 Lambeth Conferences.

The purpose of this section is to (re)frame the history of the Episcopal Church as it pertains to ministry to, with, and among LATINX people and communities by providing some key historical contexts that inform how we got to the "Institutionalization of LATINX Ministries." Ultimately, this historical section is meant to provide information that supports the work of dismantling the structures and legacies that have prevented the Episcopal Church from reaching its full potential in making the Episcopal Church a place where LATINX people and communities are not only "welcomed" of Mary and Elizabeth would have different emphases depending on whether they were written from an Anglican or Roman Catholic point of view. From a Roman Catholic perspective, Queen Mary was not "Bloody Mary." It would become even more complicated if we were to view the history of the Church of England through Puritan, Scottish Presbyterian, Irish Catholic, Quaker, or Methodist lenses.

Therefore, choosing a starting point for the framing of the history of the Episcopal Church's ministry to, with, and among LATINX people and communities is fraught with the possible conflation of chronology with the theology/ideology and the practical needs that have guided the current context of ministry to, with, or among LATINX people and communities, specifically since the late 1960s. Or, in other words, it may seem arbitrary to some!

Moreover, there are few types of histories that I will not deal with in depth, especially since each could be its own monograph. First, the history of the Episcopal Church in each place it has been or is currently located.[11] I will not delve into the specific history of the church in Puerto Rico, or Colombia, or México, or New Mexico, or Michigan. My focus is in the majority English-speaking United States context.

In significant ways, the way the Episcopal Church has functioned or functions in these other areas is different from the dynamics that occur in the United States given the differing majority/minority realities. The Episcopal Church's ministry in Spanish-speaking contexts or among people in majority Spanish-speaking countries is different than TEC's ministry in an English-language milieu while reaching out to LATINX people and communities, whether Spanish-speaking or not. In fact, where there is an area of similarity it may be in ministering to English-speaking people and communities in a majority Spanish-speaking context with the comparable majority/minority language dynamic in the United States. Yet the analogy quickly fails once this is analyzed in terms of class and power, and different reasons and histories for these communities being in Spanish-speaking countries.

Second, I will not delve deeply into the specific history of ministry, to, with, and among LATINX people and communities in each diocese of the Episcopal Church; I will only reference them as appropriate. Third, although there are key figures in the development of the Episcopal Church's LATINX ministry, and I do quote Arrunátegui at length and have relied on information from Rev. Anthony Guillén, the current missioner to LATINX communities, this history is ultimately an institutional history.

# Notes

\* Portions of this historical section were presented at "Theologizing *Latinamente*: A Conference on Latino Cultures, Liturgies, and Ethics," Seminary of the Southwest, Austin, TX, October 12, 2018; a related article is published in the November 2019 issue of the *Anglican Theological Review* 101, no. 4 (Nov. 2019): 603–24: "Dismantling the Discourses of the 'Black Legend' as They Still Function in The Episcopal Church: A Case against LATINX Ministries as a Program of the Church."

1. Herbert Arrunátegui, ed., *Hispanic Ministry: Opportunity for Mission*, 3rd ed. (New York: Office of Hispanic Ministry of the Episcopal Church Center, 2001).

2. Arrunátegui, *Hispanic Ministry*, 13–14.

3. Walter D. Mignolo and Catherine E. Walsh, *On Decoloniality: Concepts, Analytics, Praxis* (Durham, NC: Duke University Press, 2018), 113.

4. Aníbal Quijano, "Coloniality and Modernity/Rationality," *Cultural Studies* 21, nos. 2–3 (March/ May 2007): 168–78; Walter D. Mignolo, "Epistemic Disobedience and the Decolonial Option: A Manifesto," *Transmodernity: Journal of Peripheral Cultural Production of the Luso-Hispanic World* 1, no. 2 (2011): 44–66.

5. Néstor Medina, "A Different Tenor: A Decolonial Primer," *Toronto Journal of Theology* 32, no. 2 (2017): 279–87.

6. Mignolo and Walsh, *On Decoloniality*, 106.

7. José Enrique Irizarry, "The Hispanic Challenge to the Diocese of New York," A Working Paper Prepared by The Committee on Mission and Strategy of the Hispanic Commission of the Diocese of New York (New York, 1988), 5.

8. For a good starting point on understanding the historiography of the religious history of the United States, see Hjamil Martínez-Vázquez, *Made in the Margins: Latina/o Constructions of U.S. Religious History* (Waco, TX: Baylor University Press, 2013).

9. Justo L. González, *The Hispanic Ministry of the Episcopal Church in the Metropolitan Area of New York and Environs* (New York: Grants Board of Trinity Parish, 1985), 14.

10. "Libro de Oración Común: The 1662 Book of Common Prayer in Spanish," accessed February 9, 2019, *http://justus.anglican.org/resources/bcp/Spanish1662/index.htm*.

11. There are 111 dioceses in the United States, Colombia, the Dominican Republic, Ecuador, Haiti, Honduras, Puerto Rico, Taiwan, Venezuela, and the Virgin Islands. Also, the Convocation of Episcopal Churches in Europe, the Navajoland Area Mission, and since 2018 the Episcopal Church in Cuba. Previously, the Episcopal Church had a presence in México, Panamá, Nicaragua, Brazil, and Liberia.

# CHAPTER 1

# LATINX Ministries

## *Before Institutionalization*

## Some Key Chronological Points

Before getting to the institutionalization of the Episcopal Church's ministry to, with, and among LATINX people and communities, I present several conceptual chronological time frames that inform this institutionalization, as understood in this book. The first is a brief look at the colonial religious history of the United States. The second is the sixteenth century and the relationship between England and Spain. The third period is the initial forays of Protestant missionaries among LATINX people and communities in the nineteenth century, specifically the Southwest of the United States, Mexico, and places that where spoils of the war of 1898. The fourth period is the Episcopal Church's increased emphasis in what I call "hyphenated-ministries," which Rev. Robert W. Prichard refers to as "specialized ministries," in the decades surrounding the turn of, and into the middle of, the twentieth century. The last era is a brief presentation on Anglicanism's early presence in Latin America.

## Colonial Religious History of the United States

From the beginning, the Christian colonial religious history of the United States has had many religious expressions. All colonists and then immigrants brought their religion with them: English Anglicanism, Catholicism, and Puritanism; Dutch Reformed; Swiss-German Mennonites; French and Spanish Catholics; and so forth.

> All of these immigrants valued their own familiar and distinctive theology, social relationships and worship practices. So churches and ethnicities were linked from colonial days. . . . Most colonists arrived in the New World with church life thoroughly embedded in ethnic culture. Most nineteenth-century immigrants to the United States continued with some version of this pattern.[1]

Although adaptation was inevitable and necessary, notwithstanding the increasingly diverse and multicultural context of the United States, only slow inroads have been made. In fact, "[t]he European pattern of national churches within denominational traditions continued . . . well into the twentieth century."[2] Similarly, Rev. Justo L. González, PhD, describes this process also as one of power and insularity:

> At the parish level, each group of immigrants saw the church as a means to preserve its culture and traditions. . . . At the national level, there were power struggles between various groups, each wishing to be governed by a hierarchy that understood and represented it.[3]

In what is now the eastern United States, all these European groups not only brought their religious traditions and adapted them to their new context, but they also brought their conceptions about Africans and indigenous populations, and, as English and Dutch, brought their rivalries against the Spanish Empire. They brought their conviction that "Protestantism was superior to Catholicism," which meant they needed to protect the colonies from encroachment of French Catholics (North) and Spanish Catholics (South).[4] The English believed in their "racial" and religious superiority.

Even in missionary efforts, the objects of mission, whether indigenous or enslaved people, were encouraged to also have racial/ethnic-specific and segregated congregations.[5] This pattern in the United States was characterized by Milton Gordon "as structural pluralism, where there is a fair amount of acculturation along with continuing separation among peoples, particularly in the religious sphere." All this while recognizing that minoritized groups "push beyond structural pluralism into cultural pluralism."[6] "Structural pluralism," or the idea of ethnic-specific churches, is seen as an important lens in evangelization and has been termed by some the "Homogenous Unit Principle (HUP)." HUP, although a debated notion, "states that people respond most effectively to the gospel in ethnic or culturally specific churches. On the one hand this means that the gospel can be embodied in any human culture. But often it has been used as a way to reduce the gospel's claims on us and on the ethnocentricity of cultures." The inevitable question is whether these "cultural and human habits"[7] can be overcome as God invites us to a more diverse expression of God's reign and image.

In addition to the predilection of ethnic-specific churches, as the United States expanded its territory to include areas previously colonized by the Spanish and French, they also brought their rivalries with and views of those competing Roman Catholic countries. The westward expansion of the United States carried with it an ideology of providential favor, "progress and liberty," and "the superiority of the white race, the Protestant faith, and democratic government based on free enterprise"—all enshrined in the dogma of Manifest Destiny.[8]

Similarly, by the time of the Treaty of Guadalupe-Hidalgo (1848) and the western geographic expansion of the United States, there was a clear contra-distinction between the Anglo-Saxons and northern European groups against, what González characterizes as "the tyranny and Catholicism of southern European races, . . . therefore people of Nordic origin had the responsibility of civilizing the 'backward' races of the rest of the world."[9]

Rev. John L. Kater quotes Melina Rankin, who in 1857 established an evangelical society in Monterrey, Mexico, as saying that

> never in any land of Papal darkness has the Word of God shown itself to be "sharper than a two-edged sword" with more certainty than in Mexico—a country where the "mystery of iniquity" has so long prevailed, and that "Wicked" one has so boldly revealed himself—"even him whose coming has been after the working of Satan with all power and signs and lying wonders." "Popery," she affirmed, "cannot exist in the light of God's Word."[10]

Another contemporaneous example is provided by Rev. Juan Francisco Martínez:

> According to [Abiel Abbot] Livermore, the Mexicans of New Mexico and California were a "mongrel race" who had cheapened the "American birth-right" by being given American citizenship. These people had inherited the "cruelty, bigotry, and superstition that have marked the character of Span-iards from the earliest times."[11]

Sadly, this type of characterization was not unique to the nineteenth century. Here is an excerpt from a letter to the editor in response to a 2003 *Episcopal Life* article about ministry to, with, and among LATINX people and communities:

> I am greatly opposed to the new developments in the church. . . . Our Mexican neighbors are charming people, but it is their culture to be takers. I would not so much mind if the mothers would immerse their children in the language of their adopted country as have *all* our immigrants of foreign lands, who immediately take this step in fitting in to their adopted society. But, no, they do not really want to belong to us but to retain their flawed former culture.[12]

All of these are elements of the discourses of the "black legend."

## The Epic Battle between England and Spain in the Sixteenth Century

The above characterizations have roots in the sixteenth century, when there were discourses in England and the Netherlands that "systematically [denigrated] the character and achievements of the Spanish people."[13] The discursive characterization of Spain and Spaniards as "backward" can be traced, in part, to Spain having become the "other" to England. The discourses of the "black legend" not only construct Spain as "backward" but, more specifically, Spain and Spaniards as morally and racially "darker" than the rest of Europe, presumably because of their constitutive Muslim and Jewish heritage, as well as their treatment of indigenous populations in the newly encountered lands.[14]

I propose that the Episcopal Church, as a colonial and imperial church, uses "Anglicanism" and its "English" roots in a way that is consonant with the discourses of the so-called "black legend," and buys into and functions as if the discourses were real and continue to be real. Therefore, the failures in ministry with and among LATINX people and communities stem, in part, from the long-standing animosity between England and Spain, summarized by these pervasive discourses. The Episcopal Church treats LATINX people and communities as less than other communities, especially white ones, because those other communities are presumably linked to England or northern Europe, and LATINX people are linked to Spain. Moreover, the Episcopal Church functions with the following underlying notions, among others: LATINX people and communities are only recent immigrants—at most, first generation—poor and in need of material "help" from the church (thus can be ministered to), uneducated, solely Spanish-speaking, of a Roman Catholic background, at best hyphenated-Americans, and can only be objects of ministry rather than agents of ministry. In other words, LATINX people are less than because of their historical connection to their "Spanish origin," which is everything that England (thus Anglicanism and the Episcopal Church) is not! The Episcopal Church inherits this from Anglicanism and the United States inherits this from England and other imperial powers that saw themselves as better than the Spanish Empire.

As Kater indicates, for centuries, since "it was 'already Christian,'" in the case of Latin America, the presence of Roman Catholicism was seen as an exception card for any evangelistic effort.[15] If we are honest, how many times have you heard, "They are already Roman Catholic," when referring to LATINX people and communities in the United States? Thus, our story begins centuries ago; there is much still to be undone. In 1998 Arrunátegui was quoted saying:

The history of the Episcopal Church of Saint Matthew and Saint Timothy, where I serve, may reflect aspects of the change described by Prichard. The genealogy of the congregation is deeply connected to the history of New York City. As a city of many immigrants, generations born in the United States have, at times, had a desire to function increasingly in English, which may be seen as a divide between grandparents, their children, and their children.

The first congregation in the genealogy of Saint Matthew and Saint Timothy's was Zion English Lutheran Church. Organized at the end of the eighteenth century, it became part of the Episcopal Church within a decade. The congregation emerged from a desire to worship in English rather than German. As the name indicates, the congregation emerged because of a change in the vernacular, and thus in the language of worship, not by reaching out to a different constituency. Notwithstanding, I like the fact that this is the first church in Saint Matthew and Saint Timothy's genealogy, because its current bilingual configuration—English and Spanish—continues that legacy. At the end of the nineteenth century, another church in the genealogy of the Saint Matthew and Saint Timothy's had a relationship with St. Ann's Church for the Deaf. As the name indicates, St. Ann's was a specialized ministry founded in 1852 and is a congregation that continues to this day in the Diocese of New York. In 2018, Rt. Rev. Andrew M. L. Dietsche established the position of pastoral missioner to the deaf to support the whole diocese. The first missioner is recently ordained deacon Rev. Eugene Bourquin.

The model for specialized ministries has continued for more than a century. What began as an awareness of the needs of a community or communities and the social action by Episcopalians to ameliorate those needs became conflated with the notion that certain communities were characterized indelibly by certain needs and not capable of their own agency. This, in fact, diminishes the agency of certain people and communities. For example, in *Episcopalians and Race*, Rev. Gardiner H. Shattuck, Jr. explains how well-intentioned white liberals in the Episcopal Church minimized the role of black Episcopalians in the civil rights and urban work of the Church.

> Although [these white liberals] were fully committed to the goals of the civil rights movement, they tended to view African Americans more as beneficiaries of the denomination's largesse than as actors in their own right. . . . [This being the] epitome of white racial paternalism.[23]

Unfortunately, this pattern continues to be repeated today and holds true for other minoritized groups.

The history of the Episcopal Church and black Episcopalians is a history of the Church's inability to confront and deconstruct its racist history, legacy, and institutional structure. The institutional history of blacks in the Episcopal Church is relevant to the way in which ministries to, with, and among LATINX people and communities are approached and function. More work needs to be done that puts these two interrelated histories in dialogue to show how they speak to the overall historiography and underlying epistemological assumptions of the Church.

## The Sin of Racism[24]

The Episcopal Church knows that it is complicit in racism and a beneficiary of white privilege. In 2006, more than two hundred years after the ordination of Rev. Absalom Jones, the bishops of the Episcopal Church wrote a brief pastoral letter, echoing the letter of 1994, about "the pervasive sin that continues to plague our common life in the church and in our culture."[25] It was akin to the empty sentiment of "thoughts and prayers" after each mass shooting in the United States. At some point the General Convention and House of Bishops need to stop issuing statements and resolutions without changing the institutional racist structures that prevent the Church from moving forward and work in the fulfillment of the mission of the Church.[26] In the current triennium the Church is again being challenged to study and address this pervasive sin; yet, until we deal with the structural sin that permeates the Church, we will never talk ourselves out of racism.

For most of its history, if not all and to this day, the Episcopal Church has been a church of the elite; if not a church of the elite in the pews, it has nonetheless been an institution of the elite, and a white elite, at that. Furthermore, there have always been nonwhite people in the Church. Robert E. Hood, in his book *Social Teachings in the Episcopal Church* writes, "The Episcopal Church has struggled with the issue of race since blacks were first baptized at Jamestown, Virginia, in 1626."[27] The Anglican Church was present in Virginia from those early days. In 1667 the Virginia assembly passed a law that baptism did not alter the enslaved status of blacks.[28] Hood notes, paradoxically, "Still, the Episcopal Church was the first white church to undertake work among the slaves through the Society for the Propagation of the Gospel (SPG) in 1701."[29] Similar sentiments were expressed by others in Delaware in 1727. English Anglican Bishop Gibson reassured slave owners that they would not be disadvantaged by instructing and baptizing their slaves.[30] It is important to note they did not intend for blacks to have agency in the Church, but to solely be "subjects for conversion and assimilation."[31]

There are some instances in which blacks became leaders in the Church. Having left St. George's Methodist Church because of racial discrimination, Rev. Absalom Jones (1746–1818), the first black person to be ordained in the Episcopal Church, founded in Philadelphia what would become the first black Episcopal congregation (1794).[32] In my estimation, stories like that of Jones and the founding of the African Episcopal Church of Saint Thomas have more to do with the individuals themselves than with the institution doing something prophetic. Can we be proud of having Jones as part of our institutional history? No. Jones is worthy of praise because of what he achieved in spite of the Church. Our accolades are for Jones, not the Episcopal Church. At the time of Jones, did anything truly get better? In fact, it was not until 1854 that St. Thomas was allowed representation at their own diocesan convention.[33]

Robert J. Magliula, in the conclusion of a master's thesis on Jones, speaks to the power structures of the Church with respect to race. Blacks can be in the Episcopal Church so long as they stay in their place. Magliula writes:

> The racism of the Episcopal Church, though subtle at times, was blatant in its exclusion of St. Thomas Church from convention. They would tolerate their difference, their blackness, by controlling and containing it. This attitude would not be surprising for Jones or his congregation. They were not naïve. Their constitution stands as a counter-statement to this type of attitude. The convention statement simply reflects the pervasive attitude of society at large. Difference could be tolerated only if controlled. The same tendency holds true in the church and society today. The life of Jones makes apparent the fact that the struggle was not between good and bad people, but with a system, which was oppressive.[34]

Looking back from the first quarter of the twenty-first century, these statements ring true to me. The Church, while keeping ethnic ministries as programs, are tolerating difference and otherness while controlling and containing it; the Church continues to be an institution that is oppressive.

In my estimation, conditions were not any better at the end of the nineteenth century than they were in the times of Jones, leading me to ponder whether Jones could have achieved what he did after the abolition of slavery. I ask this considering the increased segregation, in society and Church after the Civil War. How then to understand the accomplishments of Rev. Alexander Crummel (1819–1898), or even the emergence of the Church in Liberia?[35] The battle was the same, yet the battleground was different. Jones was an abolitionist for the country. After the Civil War, those that had been abolitionists like Crummel needed to call the Church to task instead.

What did the denomination have to show for the work of the SPG and the Church's inability to take a strong stand against slavery? After emancipation, most blacks left the Episcopal Church. Not only did the Church not take a strong antislavery stand, it did nothing to open the structures of the Church so that blacks were emancipated in the Church. The Church settled back into its most comfortable state as a white institution. As with most white institutions in the United States, the Episcopal Church has never truly dealt with the legacy of slavery and the Civil War, which left it divided geographically, politically, theologically, and liturgically. The end of the Civil War required the Church to find some sort of comfortable "state" between North and South, and black and white. Unfortunately, that state was not characterized by integration, but by increased measures of segregation.

In July 1883, Southern bishops met in what would be called the "Sewanee Conference" and wrote a resolution for the upcoming General Convention. The failed resolution proposed separate and subordinate "missionary districts" within dioceses for black members. The proposed "Sewanee Canon" allowed for black leadership but gave no guarantee of diocesan representation. The stated reason for the proposed canon was the "peculiarity of the relations of the two races, one to the other, in our country, because of their history in the past and the hopes of the future, there is needed special legislation, appointing special agency and method for the ingathering of these wandering sheep into the fold of Christ."[36]

The use of "peculiarity" here must be understood as racist, given its common use in expressions to do with race. Magliula comments on this when the diocesan convention of Pennsylvania consented to a petition to ordain Jones from St. Thomas' Church, yet did not allow them to have representation at the convention.[37] For the Sewanee Canon, the only dissenting Southern bishop was the Rt. Rev. Richard Hooker Wilmer of Alabama, who expressed that separation by color "would be contrary to the mind of Christ, inconsistent with true Catholicity and detrimental to the best interest of all concerned, to provide any separate and independent organization or legislation for the peoples embraced within the communion of the Church."[38]

The outrage of black Episcopalians to the Sewanee Canon galvanized in the creation of the Conference of Church Workers Among Colored People (CCWACP) convened by Crummel in September 1883. In the years that followed, Crummel continued to speak to the Church's reticence to respond to prophetic words:

> The further it is pushed, the more evident becomes the fact of some past mistakes in its working, and of hesitating doubt as to its future development. The

work, then, from its very nature, calls now and then for revision, for the rectification of imperfect plans, and the creation of new and more popular modes of operation.[39]

Yet the Church continually balks at "revision and rectification." The treatment of black Episcopalians after the Civil War maintained the same mission-field mentality it had held since the time of missionary efforts by the SPG and continues even to this day.

Sharing the episcopate has never been a strong suit of the Episcopal Church and its white male bishops. The first black bishops were elected for oversees missionary districts: Rt. Rev. James Theodore Holly for Haiti in 1874 and Rt. Rev. Samuel David Ferguson for Liberia in 1885. Vestiges of the sentiments of the Sewanee Canon continued to permeate the Church through the first half of the twentieth century, as can be seen in the 1918 consecration of two black bishops, Suffragans for Colored Work in Arkansas and North Carolina: Rt. Rev. Edward Thomas Demby and Henry Beard Delany, respectively. As suffragans, they could not impinge on the diocesan bishop's authority nor have real authority to conduct their work in the very communities they served.[40] Black bishops for the Church, not just black communities, were elected beginning in the 1960s; the first of that generation was Rt. Rev. John M. Burgess, elected suffragan for Massachusetts in 1962.

Rather than being an agent of change, the Episcopal Church has changed only when outside forces have been too great to ignore. Rev. Harold T. Lewis, in assessing the Episcopal Church's reactionary involvement in civil rights movements, writes:

> Thus, the society to whose drumbeat the Church had consistently marched was once again dictating the Episcopal Church's moral and social agenda. . . . The Episcopal Church, at various stages in its history, has been prodded into action not by a particular group, but by a social condition so prevalent that to ignore it would render the Church liable to allegations of imperviousness.[41]

After World War I, in response to urban riots, the Episcopal Church began the slow process—yet to be completed—of addressing the social injustices that were inflicted on blacks, rather than solely seeing blacks as "subjects for education and conversion."[42] The discursive journey toward the equal treatment of blacks was always confronted by the continued reality of their treatment. In other words, blacks are still not treated equally in the Church. The words found in reports, such as one to the 1934 General Convention, do not match the reality. The report insisted that the Negro in the Episcopal Church be regarded without distinction in the church's liturgical and spiritual life. . . . [Yet,] said little about including blacks in the church's political offices and social institutions. . . . Furthermore, the Commission treated the issue of race as a leadership issue for the church rather than a theological and ethical issue for church teachings.[43]

Treating it as a leadership issue absolves the institution and places the burden on the minoritized community. The reality was that segregation in society continued to be mirrored in the Church. To address this, in 1943, Executive Council created the staff position of executive secretary for Negro work, a precursor to what in the 1970s would become part of Ethnic Ministries.[44] In 1946, the Bi-racial Joint Commission replaced the CCWACP. Importantly, Lewis reminds us that integration, however, was not the goal; "Negro work was still seen as a separate and distinct activity,"[45] and continues to hold true for all ethnic ministries today.[46] Again, the Church's discourse was increasingly about the "intrinsic worth of every person," the idea of equal opportunity, and the stance that "the Negro must be treated as a man and citizen, and not as a Negro."[47]

Alongside major historical events in the United States, the 1950s seemed promising regarding race relations in the Episcopal Church. Segregation in the Seminary of the University of the South (Sewanee) ended in September 1953.[48] The Brown vs. Board of Education decision in 1954 pushed the Episcopal Church to shift from a tacit endorsement of continued segregation to a view that called for integration.[49] Even the General Convention of 1955 was moved from Houston, Texas, to Hawaii "because the Bishop of Texas . . . could not ensure integrated hotels for all the church's delegates." In 1956, the Church's staff issued "Guiding Principles for Negro Work," which called for full integration in worship and all institutional aspects of the Church.

The Episcopal Church's ambivalence toward segregation and slow awakening to civil rights can also be seen in its sluggishly changing stance regarding civil disobedience, which was condemned as late as the General Convention of 1958.[50] The Church did not have a clear understanding of why there could be liberation movements that advocated the use of disobedience, or even violence, as necessary. It could be said that still holds true today. In Hood's assessment, "The bishops' posture during these turbulent years was support for the existing rule of law without asking the critical questions about its implementation and enforcement by white authorities in the racially segregated society of the South."[51]

At that time, integration became the principal stance of the Church about race relations. Reflective of this attitude was the formation of the Episcopal Society for Cultural and Racial Unity (ESCRU) in 1959. The guiding tone for

ESCRU was encompassed by Psalm 133:1: "How good and pleasant it is, when brethren live together in unity!"[52]

ESCRU emerged at the same time as sit-in protests were taking place in the South.[53] The sit-ins and other protests were very important because they addressed issues around segregation and public accommodations.[54] Although changing, the Church in the 1940s and 1950s was not of one mind. In 1960 the Church, invoking William Temple's dictum on democracy and the rights of minoritized communities, finally provided a "theological rationale for civil disobedience against unjust laws."[55] Furthermore, the 1963 Whitsunday sermon by Presiding Bishop Arthur C. Lichtenburger was essential and prophetic, especially the oft cited reproach of the Church that included the statement, "discrimination within the Body of the Church itself is an intolerable scandal."[56] This lead to the passing, in 1964, of a General Convention resolution which stated:

> Every communicant or baptized member of this Church shall be entitled to equal rights and status in any Parish or Mission thereof. He shall not be excluded from the worship or the Sacraments of the Church, nor from parochial membership because of race, color, or ethnic origin.[57]

Just as it was clear that economic justice, self-determination, and self-respect—in short, dignity and agency—were sought, the challenges that black Episcopalians experienced continued in the 1960s, when the values of integration as espoused by ESCRU had still not afforded "access" to the power structures of the Church, and black Episcopalians, ordained and lay, continued to be on the sidelines; even sidelined from the very decision-making for work done in their own communities.[58] That's white liberalism for you.

In 1964, Rt. Rev. John Hines, bishop of Texas, was elected as presiding bishop. Hines understood that "whites were as much a part of the problem as the structures and prejudices that oppressed and marginalized people living in urban ghettos."[59] Yet, the work that needed to be done could not be the sole effort of white Episcopalians. The very structure of the Church, amid the fight for racial justice, continued to exclude its own constituency: black Episcopalians.

We still live in a time in which our society has yet to fully grapple with the sin of racism. The Church is still complicit in this sin. Our Church continues to find its center in whiteness; everything else is a problem or a challenge to be dealt with. As is the case with LATINX people today, the "black challenge" after emancipation could have been conceived as one of numbers and demographics; yet the Church saw itself as so different from blacks that it could never wrap its head around what to do with blacks in their midst. There have been prophetic moments, for sure, but the structures of the Church are still the same.

There are two related characteristics of institutions that threaten the advancement of the Church and its mission. One is the way institutions manage to perpetuate themselves and look out for their own self-preservation. The other is the way institutions tend to settle back into their most comfortable state. Questions arise:

- How does the Episcopal Church guarantee its own preservation in ways that are not mission-centered?
- What is the Episcopal Church's most comfortable state? (State is markedly different than stasis—equilibrium, balance, or via media—although stasis also implies lack of movement.)
- Is the Church's legacy of hyphenated-ministry related to its inability to overcome its racist history and heritage?
- Are we still trying to live up to the Church that stood against the segregationist intentions of the "Sewanee Conference"?

Many of the books cited in this section are silent on LATINX people and communities, yet many of the observations regarding blacks in the Episcopal Church hold true for these communities as well. The reality is that there is much to learn about the Episcopal Church's treatment of LATINX people and communities through the matrix of race and the history of the Church with respect to its black membership and the sin of racism. I am deeply aware, as well, that I am silent about many other communities, especially Asian and Indigenous people and communities. These communities are also contained/controlled under the ethnic ministries umbrella in the Church.

## Protestantism in Latin America

I will continue interweaving the history of black Episcopalians and racism in the next chapter when I pick up the story in 1967. Here is a brief interlude with another piece of the puzzle: Anglicanism and the Episcopal Church in Latin America from the nineteenth century through the 1960s.

Since the sixteenth century there have been Protestants in Latin America. Until the beginning of the nineteenth century, and independence and liberal movements, most of them were individuals with a sporadic presence of small groups—immigrants and foreign business communities. Through the influence of trade, foreign churches were allowed to exist, although "permission for wealthy foreign Protestants to worship in public was one thing. Allowing the local Spanish and Portuguese people to form such congregations was quite another."[60] By the turn of the twentieth century there were enough Protestants, albeit still immigrants or foreign nationals, that it "helped open the doors for local citizens to become Protestants."[61] The inroads made by Pentecostalism shortly after what became known as the Azusa Street revival circa 1906 is but one example of the propitiousness of the time.

Yet, this would be a missed opportunity for Anglicans, who still saw Latin America as a Roman Catholic continent. Rev. Isaías A. Rodríguez describes this in the following way: "when plans were being formulated for the 1910 World Missionary Conference, to be held in Edinburgh, Scotland, the Anglican Communion insisted on the need to exclude missionary work in Latin America because it was considered a Roman Catholic territory."[62]

Two decades later there was enough of a Protestant presence that a prominent writer, and Protestant, Gonzalo Báez Camargo (a.k.a. Pedro Gringoire) wrote in 1930:

> To those who do not look at it, or who do not pay close attention, Hispanic America would seem to be profoundly and totally Catholic. Those who are professional users of the cliché and the common place, and the lyric proclaimers of a retrograde Latin America, would seek to prove that we Hispanic Americans are inevitably Catholic by birth, by tradition, and by geography. Or they would say that at least we ought to be, using no better reasons than our affinity of Catholicism with our blood, our routines, and our environment. However, a more attentive examination, without having to go too deep shows the complexity of the religious phenomenon in Hispanic America.[63]

It is easy to see here the criticism of "black legend" discourses. In fact, there was somewhat of an Anglican/Episcopal presence for over two centuries. What had not happened was the "contextualization of Anglicanism" that would emerge in the second half of the twentieth century.[64] Until this contextualization, the Anglican/Episcopal presence was primarily in the form of chaplaincies to English-speaking Anglicans/Episcopalians working in Latin American countries, both a chosen and imposed "ethnocentric focus,"[65] which could be seen, in part, as related to the discourses of the so-called "black legend." For example, David Rock cites Rt. Rev. Edward Every, who "lamented that South Americans would never match British standards for 'moral reasons: our sturdiness of character and racial superiority—the superiority of our civilization.'"[66]

To be fair, this was not a shared sentiment by all South America Missionary Society (SAMS) missionaries; a small minority already had a contextualized sense of ministry.[67] Rock argues that Anglicanism in South America through the First World War "drew closer to potential Latin American constituencies if only as yet to a limited degree. . . . [It remained] an ethnically exclusive institution serving the interests of the British commercial and investment economies."[68]

Models and foci of ministry increasingly changed after the Second World War. More specifically, after deliberations at the Lambeth Conference of 1958, "contemporary Latin American Anglicanism can be said to have been born— or re-born." Latin America finally was seen as a "field for evangelistic work" and was no longer "the neglected continent."[69] This was a shift "from earlier reticence on the part of many Anglicans to actively evangelize among even nominally Roman Catholic peoples."[70] The exception to this were Anglican missionaries that worked among non-Christian indigenous communities.

> In obedience to the Divine Commission, we have been ministering for nearly two centuries in Latin America in the name of the Lord. Today, in response to a fresh prompting of the Holy Spirit, we are renewing our dedication to this ministry on a larger scale in the face of drastic and dynamic changes in Latin America, through which the Lord of the whole earth is as ever working out His purposes.[71]

One response in the Episcopal Church was the creation of Province IX in 1964.[72]

Until the 1960s, the primary missionary effort was by the Church of England and the Episcopal Church, joined, at times, by the Anglican Churches of Canada and Australia. After 1958, there was a clear goal of autonomous national churches. The first to achieve this was the Anglican Episcopal Church of Brazil in 1965, Igreja Episcopal Anglicana do Brasil (IEAB).

As a result of the 1958 Lambeth Conference resolution, the first Latin America consultation dealing with this region as a missionary field was in 1963 (Cuernavaca, México). Participating in the consultation were "two dozen bishops, theologians, and missionary leaders with the Archbishop of York as chairman." There were representatives from the United States, Canada, West Indies, Latin America, and missionary societies.[73] The primary objective that emerged in the Cuernavaca consultation was "the development of Latin American churches, expressive of the genius of their own countries and of the unity of the Anglican Communion, and ministering alike to the needs of their societies [and the wider world]."[74] Of concern were programs in theological education, the development of strong congregations, encouragement of autonomy, and autochthonous structures.[75] One of the ways the issue of theological education was addressed was by the opening, in Puerto Rico, of the Episcopal Seminary of the Caribbean in 1961. A second consultation occurred in 1966 in Sao Paolo, Brazil, and a third in May 1968, in Paraguay, ahead of that year's Lambeth Conference.

For the better part of the second half of the twentieth century, Anglican/ Episcopal churches in Latin America have dealt with the reality of autonomy and contextualization, including issues surrounding Anglican identity.[76] A desire to have an Anglican Identity that was not colonial—or imposed. In the Paraguay meeting, "one thing was clear: although there would be variety among Anglican churches throughout Latin America, they did not want them to look like colonial enterprises." This was articulated in 1968 as the desire to have "an indigenous Church in each nation of the region, priority to be given to urban evangelism, a special emphasis on ministry in institutions of higher education, and ecumenical witness."[77] In 1987, the Latin American Anglican Congress (CALA) described Latin American Anglicanism "as a way of participating in history, reflecting local tradition and looking for an ecclesial indigenization incarnate in each country."[78] At this congress, Rt. Rev. James Ottley, bishop of Panamá, encouraged the "listening to and supporting the poor and marginalized . . . and urged Anglicans in Latin America to participate in the empowerment of the poor majorities, giving up the paternalism all too often associated with social ministry in favour of encouraging local initiative and creativity at the grassroots level."[79]

The contextualization of Anglicanism and the emergence of autonomous churches also led to a change in the language of worship from English to Spanish, which had a profound impact on Anglicans in Latin American dioceses that traced their roots to the English-speaking West Indian Anglican traditions. Akin to other areas of the Global South, the story of Latin American Anglicanism grapples with the tension of an English-speaking (Anglophile) heritage and a local, autonomous and contextual tradition often expressed in Spanish or Portuguese. In other words, this is a "struggle to become Churches deeply rooted in their own context—claiming and exercising the right to their own theological method, their own interpretations of scripture, their own structures and liturgies and music, and their own engagement with the deep realities of their homeland—goes on."[80]

This process is also affected by a variety of Communion-wide tensions: evangelical and Anglo-Catholic traditions, racism, the ordination and leadership of women, and homosexuality. The 1998 Lambeth Statements and the consent to the election of Rt. Rev. Gene Robinson in 2003 proved to be a watershed moment in relationships across the global Anglican Communion.[81]

Notwithstanding the late institutional work described above or how historically unorganized and sparse ministry was with local populations, given robust commercial networks and interests, the Episcopal Church still had a presence in other Spanish-speaking contexts since the late nineteenth century. The Church of England also made some inroads into Spanish-speaking countries or colonies in the nineteenth century, including Puerto Rico beginning in the 1870s.[82] In fact, however reticent, the Episcopal Church has had a presence, eventually formal, from Mexico through Central America beyond the Panama Canal to Colombia, Venezuela, and Ecuador, as well as Cuba, Haiti, Dominican Republic, and Puerto Rico.

International jurisdictions, mostly missionary districts, associated with the Episcopal Church in the first half of the twentieth century generally had non-native bishops. Through the 1960s there had been a dozen bishops of LATINX or Spanish descent to exercise ministry as bishops in Latin America and the United States: four in Mexico, three in Brazil, two in Puerto Rico, one in Costa Rica, one in Cuba, and one elected (not appointed) in the continental United States.[83] This last one, Rt. Rev. Victor Rivera, originally from Puerto Rico, was the first to have been elected locally through a diocesan process rather than by the House of Bishops. Rivera was elected as the third bishop of the Diocese of San Joaquin. Although a Spaniard, I count as the first LATINX Rt. Rev. Manuel Ferrando, who was appointed in 1924—the first and only (to date) suffragan for Puerto Rico. The first diocesan LATINX bishop was Rt. Rev. Efraín Salinas y Velasco, suffragan for México in 1931 and diocesan in 1934.[84]

The areas where local bishops—LATINX, Brazilian, and Spanish-speaking—were first appointed coincide with the areas where churches were able to become autonomous or develop quicker contextual ministries: Brazil (1965), Cuba (1966), Costa Rica (1967/1978), Puerto Rico (autonomous 1978–2002), and México (1995). This may also be part of the maturity and rootedness in these places. Of note is that the bishops of San Joaquin and Costa Rica were also Puerto Rican and had family members who later became bishops.[85]

There were broader movements that informed the evangelistic work by Anglican/Episcopal churches that included the broad effects of the Second Vatican Council, the emergence and maturity of liberation theologies with base communities and the "preferential option for the poor," the reaction against coloniality and apartheid, and the embrace of civil rights movements. The political realities and struggles of the various countries from the late 1960s forward also influenced the type of Anglicanism that matured in various areas and its relationship to the local context.[86]

## Diocese of New York Prior to 1967: A Brief Interlude

As seen in the brief presentation on Latin America, evangelism efforts prior to 1958 were not strategic or coordinated, and those being ministered to were not necessarily the local Spanish-speaking populations. Prior to the

institutionalization of ministry to, with, and among LATINX people and communities in the United States, many of the efforts were for the most part sparse,
sporadic, and based on individual efforts.

Although the Episcopal Church did not have a nineteenth-century presence in the Southwest of the United States, there were occasional examples of
missionary forays. There were also isolated examples of congregations in other
areas of the United States. The first Spanish Episcopal church was in Manhattan, New York. The Church of Santiago was founded in May 1866 by a group
of twelve including former Roman Catholic priests Rev. Dr. Hawks and Rev. A.
H. de Mora and incorporated into the Diocese of New York in November 1867.
Rev. de Mora was the first rector, although quickly succeeded by Rev. Henry C.
Riley (1835–1904) from Chile, and in 1969 by Rev. Joaquín de Palma (1823–
1884), a Cuban-born priest. This community never had its own building and
over the years worshipped at various Episcopal churches: Trinity Chapel, the
old French Church de St. Esprit on West Twenty-Second Street and Church of
the Annunciation on West Fourteenth Street.[87] De Palma also did pastoral work
in Brooklyn. De Palma often described the congregation as a missionary effort
not only for the thousands of Spanish speakers already in New York City, but
given the reality of back and forth travel to Spanish-speaking countries these
committed Protestants were missionaries as well. As noted before, some emerging churches in México in the second half of the nineteenth century looked to
build relationships with the Episcopal Church in the United States. There were
other early Episcopal connections between Florida and Cuba.

In the twentieth century, some sustained/continuous ministries began
to emerge. In a part of Manhattan, in the Diocese of New York, with a
long-standing history of Puerto Rican migration, the oldest continuously functioning ministry to LATINX people and communities is that of St. Edward the
Martyr in *El Barrio*. This ministry corresponded with the presence and needs
of the large Puerto Rican community in the vicinity of the church. The first
services in Spanish were offered in late 1938 by Rev. Cintrón.[88] From this
community, decades later, came the first Spanish-speaking permanent deacon
in this diocese.[89] Ministry to the Puerto Rican community was further institutionalized in various churches in New York City during the 1950s.

The connections between the Episcopal Church in New York and that of
Puerto Rico were unavoidable. The Rt. Rev. Charles F. Boynton, the fourth
appointed bishop of Puerto Rico (co-adjutor 1944; diocesan 1948–1950),
became suffragan bishop of the Diocese of New York in 1951. In 1952, St.
Edward the Martyr was declared a mission of the diocese and had a Puerto
Rican priest on staff, Rev. Esteban Reus García, who had worked with Bishop

Boynton in Puerto Rico.[90] Another priest-in-charge of St. Edward the Martyr, from 1955 to 1961, the Rev. Donald F. Gowe had worked in Ponce, Puerto Rico, for eighteen years as priest, physician, and medical director of (Old) St. Luke's Hospital.[91]

The second-oldest continuous ministry to LATINX people and communities in the Diocese of New York is the church I serve, the Church of Saint Matthew and Saint Timothy on Manhattan's Upper West Side. Worship in Spanish was offered beginning with the tenure of Rev. James A. Gusweller in 1956. Again, given the demographics of New York City at the time, that community was largely Puerto Rican. The neighborhood of the Church was very different from what it is today. West 84th Street was voted the worst block in New York City in 1961.

Gusweller wrestled the highest civil authorities of the city to improve the life of the residents of the parish, fighting against slumlords and corrupt police, and was admired by many. Gusweller effected great change in the lives of people in the neighborhood. A July 1961 *New York Times* article enumerates the problems of the block: "Drunkenness. Unemployment. Gambling. Overcrowding. Prostitution. Homosexuality. Narcotics addiction. Despair."[92] Gusweller continued this work even after the loss of the church facility by fire in December 1965. The current church building was dedicated in 1969 and was built not just for worship but also for community programs. Gusweller was integral in the development of settlement houses and the next rector, Rev. Jay H. Gordon, continued that legacy through the programs offered by the St. Matthew and St. Timothy's Neighborhood Center, a separate nonprofit that was under the control of the Church until 2005.[93]

## A Watershed Year: 1968

In order to more narrowly focus on the institutional history within the Episcopal Church in chapter 2, I will briefly present here a broader context of the momentous late 1960s and 1970s. In a collection of photographs, *The Guardian* newspaper characterized 1968 as "the year that changed history."[94] The number of political and social events of great consequence in 1968 are staggering. Assassinations (MLK and RFK), invasion (Czechoslovakia by Russia), the Apollo 8 mission, the Vietnam War, the election of Richard Nixon, a North Korean–United States standoff. Similarly, there were key moments for the Church. In May, six Latin-American Anglican bishops met in Paraguay and formulated a resolution for the upcoming Lambeth gathering. The resolution presented at the 1968 Lambeth Conference read:

Resolution 64: The Role of the Anglican Communion—The Anglican Presence in Latin America

The Conference records its conviction that, in the light of the growing importance of Latin America and the rapid social, economic, political, and religious changes there taking place, there is an urgent need for an increasing Christian witness and involvement in which the Anglican Churches must make their unique and full contribution.

The Conference rejoices in the growth and indigenisation of Anglican witness in Latin America since Lambeth 1958 and in the increased participation and awareness of some parts of the Anglican Communion, and hopes that this participation and interest will extend to the whole Anglican Communion.

The Conference recommends that the member Churches of the Anglican Communion should place prominent emphasis upon Latin America in their missionary education, their prayers, and their commitment to the world mission, as outlined in the document entitled "The Anglican Communion and Latin America."[95]

In August, Latin American Roman Catholic bishops met in Medellín, Colombia, and articulated collectively the foundations of what would be termed "liberation theology." The rapid social, economic, political, and religious changes in Latin America were described as follows in the Medellín document:

Remembering. . . . the characteristics of the present moment of our countries in the social order. From an objective point of view: a situation of underdevelopment, betrayed by massive phenomena of marginality, alienation and poverty, and conditioned, ultimately, by structures of economic, political and cultural dependence with respect to the industrialized metropolis that hold the monopoly of technology and science (neo-colonialism). [And,] from the subjective point of view: the awareness of this same situation, which provokes in large sectors of the Latin American population attitudes of protest and aspirations of liberation, development and social justice.[96]

It is clear, then, to see that the emergence of liberation theologies was not disconnected from the broader political, cultural, and ecclesial contexts of Latin American countries. Furthermore, it can be seen as the praxis of the spirit of the Second Vatican Council (1962–1965).

I present these aspects of liberation theology here, because, as I show, there was a disconnect between these prophetic ideas and the actual institutionalized work of the Episcopal Church with respect to LATINX ministries in the United States. An outline of liberation theology and the importance of *comunidades eclesiales de base* (CEBs) is found in the texts related to the Second Episcopal Conference of Latin American Bishops (RC) that met in 1968 in Medellín, Colombia, and the Third Episcopal Conference of Latin American Bishops that met in 1979 in Puebla, Mexico. For the purposes here, it is important to consider whether the Episcopal Church missed its own opportunity to enact liberative theologies that would have been among the people and would have, in part, shown our own preferential option for the poor. On the other hand, we can ask how does the spirit of ecclesial base communities speak to the Episcopal Church today?

As will become clear, the works of Rev. Herbert Arrunátegui, González, and future bishop Rt. Rev. Wilfrido Ramos Orench from the mid-1980s are clear on the place liberation theologies should have as the *loci theologici* of the Episcopal Church in its ministry with and among LATINX people and communities. This foundational piece was missed by the overemphasis on "outreach" under the guise of ministry "to" these communities. If the Church had prophetically welcomed the vast influx of Latin American people that came in the 1970s and 1980s—many fleeing from oppressive regimes, war, and violence—the Church would have perhaps welcomed people versed in the model of base communities with its emphasis on education, agency, and evangelism. This could have created the fundamental theological structure of many new congregations with LATINX people. If the Church had prophetically welcomed people from Central America, and gained a deeper understanding of the situation in what today is termed the northern triangle, the Episcopal Church would more likely have the infrastructure and knowledge base to address the fear-mongering that is being perpetuated by the current situation at the southern border of the United States. Inaction in the 1970s and 1980s prevented the Church from engaging in a liberative praxis into the twenty-first century: a missed opportunity with decades-long consequences.

From an Episcopal point of view, the emergence in the United States of liberation theologies, which account for different minority/majority contexts and oppressive models, has been gravely delayed. The Episcopal Church did not respond to the Southwest United States in the second half of the nineteenth century, nor to the vast immigration waves starting in the 1970s. Now, decades later, in the Episcopal Church, we have yet to engage in an "Anglican/ Episcopal" translation/interpretation of liberation theologies in Latin America to liberation theologies in the United States. Moreover, our work is not only disconnected from liberation theologies, but also from the gospel and the mission of the Church by its obstinate focus on demographics and marketing, which continues to allow the Church to control and contain LATINX people and communities.

## Defining Comunidades Eclesiales de Base (CEBs)

In order to stay within the United States geographical confines in chapter 2, although I am getting ahead in the chronology of this book, base communities may be the key to congregational development in the Episcopal Church. And since these developed out of the Medellín and Puebla meetings, I will introduce them here. Liberation theologies respond to the need of marginalized communities. Base communities are units that help people create agency in their own liberation. These theologies emerged in countries where these marginalized and oppressed communities represented most of the population. Thus, minority groups in power were agents of oppression for the majority.

Outside of the Episcopal Church, since the 1970s in the United States, liberation theologies have been adapted to offer models of liberation for marginalized communities that are, in fact, minority communities. Both approaches aim to liberate those that are oppressed by giving them agency in determining their future. Many theologians who write from the LATINX perspective have developed important lenses though which to understand the experience of LATINX people in the United States. This theologizing from a LATINX perspective has been limited in the Episcopal Church. Put differently, Anglicanism from the LATINX perspective is just, finally, on the cusp of emerging. As a way of introduction, CEBs are defined as

> a local, or of similar background, community, that corresponds to the reality of a homogenous group, and that it has an affectionate treatment among its members. In consequence, the pastoral work of the Church is oriented toward the transformation of these communities into "God's family," starting by being present in them as yeast in a nucleus, albeit small, that constitutes a community of faith, hope, and charity. The Christian base community is the first and fundamental ecclesial nucleus, that ought, in its own level, to be responsible for the richness and expansion of the faith, as well as in worship, which is its expression. The community is the initial cell of the ecclesial structure, and focus of evangelizations, and currently essential factor in human development and advancement.[97]

The task, which I further discuss in chapter 5, is to begin to imagine the ways CEBs can work in Episcopal Churches committed to ministry among LATINX people and communities and other marginalized groups.

CEBs are places of sacramental community with the deep purpose of liberation—a liberation that leads to agency and the full realization of all people. They are supportive liberative groups that function within a sacramental context and ultimately aim to share the Good News of God in Christ with others. They seek the formation of the greatest number of ecclesial communities in parishes, especially in rural areas or among those marginalized in urban areas. They are communities based on the Word of God, and made, when possible, in the Eucharistic celebration, always in communion with the bishop and under their auspices.

> The community is formed as its members cultivate a sense of belonging—a sense of "us"—that leads them in solidarity toward a common mission and to accomplish active, conscientious, and fruitful participation in the liturgical life and communal coexistence. It is imperative to live as community, inculcating a common objective: to attain salvation through living out faith and love.[98]

This brief introduction gives us a glimpse into the radical transformative power of base communities. As will be seen in chapter 2 regarding the General Convention Special Program and with the following story about Archbishop Oscar A. Romero, a barrier to the Episcopal Church showing solidarity with oppressed communities through embracing base communities is that it calls for the sharing and relinquishing of power and resources, and this is above all a fundamental threat to the institutional Church.

In the November 2018 issue of *The Atlantic* there was an article about the canonization of Archbishop Oscar A. Romero in October 2018, a process that developed over close to four decades. March 24, 1980. Why did the canonization take so long for this martyr?

> Nearly four decades later, Pope Francis has declared Óscar Romero a saint. An archbishop murdered at the altar, in the manner of England's Thomas Becket, would seem a simple case. But Romero's path to canonization . . . has been tortuous. More than 100,000 people thronged the cathedral plaza in San Salvador for Romero's funeral, and yet the papal representative to El Salvador and all but one of the country's remaining bishops stayed away, cowed by the regime and the Vatican alike. As the murdered man became the face of a "people's Catholicism" in Latin America—a saint by acclamation—Pope

John Paul II and Pope Benedict XVI slow-walked the official canonization process, precisely because of what the archbishop represented.[99]

It is clear to me that the issues of power and control of resources are at the center of the Church's inability to be prophetic and focus on its reconciling mission. In the following chapter, I focus on the institutionalization of LATINX Ministries and the impact and history of the short-lived General Convention Special Program.

As we will soon see, once ministry to LATINX people and communities was institutionalized, it became a program of the Church. As a program of the Church, it cannot go the way of liberation theologies, because in essence that would require its own liberation and unshackling as a program, and full participation of nonwhite people in the Church. Therefore, the Church continues to control and contain the potential, possibilities, and promise LATINX people and communities have. Liberation theologies are a threat to institutions and institutions will look to restrain its message, as seen in the history of the canonization of Archbishop Romero. Chapter 2, then, is the story of how this institutionalization happened and how it functions today in the Church. Put differently, will the Church see the "Hispanic challenge as an occasion for rejoicing, while we allow that the poor and disenfranchised of this country to evangelize us"?[100]

## Notes

1. Mark Lau Branson and Juan Francisco Martínez, *Churches, Cultures and Leadership: A Practical Theology of Congregations and Ethnicities* (Downers Grove, IL: InterVarsity Press, 2011), 13. Accessed February 9, 2019. ProQuest Ebook Central.

2. Branson and Martínez, *Churches,* 14.

3. Justo L. González, *The Story of Christianity, Volume II: The Reformation to the Present Day,* rev. ed. (New York: Harper Collins, 2010), 324.

4. González, *Story,* 329.

5. See Branson and Martínez, *Churches,* 15.

6. Branson and Martínez, *Churches,* 16. They cite Milton Gordon, *Assimilation in American Life: The Role of Race, Religion, and National Origins* (New York: Oxford University Press, 1964).

7. Branson and Martínez, *Churches,* 17.

8. González, *Story,* 336.

9. González, *Story,* 337.

10. John L. Kater, "Through a Glass Darkly: The Episcopal Church's Responses to the Mexican *Iglesia De Jesús* 1864–1904," *Anglican and Episcopal History* 85, no. 2 (June 2016): 197.

11. Juan Francisco Martínez, *Sea la luz: The Making of Mexican Protestantism in the American Southwest, 1829–1900* (Denton: University of North Texas, 2006), 14. Taken from Abiel Abbot Livermore, *The War with Mexico Reviewed* (Boston, MA: American Peace Society, 1850). "By introducing into the rights and privileges of American citizens a horde of 'outside barbarians,' the mongrel races of New Mexico and California, they have cheapened the American birthright, and loosened the very cornerstone in our fabric of Federal Freedom," 177.

12. Alice June Lindsay (Tucson, AZ), letter to the editor in *Episcopal Life,* 14, no. 6 (June 2003): 29; in response to Victor Ruiz, "Opportunity Knocks," *Episcopal Life* 14, no. 2 (February 2003): 1, 6–9. In turn, another letter, by Evelyn Morales, responded to the June letter, "Immigrant Success Story: Church Biggest Influence in Family's Acculturation," *Episcopal Life* 14, no. 8 (November 2003): 28.

13. William S. Maltby, *The Black Legend in England: The Development of Anti-Spanish Sentiment, 1558–1660* (Durham, NC: Duke University Press, 1971), 3; see also Maltby, *The Rise and Fall of the Spanish Empire* (New York: Palgrave Macmillan, 2009), 117.

14. A good start to understand the discourses of the "black legend" is A. Gordon Kinder, *Creation of the Black Legend: Literary Contributions of Spanish Protestant Exiles* (Valletta, Malta: Midsea Books, 1996); María DeGuzmán, *Spain's Long Shadow: The Black Legend, Off-Whiteness, and Anglo-American Empire* (Minneapolis: University of Minnesota Press, 2005); Barbara Fuchs, *Exotic Nation: Maurophilia and the Construction of Early Modern Spain* (Philadelphia: University of Pennsylvania Press, 2009); Margaret R. Greer, Walter D. Mignolo, and Maureen Quilligan, eds., *Rereading the Black Legend: The Discourses of Religious and Racial Difference in the Renaissance Empires* (Chicago: University of Chicago Press, 2007); and Carla E. Roland "Why Can't They Be More Like Us?: Baptism and Conversion in Sixteenth-Century Spain" (PhD diss., University of Exeter, 2017).

15. John L. Kater, "At Home in Latin America: Anglicanism in a New Context," *Anglican and Episcopal History* 57, no. 1 (1988): 5

16. ENS, "The Future of Hispanic Ministry," March 19, 1998 [98-2119].

17. John L. Kater, "Latin American Anglicanism in the Twentieth Century," in *Oxford History of Anglicanism, Volume V: Global Anglicanism, c. 1910–2000,* ed. William L. Sachs (Oxford, England: Oxford University Press, 2018), 98.

18. The Iglesia de Jesús was a non–Roman Catholic church that emerged in Mexico after Benito Juárez guaranteed religious freedom in 1859. See Kater, "Through a Glass Darkly," 194. This Iglesia de Jesús is different than the one I reference for Puerto Rico. For a collection of digitized and transcribed documents on Anglicanism in Mexico see *http://anglicanhistory.org/mx/*. Many of the articles have been uploaded through the efforts of Wayne Kempton, archivist for the Episcopal Diocese of New York.

19. Kater, "Through a Glass Darkly," 225. Emphasis in original.

20. BCP, 877: "The Historic Episcopate, locally adapted in the methods of its administration to the varying needs of the nations and peoples called of God into the unity of His Church."

21. Robert W. Prichard, *A History of the Episcopal Church. [Complete Through the 78th General Convention]*, 3rd rev ed. (New York: Morehouse Publishing, 2014), 178; *A History of the Episcopal Church*, rev. ed. (Harrisburg, PA: Morehouse Publishing, 1999), 173, 175.

22. Prichard, *History* (rev. ed.), 180; and Prichard, *History* (3rd rev. ed.), chapter 8, section "Special Ministries and Segregation."

23. Gardiner H. Shattuck Jr., *Episcopalians and Race: Civil War to Civil Rights* (Lexington: University of Kentucky Press, 2000), 170–71.

24. ENS, "House of Bishops Pastoral Letter on Sin of Racism, March 1994," April 21, 1994 [94090].

25. ENS, "The Sin of Racism: A Call to Covenant," March 21, 2006 [032206-3-A].

26. Pastoral letters of 1994 and 2006. Some General Convention resolutions are 1979-B052 and D083; 1991-A199; 1994-A047, D132, and D136; 2000-A047 and B049. More broadly: a search of the term "Racism" in the Acts of Convention in the digital Episcopal Archives yields sixty-nine resolutions.

27. Robert E. Hood, *Social Teachings in the Episcopal Church* (Harrisburg, PA: Morehouse Publishing, 1990), 102. I recognize that this statement is technically anachronistic.

28. Prichard, *History* (3rd rev. ed.), 23; Rebecca Anne Goetz, *The Baptism of Early Virginia: How Christianity Created Race* (Baltimore, MD: Johns Hopkins University Press, 2012), 97–98.

29. Hood, *Social Teachings*, 103.

30. Robert J. Magliula, "Absalom Jones: A Biographical Study" (MDiv thesis, Union Theological Seminary, 1982). Magliula cites Faith Vibert, "The Society for the Propagation of the Gospel in Foreign Parts: Its Work for the Negroes in North America before 1783," *Journal of Negro History* 18, no. 2 (April 1933): 208.

31. Hood, *Social Teachings*, 110.

32. Jones was ordained as deacon on August 6, 1795, by the Rt. Rev. William White, and as priest in 1804. The Episcopal Church celebrates Jones with a lesser feast on February 13.

33. Magliula, "Absalom Jones," 52.

34. Magliula, "Absalom Jones," 63.

35. Crummel was ordained in the 1840s in Massachusetts. Crummel was the first black person to graduate from Cambridge University and spent twenty years in Liberia before returning to the United States in the 1870s.

36. "An Account of a Conference Held at Sewanee, Tenn., July 25 to 28, 1883, on the Relation of the Church to the Coloured People," in *Documents of Witness: A History of the Episcopal Church, 1782–1985*, ed. Don S. Armentrout and Robert Bloak Slocum (New York: Church Publishing, 2000), document #45, 196–200. From *Journal of General Convention*, 1883, 595–600.

37. Magliula, "Absalom Jones," 52–53.

38. Richard Hooker Wilmer, "Contrary to the Mind of Christ," in Armentrout and Slocum, *Documents of Witness,* document #46, 200–201.

39. Alexander Crummell, "Modifications of Methods of Work Among the Colored People, 1897," in Armentrout and Slocum, *Documents of Witness*, document #35, 152–55.

40. Shattuck, Episcopalians and Race, 24–25.

41. Harold T. Lewis, *Yet With A Steady Beat: The African American Struggle for Recognition in the Episcopal Church* (Valley Forge, PA: Trinity Press International, 1996), 161, 162, 163.

42. Hood, *Social Teachings*, 111.

43. Hood, *Social Teachings*, 112.

44. Hood, *Social Teachings*, 113; Lewis, *Yet With A Steady Beat*, 139.

45. Lewis, *Yet With A Steady Beat*, 141; Hood, *Social Teachings*, 114.

46. The black staff position was suspended between 1967 and 1973 and then reinstated when the section for Ethnic Ministries was created in 1973.

47. Hood, *Social Teachings*, 114.

48. Donald S. Armentrout, "A Documentary History of the Integration Crisis at The School of Theology of The University of the South, 1951–1953," *Sewanee Theological Review* 46, no. 2 (Easter 2003): 172–212. Woody Register, "'The Real Issue': A Reconsideration of the Turbulent Desegregation of Sewanee's School of Theology, 1952–1953, Part I," posted on December 11, 2018, in *Meridiana: The Blog for the Sewanee Project on Slavery, Race, and Reconciliation, http://meridiana. sewanee.edu/2018/12/11/the-real-issue-a-reconsideration-of-the-turbulent-desegregation-of-sewanees-school-of-theology-1952-1953-part-i/.* Accessed February 28, 2019. Register makes a very good observation about the use of the term "crisis" to describe the events at Sewanee, since this gives privilege to the white point of view (epistemology).

49. Lewis, *Yet With A Steady Beat*, 148. Shattuck, *Episcopalians and Race*, 67–68.

50. Shattuck, *Episcopalians and Race*, 159.

51. Hood, *Social Teachings*, 117.

52. Shattuck, *Episcopalians and Race*, 98, 101.

53. Shattuck, *Episcopalians and Race*, 102.

54. Hood, *Social Teachings*, 109, 119.

55. Hood, *Social Teachings*, 119. Shattuck, *Episcopalians and Race*, 102–3: "It can be known whether Democracy is true to its own root principle . . . by the careful regard which it pays to the rights of minorities."

56. As quoted in Lewis, *Yet With A Steady Beat*, 149; Harold T. Lewis, "By Schisms Rent Asunder? American Anglicanism on the Eve of the Millennium," in *A New Conversation: Essays on the Future of Theology and the Episcopal Church,* ed. Robert Boak Slocum (New York: Church Publishing, 1999), 7; Shattuck, *Episcopalians and Race*, 150.

57. As quoted in Hood, *Social Teachings*, 121. This resolution had failed to pass in 1949.

58. Shattuck, *Episcopalians and Race*, 166.

59. Hood, *Social Teachings*, 122–23. Shattuck, *Episcopalians and Race*, 171.

60. H. McKennie Goodpasture, ed., *Cross and Sword: An Eyewitness History of Christianity in Latin America* (Maryknoll, NY: Orbis Books, 1989), 150, 183.

61. Goodpasture, *Cross and Sword*, 183.

62. Isaías A. Rodríguez, "A Reflection Concerning Anglicanism and the Hispanic World," in *Our Ninety-Five Theses: 500 Years after the Reformation* (Orlando, FL: Asociación para la Educación Teológica Hispana, 2016) Kindle edition. The author shared a word document of this article with me.

63. Gonzalo Baéz Camargo, a Methodist, wrote *Hacia la renovación religiosa en Hispano-América* (Mexico City: Casa Unida de Publicaciones, 1930), 9. As translated in *Nuestra Fe: A Latin American Church History Sourcebook*, ed. Justo L. González and Ondina E. González (Nashville, TN: Abingdon Press, 2014), 159.

64. Phrase used by Kater, "Latin American Anglicanism," 114.

65. As quoted by David Rock, "Anglicanism in Latin America, 1810–1918," in *Oxford History of Anglicanism, Volume III: Partisan Anglicanism and its Global Expansion, 1829–c.1914*, ed. Rowan Strong (Oxford, England: Oxford University Press, 2017), 367. In Argentina there was a treaty in 1825 that "prohibited contact between the Anglican Church and the Latin American population," 386. See also Kater, "Latin American Anglicanism," 114. At times other types of prohibitions also existed, according to Prichard, *History* (rev. ed.), 226. N28: since 1910 Mexican "law forbade foreign clergy from serving native congregations."

66. Rock, "Anglicanism in Latin America," 384–85. Appointed bishop of the Falkland Islands in 1902.

67. For example, William Case Morris. See Rock, "Anglicanism in Latin America," 386.

68. Rock, "Anglicanism in Latin American," 387.

69. Stephen F. Bayne, Jr., "Latin American Mission," *The Living Church* 146 (February 24, 1963): 18.

70. Kater, "Latin American Anglicanism," 103; Prichard, *History* (rev. ed.), 219. See also Kater, "At Home," 5, 9.

71. Quoted in Bayne, "Latin American Mission," 18.

72. Prichard, *History* (rev. ed.), 219.

73. Bayne, "Latin American Mission," 19.

74. Kater, "Latin American Anglicanism," 103; see also Humberto Maiztegui, "Homosexuality and the Bible in the Anglican Church of the Southern Cone of America," in *Other Voices, Other Worlds: The Global Church Speaks Out on Homosexuality*, ed. Terry Brown (London, England: Darton, Longman and Todd, Ltd., 2006), 246–47.

75. Kater, "Latin American Anglicanism," 103; see also "At Home," 13; SPCK, *The Anglican Communion and Latin America: The Report of a Consultation at Sao Paulo, Brazil, 24–28 January 1966* (London, England: SPCK, 1966), iv, 3.

76. Kater, "Latin American Anglicanism," 105, 114. This is in part a response to Article 34 of the Thirty-Nine Articles that enshrines in our tradition the idea of "autonomy."

77. Kater, "Latin American Anglicanism," 106; see also "At Home," 13; SPCK, *Anglican Communion and Latin America*, 2.

78. Maiztegui, "Homosexuality," 247.

79. Kater, "Latin American Anglicanism," 112.

80. Kater, "Latin American Anglicanism," 122.

81. This is particularly true for the churches of the Province of the Southern Cone (renamed in 2014 as The Anglican Church of South America and currently includes Argentina, Bolivia, Paraguay, Peru, and Uruguay); also for churches/provinces that have affiliated themselves with GAFCON (Global Anglican Future Conference) or similarly for ACNA (Anglican Church of North America). See Maiztegui, "Homosexuality."

82. From the Anglican Province of the West Indies, Churches in Ponce (Santísima Trinidad) and Vieques (Todos los Santos).

83. México: Rt. Rev. Efraín Salinas y Velasco (1931/1934); Rt. Rev. José G. Saucedo (1958); Rt. Rev. Leonardo Romero (1964); Rt. Rev. Melchor Saucedo (1964); Brazil: Rt. Rev. Athalicio T Pithan (1940);

Rt. Rev. Louis Melcher (1948); Rt. Rev. Plínio Lauer Simões (1956); Puerto Rico: Rt. Rev. Manuel Ferrando (1923); Rt. Rev. Francisco Reus-Froylán (1964); Cuba: Rt. Rev. Romualdo González-Agueros (1961); Costa Rica: Rt. Rev. José A. Ramos Orench (1969); Diocese of San Joaquin: Rt. Rev. Victor Rivera (Elected 1968). Since the 1970s there have been more LATINX bishops consecrated.

84. Although the Iglesia de Jesús in México was not yet a missionary district of the Episcopal Church, it must be considered that the first LATINX bishop was in fact the Rt. Rev. Henry (Enrique) Chauncey Riley originally from Chile and ordained in the Diocese of New York, and consecrated on June 24, 1979 at Trinity Church, Pittsburgh, for the Valley of Mexico, where he had been since 1869. Riley, briefly was rector of the Church of Santiago in New York City in 1866.

85. Rev. Bavi Edna "Nedi" Rivera (2005-Olympia); Rev. Wilfredo Ramos Orench (2000-Connecticut).

86. See SPCK, *Anglican Communion and Latin America*, 4.

87. "Death of the Rev. Joaquin de Palma," *The New York Times*, July 14, 1884, accessed June 22, 2018. "The Church of Santiago," *The Church Journal*, March 30, 1870. See also Juan Ramón de la Paz, "La Historia de la Iglesia Episcopal de Cuba" (STM Thesis, Seminario Evangélico de Teología de Matanzas, Cuba, 2001). See also *The Centennial History of the Protestant Episcopal Church in the Diocese of New York, 1785–1885* (New York: Diocese of New York, Committee on Historical Publications D. Appleton, 1886), 210, 339, 281 notes Rev. De Palma's ministry. To my knowledge the Church of Santiago had five rectors with de Palma's ministry being the longest. The congregation discontinued services by 1894. My gratitude to Wayne Kempton, Diocese of New York's archivist for access to archival material about the Church of Santiago. It would take more than a century for another "LATINX" rector in the diocese, and the first female LATINX rector 150 years later, in 2010. In 2019, there is still only one LATINX rector in the Diocese of New York.

88. Judith Mason, "History of the Church of St. Edward the Martyr" (New York: n.p., 1982), 8. My gratitude to Wayne Kempton, Diocese of New York's archivist for access to this resource.

89. Rev. John Morelli was the first Spanish-speaking deacon ordained in the Diocese of New York. Since then, four other Spanish-speaking deacons, also of Puerto Rican descent, have been ordained: Rev. Nydia Flores (St. Augustine's, 1997); Rev. George Díaz (St. Mark's in the Bowery, 2005); Rev. Luis A. Rivera (Congregation of Our Savior at the Cathedral of St. John the Divine, 2015); Rev. Pedro L. Rodríguez (St. James' Fordham, 2018); currently Chris Colón is a postulant to the permanent diaconate (St. Mary in the Highlands).

90. Rev. Reus García was the father of Rt. Rev. Francisco Reus Froylán, first Puerto Rican bishop (appointed by House of Bishops) of the Diocese of Puerto Rico. Mason, "History of the Church of St. Edward the Martyr," 11.

91. Mason, "History of the Church of St. Edward the Martyr," 13; Rivera Torres, *Documentos*, 61.

92. McCandlish Phillips, "A 'Trouble' Block Feeds on Misery. Drunkenness, Joblessness and Addiction Thrive on West 84th Street. 'Ghetto of Sociopaths.' Minister Blames Bias and 'Criminal Landlords'— Urges City to Act." *The New York Times*, Friday, July 7, 1961, 27, *https://timesmachine.nytimes.com/times machine/1961/07/07/97678424.html?action=click&contentCollection=Archives&module=LedeAsset& region=ArchiveBody&pgtype=article&pageNumber=27*; "Rev. James A. Gusweller," WNYC Public Radio interview, December 28, 1958, Audio courtesy of the NYC Municipal Archives (LT8289); WNYC Collection (72125), *https://www.wnyc.org/story/rev-james-a-gusweller/*.

93. In 1964 there were two extensive articles on the ministry of Gusweller published in the Profile section of *The New Yorker Magazine*: see Robert Rice, "Church-I," *The New Yorker Magazine* 40, no. 24 (August 1, 1964): 41–60; and, "Church-II," *The New Yorker Magazine* 40, no. 25 (August 8, 1964): 37–73.

94. "1968: The Year That Changed History," *The Guardian*, January 17, 2008, *https://www.theguardian. com/observer/gallery/2008/jan/17/1*.

95. Resolution 64 from "Lambeth Conference Resolutions Archive 1968," *http://www.anglicancommunion.org/media/127743/1968.pdf*.

96. Consejo Episcopal Latinoamericano (CELAM), *La iglesia en la actual transformación de América Latina a la luz del Concilio II*, 3rd ed. (Santafé de Bogotá, Colombia: Secretariado General del CELAM, 1969), Section X.1.2. (My translation). "Recordemos, una vez más, las características del

momento actual de nuestros pueblos en el orden social: desde el punto de vista objetivo, una situación de subdesarrollo, delatada por fenómenos masivos de marginalidad, alienación y pobreza, y condicionada, en última instancia, por estructuras de dependencia económica, política y cultural con respecto a las metrópolis industrializadas que detentan el monopolio de la tecnología y de la ciencia <neo-colonialismo>. Desde el punto de vista subjetivo, la toma de conciencia de esta misma situación, que provoca en amplios sectores de la población latinoamericana actitudes de protesta y aspiraciones de liberación, desarrollo y justicia social." Hereafter *Documento de Medellín*.

97. CELAM, *Documento de Medellín*, Section XV.3.10. (My translation). ". . . una comunidad local o ambiental, que corresponda a la realidad de un grupo homogéneo, y que tenga una dimensión tal que permita el trato personal fraterno entre sus miembros. Por consiguiente, el esfuerzo pastoral de la Iglesia debe estar orientado a la transformación de esas comunidades en "familia de Dios", comenzando por hacerse presente en ellas como fermento mediante un núcleo, aunque sea pequeño, que constituya una comunidad de fe, de esperanza y de caridad. La comunidad cristiana de base es así el primero y fundamental núcleo eclesial, que debe, en su propio nivel, responsabilizarse de la riqueza y expansión de la fe, como también del culto que es su expresión. Ella es, pues, célula inicial de estructuración eclesial, y foco de la evangelización, y actualmente factor primordial de promoción humana y desarrollo."

98. CELAM, *Documento de Medellín*, Section VI.3.13. (My translation). "La comunidad se formará en la medida en que sus miembros tengan un sentido de pertenencia <de "nosotros"> que los lleve a ser solidarios en una misión común, y logren una participación activa, consciente y fructuosa en la vida litúrgica y en la convivencia comunitaria. Para ello es menester hacerlos vivir como comunidad, inculcándoles un objetivo común: el de alcanzar la salvación mediante la vivencia de la fe y del amor."

99. Paul Elie, "The Martyr and the Pope," *The Atlantic,* November 2018, 62–68.

100. "Un Manifesto Hispano," in *Reflexiones Teológicas: Modelos de Ministerios, Revista Teológica de la Comisión Hispana de la Diócesis de Nueva York* 2 no. 2 (Jan.–Jun. 1989), 37.

people and communities, as well as antiracism initiatives, are approached by the Episcopal Church to this day: as programs and not as integral to all aspects of the Church. Again, the Episcopal Church's continued inability to confront racism is still a stumbling block, not just for black Episcopalians, but for all minoritized ethnic and racial groups in the Church. One eventual reaction to Hines and the GCSP was the election of Rt. Rev. John M. Allin as presiding bishop.

Rev. John L. Kater reminds us that the immediate impetuses of the GCSP were the 1967 summer riots when:

> new and bitter violence erupted in ghettos across the United States, with the worst toll of death and destruction recorded in Newark and Detroit. Moved by the rioting [Hines] made several private trips into nearby ghetto areas accompanied by black members of the Executive Council staff. Described by one of those who accompanied him as "one of the few whites in the Church who were both sensitive to the issue and also had some power," Hines became convinced that the Church must make some substantial institutional response to the urban crisis.[3]

As a result, Hines created an ad-hoc committee in preparation for the upcoming 1967 General Convention. The presiding bishop's understanding of the plight of the urban poor echoed what Sterling Tucker of the Urban League in Washington explained (as summarized by Rev. Gardiner H. Shattuck Jr.): "[T]he white leadership of the major American denominations needed to do more than merely wring their hands and decry the existence of poverty; they also needed 'to take a stand in the streets' with the poor and place the management of the ghetto in the hands of those who lived there."

Furthermore, as Shattuck continues, the report of Hines's ad-hoc committee indicated that

> whatever funds the Episcopal Church committed to alleviating poverty should be given away entirely "without strings" to representatives of the poor people themselves. Although this process might be an extremely painful one for white church members, who would have to relinquish control over their money, it would help purge whites of racism and simultaneously empower African Americans.[4]

Entering the 1967 General Convention, Hines understood how radical the GCSP would be since it called for the relinquishing of resources and power. Without hesitation, Hines brought the issue front and center at the Convention in Seattle, requesting $3 million annually.

Among its aims will be the bringing of peoples in ghettos into areas of decision making by which their destiny is influenced. It will encourage the use of political and economic power to support justice and self-determination for all . . . [by providing money] to community organizations involved in the betterment of depressed urban areas, and under the control of those who are largely both black and poor, that their power for self-determination may be increased and their dignity restored.[5]

Presiding Bishop Hines requested the funds for "assisting the poor to organize themselves so that they may stand on their own feet, rise out of their degradation, and have a full share in determining their own destiny."[6]

Approved by large majorities of both houses, all these aims were consonant with the articulation of ideas in contemporaneous liberation theologies in Latin America. In David L. Holmes's estimation, "under [Hines's] leadership, the Episcopal Church became more involved in social concerns than at any time in its history." This led to the quest for social and economic justice.[7]

There are several inauspicious things about this beginning that were inherently counter to the aims of Hines through the GCSP. Among them was the fact that although the Church funded the GCSP, it did not require Church structures to change one bit; in other words, it functioned within the same faulty structures. Bishops and others might have been upset at how resources were being spent, but the GCSP did not lead to structural changes; in fact, it ultimately further cemented them. Thus, even if giving the money away "without strings" was hard, it did not change anything for the Church itself. Second, Hines envisioned bringing people in the urban "ghettos into areas of decision making," yet black Episcopalians, lay and ordained, were mostly excluded from this "decision making" inside the Church and were generally not included in the implementation of the GCSP in communities where they already had a presence.[8]

Hines called the Church to a special convention, rare in its history, in early September 1969 to discuss the progress of the GCSP. By then many Episcopalians, many of whom did not understand the relationship of racism and power, had become increasingly uneasy with and fearful of the perceived ties of the GCSP to Black Power and Black Nationalist movements and began trying to limit the funding and structure of the GCSP.[9] To intensify matters, the Black Manifesto (which came out of a gathering of the Black Economic Development Conference) demanding $500 million dollars in reparations from white Christian churches and Jewish synagogues had been delivered to the Episcopal Church Center on May 1, 1969, and had been rejected by the Executive Council a few weeks later.

This brief presentation on the GCSP barely scratches the surface of the various issues informing the action and inaction of the Church. Below, I will bring in more details about the emergence of institutional structures for ministry to, with, and among LATINX people and communities, and interweave with more about the GCSP. In the meantime, it is important to note many other momentous events through the mid-1970s: the founding of the Union of Black Episcopalians (UBE, 1968),[17] women's leadership as deputies and through ordination, prayer-book revision, declarations on homosexuality. In 1973 the "Black Desk" was re-established and, in addition to the new "Hispanic Desk," one for Asian Americans and another for indigenous people and communities were created. These together are today's "Ethnic Ministries" of the Episcopal Church.

I should note here two important issues of nomenclature: first the denoting of Black Desk or Hispanic Desk is problematic because it nominalizes "Black" and "Hispanic," thus othering these groups. Second, the denoting of "desks" in itself is revealing, given that they were called "desks" because the various missioners and their staff did not have individual offices; they all worked together in one office and had a particular "desk" assigned.[18] In essence, those in ethnic ministries were relegated to a bullpen and not to starting roles.

Sadly, as was the case with the GCSP, the need was there, the intention was good, and the work was, in part, prophetic; yet as things became institutionalized, ministry to, with, and among LATINX people and communities became another program of the Church. Programs are tools on the shelf that can be used or not. Once something is a program, a "thing" reified and packaged, it can be purchased—bought into, or not. It is sinful for certain groups of people in this Church to be treated as commodities.

## 1967 to Today: Momentous Changes; Irreversible Changes

As UBE moved parallel to the GCSP and ESCRU, the GCSP was not the only program that addressed LATINX people and communities. There were other efforts and signs of institutionalization in the 1960s and some functioned parallel to, or supplanted, the GCSP.[19] Yet, as evidenced by the importance I have given to the history of the GCSP, its fate and the ministry to, with, and among LATINX people and communities are intertwined. Therefore, as we continue the chronology of ministry to, with, and among LATINX people and communities, I will weave in an analysis in places where I think the demise of the GCSP impacted these ministries in the Episcopal Church.

In 1971 the staff position of "Hispanic Officer" was established as part of the Executive Council. The position was held by Rev. Jorge Juan Rivera Torres of Puerto Rico until 1973. In 1972, Executive Council approved the charter of a fifteen-member National Commission on Hispanic Affairs (NCHA), later called National Commission on Hispanic Ministries (NCHM).[20] It was established as a continuing and expanding program of the Church with the following purposes: fulfill the needs and aspirations of LATINX people and communities and to serve the ministry among LATINX peoples within and outside the Church.[21]

The Commission was tasked to review the Church's work and involvement with LATINX peoples, and recommend developments, plans, and programs to Council and future General Conventions. Moreover, the Commission, with specific guidelines, was directed to review and approve grant requests originating from the Commission and make recommendations concerning all other grants affecting LATINX peoples. The Commission needed to stimulate the development of the process of *concientización*—putting the burden of educating the majority Church on the minoritized community. Finally, they were instructed to encourage the involvement of local congregations and community groups in this work.[22] All of these things are still mandates of the current LATINX ministries office.

From the beginning, ministry to, with, and among LATINX people and communities was envisioned and functioned as a "program." The Commission, therefore, only made recommendations for grants, but were not decision makers. Furthermore, LATINX people themselves were burdened with educating the Church, albeit in language that echoes the ideals of liberation theologies: the idea of *concientización* or "consciousness raising." I ask, though, was this *concientización* ever meant to actually change the institution of the Church and lead to a liberative fulfillment of its mission?

From 1968 to 1973 the GCSP, under the leadership of Mr. Leon Modeste, made grants totaling more than seven million dollars. The 1973 General Convention underfunded the GCSP ($650,000 for the triennium) and renamed it Community Action and Human Development, which Hood analyzes as "intending to weaken its independence." Some emphasis was shifted to much smaller grant programs "for racial and ethnic minorities [which] were combined under the title *Mission Service and Strategy*" (MSS) ($2 million for the triennium).[23] The seeming change in structure guaranteed greater control. These changes were described in an unpublished report:

> The General Convention of the Episcopal Church . . . established a new staff section to coordinate the church's program and grant concerns for racial and ethnic minorities. The new section, to be known as Mission Service

and Strategy, will coordinate the program and administrative grants currently managed by the GCSP, the National Committee on Indian Work, the National Commission on Hispanic Affairs, and new work to be undertaken with Black and Asian Episcopalians.[24]

In fact, outreach was now "restricted to work and mission under direct Episcopal auspices."[25] The GCSP officially ended at the Executive Council meeting of December 1973, just months before Hines's resignation.

A more benign history of the GCSP would see the continuing work among minoritized groups as a positive action by the Episcopal Church. To be clear, my presentation on the GCSP is not an assessment on whether it was the best way to achieve the goals of empowerment and liberation by the Episcopal Church. What I am aiming to show is that the Church has a way of using power and resources that inherently goes against those goals, and benefits from keeping black, LATINX, and other minoritized people on the margins through the sole focus on programs of the Church; through their commodification.

No one has ever accused the Church for being too consistent in its policies. But while certain programs were being abolished, shifted, or defunded, the Executive Council, in 1972, set a priority of minority empowerment "as the major objective in mission and ministry."[26] All this jockeying and continual restructuring took place without actually changing the structures of the Church. In 1973 the General Convention approved a plan that both created what we now understand as "Ethnic Ministries"—ministries with Black, LATINX, Asian, and Native American people—and, in essence, terminated the GCSP. Structurally, "Ethnic Ministries" was put into one budget item of the Church.[27] The restored "Black Desk" that had been vacant since 1967 also assured that the funding of this work would be under the greater control of the Church—it would be further institutionalized and made into programs across the board.

I want to highlight the incongruency or hypocrisy here. The demise of the GCSP uncovered a Church and its leadership that wanted to control resources and access to power. We do this all the time. Imagine how many times you've heard something to the effect of, "I don't give money to (fill in the blank), because I don't want them to spend it on (fill in the blank)." In short, I don't want my resources wasted or used in a way I don't agree with. This control clashes with the right of the receiving person to do with their life what they choose, affording others the same dignity we want afforded to ourselves. Somewhere in the middle is a position that resources problems and challenges appropriately, while prophetically surrendering control, and believing that, if we have done the discernment, God can direct the rest. We may not always get it right, but we cannot start from a place that is wrong and think things will change toward the good.

## The Demise of the GCSP

One overt reason for the demise of the GCSP was that some in the Episcopal Church frowned upon the stances and tactics of some of the grassroots organizations that received grants. Some were associated with late 1960s Black Power and Black Nationalism movements. Many in the Episcopal Church were unable (or unwilling) to understand the dynamics of power and racism, as well as their own role in those dynamics. Kater concludes a 1979 article on the GCSP with a sad assessment regarding this era:

> But if the Church's flirtation with self-determination came to an end, it is not yet clear if its traditional social theology has survived. There is little internal impetus towards a substantive role for the Episcopal Church in the social crisis of the present; and it is uncertain whether another period of rapid change would call forth a reassertion of the theological categories of the past for interpreting the Church's place in society. In the meantime, the challenge lives on in a world where justice and unity and freedom remain unfulfilled dreams.[28]

It is my belief that this sentiment still holds true four decades later. From another angle, Rev. Harold T. Lewis describes the nature of the Episcopal Church:

> As "a non-prophet organization," that is to say, a body that has not historically, set a moral example for the nation to follow but rather has taken its lead from the mores of the nation with which it has had a unique, symbiotic relationship since they both came into existence, almost simultaneously, at the end of the eighteenth century.[29]

Grants from the GCSP were wide-ranging, including grassroots organizations that sought to empower Latinx people and communities, and like the attitude toward some black organizations, many in the Church also frowned on the ideology and work of some of those Latinx groups. The GCSP aimed to address issues of poverty and agency in many minoritized communities. Yet the Church was also dealing with other civil rights issues at the same time. None of these were occurring in a vacuum or isolated from greater events and one another.

For more than a century, parallel to efforts of abolition, desegregation, and civil rights were efforts to allow women to exercise leadership in the Church, which can be seen in the history of deaconesses in the Church (1889 General Convention), the first female priest (Florence Li Tim-Oi ordained in 1944), the first woman ordained as deacon (Phyllis Edwards in 1965), women lay readers and chalice bearers (General Convention 1969), women's participation as deputies to General Convention (1970), the Philadelphia Eleven in 1974 and the subsequent battle to validate their ordination, and the approval of women's ordination at the 1976 General Convention.[30] The first ordination, to the priesthood, after the 1976 change in the ordination canon was that of Rev. Jacqueline Means (January 1, 1977).

As happened with women in leadership in the Church, I believe that some of the issues that contributed to the demise of the GCSP have to do with power and distribution of resources. One of the threats posed by women's ordination to the priesthood was that it meant women could access the episcopacy and thus the power structures of the Church. As a matter of fact, when the vote came through in 1976, some of those ordained in 1974 understood, upon reflection, that a change in the Canon was not enough.

> It was no longer enough for them to be allowed access to the church. They wanted a drastic change within the institution regarding its sexist treatment of all women, whether those women wanted to be priests or not. Many wanted changes in the liturgy to reflect a much broader image of God. And some voiced deep concern over a group, predominantly a male group, voting on their validity to their calling.[31]

The General Convention's validation of their priesthoods can be seen as being indicative of symbolic change rather than substantive change . . . "allowing a few token women into the sacred male ranks of priesthood and episcopacy, but maintaining its misogynist posture toward lay women at the grass roots level."[32]

The issue of gender was not resolved in 1976, and many of these women were not able to fully exercise their ordained ministries.[33] As with the failed experiment of suffragan bishops for black constituencies and statements on equal participation in the Church, the structures were not altered in such a manner that truly changed the institution, nor the reality of the experience of minoritized groups. It was a placation, not a transformation.

During the 1970s, the Episcopal Church also dealt with issues of sexual orientation, especially as related to marriage and ordination of noncelibate people in same-gender relationships. The oft cited 1976 General Convention resolution A069, which stated that "homosexual people are children of God who have a full and equal claim with all other people upon the love, acceptance, and pastoral concern and care of the Church," has been foundational in the quest for the rights of lesbians and gays in the Church.[34] As a matter of fact, everything since has been a convoluted process of preventing full inclusion while seemingly being careful (or bound) to not go against the statement in A069 that lesbians and gays are children of God.

The history of the GCSP, as summarized by Kater, and its eventual dismantling continue to inform the direction the Episcopal Church takes toward "ministry to" certain communities, and it continues to dictate an ideology (disguised as theology) of control over resources that only makes the Church "feel good" about engaging certain communities rather than empowering people and communities to seek their own agency and liberation. The grant structure of the budget of the Episcopal Church is an example.

Although I see the GCSP as the precursor of Ethnic Ministries in the Episcopal Church, their processes were parallel and not necessarily subsequent to one another. Even with the GCSP on its last legs, the institutionalization of ministry to, with, and among Latinx people and communities continued. All the while, the specter of the GCSP continued to impact the MSS grant process; its demise continued to inform the distrust of minoritized ministries. As a result, even without the GCSP, the decision-making process by those in power was still informed by the challenges the GCSP posed to the Church. With this history of the GCSP as background, I move to a more specific history of the Latinx Ministry Office at the Episcopal Church Center.

## Institutionalization of Latinx Ministries

In the Episcopal Church, outside of Spanish-speaking countries and colonies, worship in Spanish was offered increasingly after World War II. Many of the clergy involved in these ministries had some connection to Episcopal/Anglican churches in Spanish-speaking countries or colonies: historically, Puerto Rico and Cuba.

Rivera Torres was the Latinx officer for two years. Rivera was succeeded by Ms. María T. Cueto, a member of the NCHA since 1971.[35] Mr. Nelson E. Canals was appointed as an associate Hispanic officer.[36] Cueto's tenure continued the systematic institutionalization of ministry to, with, and among Latinx people and communities. During Cueto's tenure there were several churchwide gatherings: a consultation in 1975, and a conference and meetings in 1976. Parallel to the work of the officer, the NCHA also developed their own work strategy and provided grants to various grassroots organizations.

At the General Convention of 1976, the NCHA, then part of the MSS, became part of the Coalition for Human Needs, which was part of the Church in Society section of the Episcopal Church Center. The Coalition was described as "the main grant-making body for minority community action groups and the Church's ethnic ministry programs."[37] This continued the grant-making legacy of the GCSP, albeit more and more under the control of the institution.

In September 1975 the First National Consultation on Hispanic Ministries was held, which included representatives from twelve dioceses. Decisions made at the Consultation included:

1. To form a committee composed of representatives from the Southwest, the West Coast, the Northeast, the Midwest, and the Southeast, to study and develop liturgical and musical materials for the Hispanic people in the U.S. . . .

2. To form a committee on Evangelism and Christian Education for Hispanic people in the U.S. . . .

3. To form a Steering Committee to coordinate the continuity of the Consultation and to meet with the National Commission on Hispanic Affairs (NCHA) to develop a permanent relationship. . . .

4. To constitute the Consultation into an ad-hoc committee for Hispanic Ministries in the U.S., and to have annual meetings.[38]

Different from the NCHA, the Consultation moved the LATINX office toward the specific needs of congregations: liturgical and musical resources, and appropriate evangelism and formation materials. Committees were created that functioned independent of and with the NCHA. Although the LATINX officer was ex-officio to the Commission, which responded to Executive Council, the NCHA worked independently, sponsoring their own consultations and developing working committees that worked specifically with LATINX ministries at the Church Center. As a follow-up to the Consultation, a steering committee, in a coordinating role, met with the NCHA and the presiding bishop in October 1975 to "discuss their concerns for the ongoing work of the Church among the Spanish-speaking communities of the U.S.," including social action ministries.[39] This would not be the last meeting with a presiding bishop, nor one that led to transformation.

The First Annual Hispanic Ministries Conference was held in Houston, Texas, in February 1976. A month later, a Theological Development Task Force met in Puerto Rico to deal with the "expansion of the theological development program." At the time of this meeting, although some congregations with LATINX ministries existed, no diocese in the continental United States had articulated organized work with LATINX people and communities as a mission objective.[40] In a vastly contradictory manner and a clear example of containment, just as the Episcopal Church decided to more systematically address LATINX people and communities, the Board of Trustees of the Episcopal Seminary of the Caribbean decided to close what had been a valuable resource for ordained leadership, domestically, in Province IX, and in Latin America. The closing of the seminary guaranteed an enduring dependency model for any ministry with LATINX people and communities.[41]

According to Rev. Isaías A. Rodríguez, at this meeting the group expressed hope that "dioceses would realize the importance of this mission and would help develop a plan oriented toward this ministry." The group expressed the need for "indigenous" clergy, the development of a hymnal that was representative of the various LATINX cultures, a lectionary for the Eucharist, and a database of materials from places where this ministry was already occurring.[42] The Task Force met again in May of 1976 in Chicago.

As I will discuss further in chapter 4, the closing of this seminary is one of the fundamental problems confronted by LATINX people and communities in the Episcopal Church in the United States and Anglican/Episcopal Churches throughout Latin America today. Crippling theological education guarantees power structures will remain unchanged and inherently guarantees limited, or "just enough" fair and equal access to the resources and power structures of the Church. This is a way in which the sins of racism and misogyny continue to systematically affect the Church well into the twenty-first century. Aside from some very broad trends in theological education over the past fifty years, I believe that part of the decline can be attributed to these institutions being unable and unwilling to adapt to changing demographics and the increased number of women and people of color enrolling in seminaries. Racism and misogyny are part of the reason we have such a decline in theological education. Put differently, the Church is structured to not support women and people of color.

Briefly, as we fast forward to 2020, I see this potentially happening with the ability of the House of Bishops to prophetically, authoritatively, and effectively lead and influence the Church. I worry that, as the number of women and people of color increases, without serious intentional structural changes, the institution will find a way to keep power and resources in the hands of white men in leadership, and this will not be in the House of Bishops. In other words, the House of Bishops will no longer be the place were white men will pursue their call or exercise their leadership. Instead, the centers of power and resources will be large wealthy parishes, and other large wealthy institutions, which can employ their resources in a hegemonic way. Yes, women and people of color belong in the House of Bishops. Yes, women and people of color belong in all of our seminaries. But, just because the faces in a group photo look more diverse does not mean that the institution has changed.

## Excursus: Maria T. Cueto, First and Only Female and Lay LATINX Missioner for the Episcopal Church

From 1975 through 1977 there were a series of events that scarred LATINX ministries at the Episcopal Church Center, with visible and invisible wounds. The handling of these events is not unrelated to the negative reactions many in the Church had toward the GCSP, which led to its demise, and the election of Rt. Rev. John Allin as presiding bishop (bishop since 1961 and presiding bishop from 1974 to 1985)—a pendulum swing, of sorts, from the Lichtenburg/Hines eras. The Church had shifted toward greater control and Allin sought to work within its established structures instead of outside them.

In 1973, Cueto succeeded Rivera as Hispanic officer; Ms. Raisa Nemikin was the staff secretary to the Commission; and Canals was the assistant Hispanic officer. Contemporaneously and unrelated to the Episcopal Church, on January 24, 1975, Fraunces Tavern in New York City was bombed, killing four people and injuring scores of others. The *Fuerzas Armadas de Liberación Nacional Puertorriqueña* (FALN) claimed responsibility for this attack and dozens of others that occurred in New York City around the same time.[43] A person of interest in the bombing, Mr. Carlos Alberto Torres of Chicago, was an Episcopalian who had been a member of the NCHA.[44]

Several grand juries were empaneled in Chicago and New York in 1976 to deal with the FALN. In November and December of that year a series of subpoenas for the Episcopal Church Center and NCHA records were made of the presiding bishop and others. On January 4, 1977, Cueto, Nemikin, and other commission members were subpoenaed to testify before the grand jury; out of conscience they all refused and served jail time.[45] Presiding Bishop Allin and Rt. Rev. Milton L. Wood did cooperate with authorities and handed over material requested by the FBI, although both were adamant that they did not "open the files" at the Church Center (a recurring accusation on how the case was handled).[46] Allin, in those first months, was on the side of cooperation with the authorities, regardless of the perceived injustices and intimidation of certain staff members of the Hispanic Office by the FBI.

Quickly, Rev. Herbert Arrunátegui was appointed the next LATINX officer, effective February 1, 1977; on March 14, Cueto and Nemikin were placed on unpaid leave.[47] Others like Rt. Rev. Paul Moore (New York), Rt. Rev. Francisco Reus Froylán (Puerto Rico), Rt. Rev. Robert DeWitte (retired Diocese of Pennsylvania), recently ordained women, and the Executive Council spoke in support of Cueto and Nemikin.

Although not overtly, Allin's response to the accusations that funding had been used for the Puerto Rican nationalist organizations, which led to the grand jury subpoenas, was emblematic of the distrust then, and the distrust of minoritized communities that continues today. Cueto and Nemikin were incarcerated for ten months. Well into 1978, Allin and Wood presented a report to the Executive Council on their termination process, and the handling of the matter. A few months later an accord was agreed by Allin and Cueto's representative regarding severance.

The ten-month imprisonment of Cueto, Nemikin, and others did not end FALN questions or the grand jury ordeal for Cueto, who was arrested again in September 1982 for refusal to testify and served another twenty-five months of a three-year sentence in federal custody. After the second period of incarceration in 1985–1986, Rev. Richard Gillett, Cueto's pastor during this time, noted that

> "it has raised questions which have still be answered." Among such questions he lists: What are the rights of privacy for the Church's increasing numbers of lay ministers, many of whom deal with sensitive pastoral matters? What is the Church Executive Council's responsibility to one of its employees arrested in what that person sees as devotion to duty and conscience? When does a person have the right to remain silent? What about abuses of the grand jury system itself, now under review by a congressional sub-committee? How many times can you be charged for the same offense?'
>
> ("Theoretically," he noted, "Maria could be charged again by a new grand jury for the same refusal.") The list culminates: What are the rights of a group which dissents from the government's position, such as those who seek independence for Puerto Rico? Or those involved in the Sanctuary movement? "Maria's case has focused the Church's attention on these questions," says Gillett, "and the Church must seek the answers."[48]

As I read about these events, more than four decades later, it seems clear that the reaction of the Episcopal Church Center was consonant with the reaction of others in authority to the funding choices made by the GCSP and reactions against the Black Manifesto. Those that were able to dismantle the GCSP also managed to take control of Ethnic Ministries.

This is by no means a full picture of all the events related to the arrests of Cueto and Nemikin, nor that of Torres, nor the nationalist movements related to Puerto Rico, but it is relevant here, not only because Cueto was the Latinx missioner, but also because the arrests are informed by power dynamics in the Church, and continue to inform the inability of the Church to share power. The structure that keeps ministry to, with, and among Latinx people and communities as a "program" of the church ensures that power and resources will not be fairly shared. The events surrounding the GCSP and the FALN inform how whole communities are treated by the Church. This is why the history of the GCSP has been so consequential.

## Back to the Chronology

Soon after the grand jury subpoenas in January 1977, Arrunátegui was appointed Latinx officer on the Executive Council staff at the Episcopal Church Center by Presiding Bishop Allin with the mandate "to work with the National Commission on Hispanic Affairs, whose purpose is to seek to fulfill the needs and aspirations of the full spectrum of Hispanic peoples in the U. S., and to serve the ministry of the Episcopal Church among them, both within and outside the Church."[49]

Later in 1977, the NCHA established that it would encourage the Church's dioceses with Latinx work to establish committees to serve as liaisons with the National Commission. The goal was for the dioceses to become aware of "the importance of promoting and developing a native clergy of Hispanic-Americans" and "to stop the drain on Province IX."[50]

The NCHA called for a conference in Miami in September 1977 where, according to Arrunátegui, the delegates would come together "to express their needs, common goals, and suggest ways in which the Commission could help the dioceses in a more effective way to develop a ministry with Spanish-speaking people." The conference would also suggest "resources that will enable those ministering to Spanish-speaking people to put into action the Christian witness."[51] The major results of the consultation were a call for a permanent structure for the development of Latinx ministries and a commitment to move quickly in producing Spanish liturgical and musical worship materials.[52]

In hindsight, these 1977 meetings show that although the Commission and the missioner were both part of the institution of the Church, they approached their work differently, with a more structural approach by the Commission and a more programmatic one by the missioner. Surprisingly, although the Latinx office was concerned with programmatic needs, many of Arrunátegui's writings were rooted in a liberative theological foundation for the overall work with Latinx people and communities.

In July 1977 the now NCHM, renamed from Affairs to Ministry—a conceptual improvement—"began to set direction for more Hispanic participation in the development of Christian educational material and the Church's worship." Also, the Commission agreed to request that the Executive Council "take care that there is Hispanic representation on the Church's committees responsible for liturgy, music and ministry." Commission members were especially concerned about seminary education and other preparations for ministry.[53] These concerns are so often repeated that they became tropic. Speaking about the Miami meeting, Arrunátegui said that what would be proposed would be "a whole new model of ethnic ministry," following parts of the model of the Episcopal Asiamerica Strategies Taskforce (EAST).

Furthermore, Arrunátegui said there was concern about the "lack of funds from the National Church. Delegates called for a greater voice in the management of their own affairs and even discussed the possibility of nongeographic bishops to the Hispanic communities"—a challenging proposition for the Church. Moreover, at this meeting, the issue of *concientización* resurfaced, this time described as a way "to establish an authentic and natural flow between the grass roots communities and the Presiding Bishop by way of the National Commission and those communities and their respective bishops." Again, this shows some of the challenges of this work as a program of the Church. Including the fact that the burden always falls on the minoritized community and not the whole Church. Grounded in ideas of liberation theologies, the Commission was called on to take a greater role as advocate for undocumented immigrants and to identify with their suffering.[54]

Echoing the meetings of the prior year, liturgical and formation needs were also identified. In response, in 1978, Arrunátegui spearheaded the efforts of translating the forthcoming 1979 Book of Common Prayer into Spanish; the translation was dedicated in 1982. In 1980 a provisional hymnal in Spanish was published.[55]

In 1979, the Third Annual Hispanic Ministries Consultation set a series of goals for formation.[56] By the time the General Convention of 1979 came around, there were twenty dioceses and fifty-two congregations with some sort of ministry to, with, or among LATINX people and communities. Most of the clergy at that time came from Province IX.[57] The General Convention mandated each diocese to undertake a survey of ministries with LATINX people and communities.

In November 1979, the survey instrument was developed by the NCHM under the direction of Arrunátegui. Questionnaires were mailed to ninety-four diocesan bishops; eighty-eight dioceses responded. Arrunátegui hoped "that the final project will be more than simply statistics. We hope to show Hispanics speaking for themselves, concerned for the lack of ministry and concerned for their brothers and sisters."[58]

The 121-page report with an extensive appendix was issued by the Task Force in 1980. The report indicated that there were now twenty-two dioceses, including congregations, who were involved in ministry to, with, or among LATINX people and communities.[59] Another twenty-six dioceses without congregations had some form of ministry to LATINX people and communities. Nine of these twenty-six, along with another seven dioceses, foresaw the development of ministry to, with, or among LATINX people and communities within five years.[60] Related to this growing ministry, Arrunátegui noted, "There are only thirty-five priests of Hispanic heritage in the eight domestic provinces of the Church and the need is urgent for well-trained, dedicated people who want to serve Christ and his Church through the Hispanic community."[61]

With the Task Force's report in hand, other more specific consultations were held, including the Hispanic Theological Consultation of 1981. Issues raised in the report of the Consultation are still echoed in what continues to hinder the promise of ministry to, with, and among LATINX people and communities in the Episcopal Church today. The theme of the consultation was "What Hispanics have to offer to the Episcopal Church in the United States." Arrunátegui presented a deep sense of LATINX Episcopalians being value added to the Episcopal Church. The report has many elements that were repeated in all Arrunátegui's reports over the next eighteen years. It was deeply grounded in liberation theologies as seen in the following statement:

> The Hispanic experience of exploitation and dependency is now bringing to our churches a living awareness of suffering, and evangelical call to solidarity with the poor, and a commitment to the struggle for liberation.[62]

Furthermore, the report insisted on the need to challenge and change the structures of the Church.

> The Episcopal Church must reexamine its own structures to eradicate areas of injustice against minorities and against Spanish-speaking people in particular. For example: we allow racism and sexism to exist in the Church: we allow unfair financial support for Hispanic congregations and unjust representation in decision-making bodies of the Church: we tolerate the presence of superficial hospitality and deprecating attitudes toward Hispanics. Therefore, we urge action to confront structural injustice wherever it exists.[63]

Unfortunately, many other reports regarding black or Latinx Episcopalians also list similar litanies of problems in access to power and resources, and problems with leadership development; all maintained by the unchanging unjust racist and misogynist structures of the Church. Nowadays these charges can still be made against the Church, notwithstanding the fact that many Latinx leaders were clear for decades on the theological foundations and prophetic call to this important ministry.

In the 1980s, the Latinx leadership in the Episcopal Church understood at the grassroots and theological levels what the mass migrations from Central America and Latinx population growth in the United States meant. This led to "Latin America in the 80s: A Challenge to Theology," a meeting in 1983 that connected the two.[64] One of the presenters, Roman Catholic Archbishop of Panamá, Marcos McGrath, described its relevance:

> This morning we will take a look at Latin America: under the concrete aspect of the theological challenge it offers to itself, to the world, and, specifically to the United States. A direct challenge, across the hemisphere; and an indirect challenge, through the Hispanic-American community in this country.[65]

McGrath not only made the connection between the United States and Central America, but also named the barriers to the conference participants, which included Presiding Bishop Allin. McGrath clearly pointed out the connection and included comments on the discourses of the "black legend."

> There are some aspects of the United States' understanding of Latin America which are prior to the theological. . . . This is at once a part and a result of a definite neglect and prejudice against Latin America in North America, like and in a way inherited from the older prejudice of northern Europe toward the Iberian Peninsula, of Spain and Portugal. It is true that both North America and Latin America have developed, since the sixteenth century, as products of a process of conquest and colonization carried on from Europe . . . [yet, from then on] the common European tree branched in very different and independent directions. . . . Much has been written about the "black legend" ("la leyenda negra") regarding Spain, a rather malevolent interpretation of everything Spanish, prevalent to the north, especially among the English and in the United States. Edgar Allan Poe's "The Pit and the Pendulum," a picture of torture by the inquisition, is a good sample. This one-sided view of history tended to decry and berate the inquisition and forget the trials for heresy in Geneva or for witchcraft in Salem, Massachusetts. It tended to lament the sufferings of Indians and blacks in Latin America, and

overlook the equal if not more disastrous abuses of them in North America. It tended to caricature the "Other Spanish Christ" as wrapped in superstition, while ignoring the dangers to Christ and to Christianity of the profit-dominated capitalism growing apace in Europe and the United States.[66]

One of the problems we face on the inter-American level, a projection of all we have discussed, both of the "black legend" and of economic colonialism, is the attitude of superiority the North American tends to adopt in face of everything and everyone from Latin America. This is, of course, projected upon the Hispanic community within the United States.[67]

McGrath's observations were rooted in pastoral experiences in Panamá, participation in the Second Vatican Council, and involvement with CELAM (Council of Latin American Bishops), including the visionary meetings in Medellín and Puebla. All those experiences were crucial because they were rooted in the lives of the disenfranchised in Latin America, leading to the development and enactment of *comunidades eclesiales de base* (CEBs: ecclesial base communities) in Latin America, and the theological foundations of liberation theologies. The GCSP in its purest form could be understood as having supported base communities in the United States's context. The sentiments expressed by McGrath are still relevant to the Church in the United States today.

The only ones not on board with liberation theologies were those who could potentially most effect change in the Church: the bishops. Similar to McGrath, in 1985, Rev. Justo L. González, having assessed the Diocese of New York and environs, said the Episcopal Church in its call to ministry among LATINX people and communities needed to understand **the two foci** of the LATINX challenge: *the challenge of numbers* and *the challenge of the poor.*[68] González was also deeply immersed in liberation theologies, or *the challenge of the poor*; the Episcopal Church, however, chose to increasingly focus on *the challenge of numbers.* González's 1985 report has been often cited, but its content has not been implemented or fully understood. Although the Church has not heeded the recommendations found in González's report, it was so salient that as recent as 2005 it was cited by Rt. Rev. Wilfrido Ramos Orench.[69]

The 1980s present a dichotomy for ministry to, with, and among LATINX people and communities between the theological grounding of these ministries and their resourcing. By this I mean that although Arrunátegui and others understood the need for a theological foundation for the work before them, the institutional Church was also bogged down with the bit-by-bit resourcing of practical needs of the dioceses and congregations—a tug-of-war between depth and superficiality, when in fact both were needed to fully root the tradition and be able to bear long-term fruit. Although two seminal reports in 1985—grounded in liberation theologies and the preferential option for the poor—were written by González and Arrunátegui, the work coming out of the ministry office was primarily for the programmatic resourcing (materials) for dioceses and congregations. This is similar to the bifurcation of focus between the Commission and the Office noted for the 1970s.

Another Latin American focused conference happened in 1985: "A Time for Understanding: Colloquium on Central America."[70] Looking back from 2020, it is difficult to read about the 1983 and 1985 Latin American focused conferences and not see a missed opportunity. The current issues at the northern border of Mexico and the northern triangle in Central America are not unrelated to actions taken by the United States more than forty years ago, and the inability of the Church to support LATINX people and communities. Not supporting LATINX people and communities in the 1970s and 1980s prevented the creation of the necessary attitudes, understandings, and structures that could be at the forefront in the Church's effort to deal with the injustice and humanitarian crisis that exists today at the southern United States border.

In 1985, Rt. Rev. Edmond L. Browning was elected to succeed Allin as presiding bishop and served until 1997. Browning's term roughly coincided with the second half of Arrunátegui's tenure as missioner. Noticeable is the fact that LATINX ministry reports from the Episcopal Church Center printed during that time had cover letters from Browning. This had not been the case during Allin's tenure, nor since.

Three major reports were issued in 1988. The first, *Now Is the Time: Report of the National Hispanic Strategic Conference*, summarized the work of four meetings in 1987 and 1988. The preface to *Now Is the Time*, written by Browning, said a lot about "potentiality" and "intentionality." Browning saw "Hispanic ministry" as one part of the "Household of Faith," which was the Church.

> In order for the Church to fulfill its call to mission through a clear vision for ministry, each part of the household must be engaged in the development and nurturing of the vision. . . . It is a process which demands continual discussion and reflection by all parts of the Church, in order that we might fulfill the vows of our Baptismal Covenant.[71]

These sentiments are agreeable to me, so long as all parts of the "Household" have equal footing and the same entrance.

When we open our doors and welcome a "pilgrim people" into full membership into our Church, we will find ourselves changed. The Church will be, in
miniature, what the Anglican Communion is throughout the world: a body
of believers "from every family, language, people and nation."[72]

The report on the conference *Hispanic Ministries: Recruitment, Training
and Deployment* was also published in 1988. I will include more about this
conference in chapter 4 under the topics of leadership development and theological education. The third report was an extensive analysis of a study com-
missioned by Browning and Arrunátegui: *A Celebration of Diversity: Hispanic
Ministry in the Episcopal Church. An Evaluation of the Current State of Hispanic
Ministries in the Episcopal Church of the United States.*[73]

In preparation for the General Convention of 1988, members of the *Coalición Hispana Episcopal* (C.H.E.) and the Hispanic Commission of the Diocese
of New York met to prepare a document to be distributed at the Detroit convention. The title of the document was *A Hispanic Manifesto*. In this manifesto
lay and ordained LATINX leaders make a call to decry the injustices that LAT-
INX people and communities suffer and challenge the Episcopal Church to
decide to side with clarity and commitment with the poor, domestically and
abroad. They frame the manifesto as a "message of hope, based in our faith in
the liberating God of the Exodus and in the resurrected Christ."[74] The manifesto describes the demographics of LATINX people and communities in the
United States, the poverty rate in these communities, even describing the root
causes of this poverty and deprivation.

> Along with other poor peoples of the world, and the growing third world
> in this country, we are the victims of a political and economic system that
> is based on greed, and produces a few rich and privileged, while producing
> a great number of poor and deprived people. There is the North-South divi-
> sion, although we prefer calling it: The abysm between Lazarus and the
> Rich Man. Through cheap labor, our people have become the enslaved of
> our times.[75]

The manifesto describes well the fact that this is about full participation in
the Church, rather than being objects of the Church's largess.

> We aim to be, and convert ourselves, in a prophetic force, in witness and
> service, serving the Hispanic presence, inside and outside of the life of the
> Church, by, and for the Hispanic people. We are committed to the renewal
> and strengthening of [the Church's] life, work and mission, making it atten-
> tive and receptive to the needs of the poor and destitute.[76]

Moreover, it calls for LATINX leadership and empowerment:

> We commit ourselves to the development of Hispanic ministries, congregations and ways of life and work, that will be of Hispanics and for Hispanics. The challenge for us and for our Episcopal Church is the empowerment of Hispanics, to develop models of church that are in the hands of and administrated by our people, including the development of new models of Hispanic ministries, both lay and ordained, that are accessible to our people.[77]

The manifesto ends with a series of calls to the Church regarding contemporary issues: to advocate for immigration reform; to establish a commission against racism within the Church; to reaffirm support for Affirmative Action; to work toward the removal of barriers based on race, sex, or economic condition; to oppose physical violence and mental torture in correctional facilities; to oppose "English Only" legislation; to support the leadership development of indigenous people; to not support any 500-year celebration of the so-called discovery; to support the rights of people to direct their lives and destinies without coercion, intervention, or other forms of control.[78] The manifesto closes with these words, "We pray that the Hispanic challenge with which we are confronted today and in the future, be an occasion for rejoicing while allowing the poor and destitute of this country to evangelize us."[79] If I could summarize the one challenge that encompasses the inability of the Church today to focus on its mission and the sharing of power and resources, it would be found in the sentiment of whether or not majority-church Episcopalians are willing to be evangelized by the poor and destitute?

A very active voice that has articulated a liberative approach to LATINX Ministries since the 1980s is Rt. Rev. Wilfrido Ramos Orench. Much of Ramos's work was influential in the development of the 1988 manifesto. The same is true for Ramos's involvement in the development of Atlanta Manifesto in 2001. Another important voice is Rev. José Enrique Irizarry from the Diocese of New York.[80] The LATINX leadership in the Diocese of New York also benefited from the support of Rt. Rev. José Antonio Ramos Orench, who served in a nonstipendiary manner in the diocese from 1981 to 1987; later as assistant bishop for Hispanic ministries from 1988 to 1989. No reports on ministry to, with, and among LATINX people and communities have been written in the Diocese of New York since 1989.

From 1975 through the 1980s there was a frenetic pace of consultations, gatherings, and meetings aimed to lay out the theological foundation for ministry to, with, and among LATINX people and communities. In the 1990s, the work reached some maturity in various areas, to the extent that some specific ministries became models to follow and were celebrated. Many of the then current successes are included in two related reports titled "Our Hispanic Ministry" (1989 and 1991).[81] Around the same time, Rev. Albert R. Rodríguez produced a report on theological education for Latinx persons in Episcopal Seminaries.[82] The next report from the Office of Hispanic Ministry came in 1998: *Hispanic Ministry: Opportunity for Mission*. To my knowledge, it was the last comprehensive report written by Arrunátegui, and again had clarity about the potential of ministry to, with, and among Latinx people and communities, and how it was not something "other" but integral to the fulfilling of the mission of the Church.

> The Church must insist on the freedom of all peoples to remain faithful to their cultural heritage, their particular language and traditions. At the same time recognizing the reality that culture is ever subject to change, the Church must take into account the diversity within the Episcopal Church.[83]

Arrunátegui captured some central tenets of Anglicanism and the Episcopal Church. Anglicanism emerged as an autochthonous expression of Christianity in England, which was further adapted to the colonial and later disestablished context of the Episcopal Church, which has continued to change to reflect changing times. Can we dare to imagine what the vernacular expression of Anglicanism is today in the United States? A vernacular that includes a diversity that already exists in the Church and an even greater diversity that already exists broadly throughout the country?

Arrunátegui outlined three things:

> a multifold mission which incorporates all people into the body of Christ through baptism, equips all people to participate in the life and mission of the Church, and strengthens and nurtures all people through sound theological understanding about the Christian faith.[84]

These things require deep thinking and execution in three areas: the mobilization of resources, leadership development, and development of a strategic vision.[85] All of them can be accomplished through Christian base communities. As we will see later, this was further developed by Rev. Juan M. C. Oliver in *Ripe Fields*. The election in 1997 of Rt. Rev. Frank T. Griswold as presiding bishop, the end of Arrunátegui's tenure in 1999, and the appointment of Rev. Daniel Caballero as the new missioner for Latinx people and communities marks a changing of the guard. The end of a century; the end of a millennium.[86]

# Y2K: The Demographic Panic

Pick up any report on LATINX people, communities, and ministries for the last fifty years and there will be some mention of changing demographics. Having been an engineer, I love what numbers can do to contextualize a particular question. This demographic concern extends to the adding of an ethnicity question in the United States Census of 1980 (albeit all the ethnicities were LATINX ones). Yet a few decades ago, demographics were not driving these ministries, but a theological foundation which started from the mission of the Church looking to include LATINX people and communities in a more intentional manner—all under the reality of changing demographics, migration, and liberation theologies. What I mean by demographics not being the driving force is that churches responded to the reality around them and they had a theological foundation and tradition that compelled them to this work. Unfortunately, amid a changing reality for all mainline Protestant churches, many congregations today are first compelled to reach out to LATINX people and communities because of changing demographics and declining Sunday attendance, rather than the fulfillment of the mission of the Church (#BCP855).

González's analysis of the foci of this ministry—*the challenge of numbers* and *the challenge of the poor*—has endured for decades, yet the Episcopal Church has chosen to deal more and more with the challenge of numbers, with an all-consuming focus on demographics, and what I call the "Demographic Panic."[87] Although a decades-long focus on liberative theologies was pursued, other interests prevailed. With the reality of the data and discourse around the census of 2000, the Church further reacted. Much like Lewis's assessment of race matters mentioned earlier, the Episcopal Church's handling of these issues has always been reactionary.[88]

Before the 2000 census, many were aware of demographics, but they did not use them as the driving point, but as one aspect that could contextualize the call to and theological grounding of these "particular" ministries. In the wider culture of the United States, the demographic shift was felt as early as the 1970s; the 1980s were already seen as the "Decade of the Hispanic."[89] Yet the full reality of LATINX demographics did not become mainstream until the 2000 census was published. Since the 1970s the theological grounding for LATINX Ministries had taken a backseat to the material/pamphlet resourcing of the Church. It was diminished even further by the demographic panic that emerged after the year 2000. Ignoring these vast communities in our evangelism was no longer tenable; it would have been foolish to not bring the Good News of God in Christ to the communities where we had a presence. Yet demographics and fear were driving the push—not the fulfilling of the mission of the Church through all the actions of ministry. González not only noted the *challenge of numbers* and *challenge of the poor*, but also wrote about the dangers of ministry driven solely by demographics:

> The first danger is that mission may tend to be conceived in essentially ecclesiocentric ways. The reason for mission and ministry then becomes, not so much the needs of Hispanics, nor even the need of the Church to have Hispanics as such within its ranks, but rather the instinct of self-preservation which the Church shares with every other institution. This in turn leads to other policies which, while perfectly natural in the case of other institutions, may be self-defeating or self-contradictory in the case of the Church.[90]

The challenge has been that the demographic panic has been perpetuated and compounded by the increasingly noticeable declines in membership in the Episcopal Church which culminated, in some ways, with the General Convention of 2000 establishing a task force to develop a 20/20 Vision, which called for the doubling of Average Sunday Attendance (ASA) by the year 2020. That made sense given that the United States population in 2000 was 282.2 million (35 million LATINX people) and was projected to be 340 million by 2020 (70 million LATINX people). The population estimate as of January 1, 2019, was 328,231,337. The population of LATINX people will about double between 2016 and 2060 (57.4 to 111 million: 65.8 to 75.5 percent U.S.-born LATINX people).[91]

Not long after the 2000 convention and shortly after Ramos Orench's consecration as suffragan of Connecticut, six bishops met on Easter Monday 2001; from that meeting came what has been called "The Atlanta Manifesto"—again, a bold choice to title their new call to action a manifesto.[92] To start the declaration, they mentioned both the General Convention and the census. They called out the Church on growing ministry to, with, and among LATINX people and communities, but not doing so as the same rate of the demographic change; for ignoring LATINX people and communities; and for false excuses. They wrote, "We cannot present defensive excuses of language or of any other kind, about being involved in this mission and ministry."[93] Although a new bishop in 2001, Ramos had been ordained for close to thirty-five years. Ramos had been a leader in Puerto Rico, Connecticut, and nationally, and had written extensively about LATINX ministries over the decades, yet, in looking at the two manifestos, a dozen years apart, you can hear the frustration at the paltry pace of the Church in engaging in this work.

Of interest to me in the latest manifesto is one of the last vestiges that the theological foundation for the declaration was still the preferential option for the poor and liberation theologies. The bishops called for a focus on mission (away from a "maintenance culture"), welcome (not just to "be like us"), commitment, and hope—to "become a Church in a **state of mission**." They added a pastoral letter which spoke of the demographic opportunity, yet placed the opportunity as an apostolic calling that both refocused the Church and opened its power structures to more diversity. The manifesto was concurred to and commended at the New Dawn Conference in Los Angeles in May 2002.[94] The manifesto demonstrates that there continued to be a clear disconnect and dissociation between the purported theological foundation for the work if the Church and the actual actions and reality of the Church.

In 2002, as part of Vision 20/20 Griswold envisioned a "restructuring" of the various sections of the "institutional Church." As reported, Griswold indicated that

> the ethnic ministries staff will focus more strongly on congregational development, rather than advocacy. That function will be shared more with the peace and justice staff, including the Washington office. Griswold also underscored the role of local congregations in advocacy work.
>
> "We have come to a new place with regard to ethnic ministries," Griswold told the council. "In a church free of the sin of racism and the other 'isms,' there would be no need for a focus upon particular ethnic groups and identities because the church, in all its variations, would reflect the fullness of Christ and the face of Christ, and be transformed by the multiplicity of languages, races and the cultural particularities incarnate in the members of Christ's risen body. But we have not yet become who we are called to be."
>
> "Given that, it has become clear that our best energies in seeking to serve the ethnic communities need to be focused on congregational development and clergy recruitment. This is in line with the vision of 20/20, the mission energies around the church, and the demographics of our nation."[95]

There is a kernel of insight in Griswold's words. In some way Griswold was trying to say that this is the life of the whole Church and not the work of some *others* as a program of the Church. Two dangers would remain. Without structural changes, ethnic ministries remain a program. Without intentionality, the few people of color would be erased in the Church under the guise of being post-racial. We know that nothing really changed. In 2005, Ramos gave the keynote address at the Latinx seminarians gathering at Virginia Theological Seminary. Again, both the Atlanta Manifesto and the address are rooted in liberation theologies. Ramos used the ideas of Latinx people being "companions of Jesus," people in diaspora and in pilgrimage. Ramos saw this ministry as one of solidarity, service, and presence—of servanthood. Notwithstanding, these statements have rarely been truly foundational to the work on the ground—which is perennially in survival mode—challenged by unjust and nonprophetic power and resource structures. Challenged by a structural dependency.

Ramos called the Church to allow LATINX people and communities to have agency in changing the Church. Ramos quoted González's *challenge of the numbers* and *the challenge of the poor* and reminded the Church of the *challenge of the poor*. Finally, Ramos called the Church to be diverse and inclusive, to practice radical hospitality, and to practice affirmation rather than assimilation, and called for **radical transparency** and **full accountability** to build mutual respect. Bishop Ramos's final two aspects were **radical discipleship** and the raising of competent leadership.[96]

In November 2005, Caballero retired as LATINX missioner and was succeeded by Rev. Anthony Guillén. Guillén continues to serve as missioner and since 2018 as director of Ethnic Ministries.[97] One of the first things that Guillén did was change the name of the ministry office to the Office of Hispanic/Latino Ministries.[98] In 2006 Rt. Rev. Katherine Jefferts-Schori was elected as presiding bishop; Jefferts-Schori was succeeded by Rt. Rev. Michael Curry in 2015.

## The Episcopal Church's Strategic Vision for Reaching Latinos/Hispanics

As we move into the last fifteen years of ministry to, with, and among LATINX people and communities, it may be helpful to pause and summarize some of the observations of the first thirty-five years. We know that ministry to, with, and among LATINX people and communities continues to function as a program of the Church, whereby the institution continues to control and limit access to power and resources. The 1970s were characterized by a furious pace of consultations and meetings, and the parallel work of two institutional entities—the NCHM and the LATINX ministries office. These two entities worked together, but at times worked on parallel tracks: one more institutional and structural, the other programmatic. It can be said that this era ended with the publishing of the results to the church-wide survey conducted in 1980, which got a grip on the state of this ministry at that time.

The 1980s were a time in which this ministry was deeply grounded in Latin American liberation theologies and the two foci of *the challenge of numbers* and *the challenge of the poor*. Of interest during this time are the symposiums connecting the situation in Latin America, especially Central America, to migration to the United States. The end of the 1980s saw a shift with strategic conferences and the beginning of highlighting the work that was yielding great fruit—telling Latinx success stories. The late 1980s brought forth the first Latinx manifesto. At that time there was also a transition to a focus on "recruitment, training, and deployment," a focus of chapter 4. The 1993 consultation expanded the work done in 1988, yet not much progress had been made, except for the *Instituto Pastoral Hispano*. Through it all, the Latinx ministries office, Forward Movement, and dioceses like Los Angeles were producing Spanish-language resources.

Through the end of the 1990s until the turn of the millennium there was a shift from speaking about "ministry" to talking about "mission"—perhaps "mission" as "mission field," hence increasing the focus on demographics. The Atlanta Manifesto and Ramos's reflections tried to hold on to a foundation in liberation theologies, but clearly, based on subsequent results it was more evident they were losing their grip on the theological foundation and liberation imperatives. This was about power and resources, and fair access to them. Nowadays there are over 400 congregations in the Episcopal Church actively involved in some work along the spectrum of ministry to, with, and among Latinx people and communities.[99]

As I mentioned at the beginning of this chapter, we have entered the realm of living church history. My style in presenting these most recent years will be through my own experiences and the contextualizing of such. I became involved with the Latinx Ministries Office when Caballero rebooted the gathering of Latinx seminarians at the seminary in Austin in 1999. From that, two of us offered to host the gathering at CDSP the following year.

I started working in churches with Latinx people in the continental United States in 2003, soon after my ordination, and began my work with the Church of Saint Matthew and Saint Timothy in September 2004. While serving St. Matthew and St. Timothy's, I attended the Nuevo Amanecer Conference in Peachtree City, Georgia, in 2008. At that conference I attended the review of the early development of the marketing work that would lead into the planning document "Creating a Welcoming Presence: Inviting Latinos/Hispanics to Worship." In many ways that conference was a learning experience; in other ways it was a disappointment.

A different transformation also began in 2008. As I was recently reminded, a small group gathered in the lobby of the conference hotel to openly discuss being part of LGBTQ+ communities, having a Latinx background, and being people of faith; from that meeting some of my work of LGBTQ+

inclusion in the Church emerged.[100] I am proud of the work of LGBTQ+ LATINX people in the Church, and the efforts made to provide workshops and plenaries that have to do with welcome, inclusion, solidarity, and belonging. Little did we know the larger conversation that would emerge at Nuevo Amanecer in 2014, 2016, and 2018. We have a way to go, but the seeds planted in 2008 have continued to yield fruit.

At the 2008 Nuevo Amanecer, I found disappointment in the workshop offerings, since I did not expect a denomination-wide conference to spend time discussing "Anglicanism or Episcopal Church 101." I could understand Anglicanism 101 being taught at the parish or diocesan level, but not at a larger conference. I was later disillusioned by the event because the marketing work was used as an all-encompassing strategic plan, when it had lost its theological grounding and was two layers removed from the mission of the Church and its ministries. It was solely about demographics and marketing. I was so disappointed that I did not attend the next Nuevo Amanecer conference in 2010.

In my opinion, when the planning document evolved into a strategic document presented at the General Convention of 2009, one could see the full realization that LATINX Ministry had lost its theological grounding and promise. The document presented was called *The Episcopal Church's Strategic Vision for Reaching Latinos/Hispanics to Worship*. Continuing with the demographic panic, the planning document saw itself as "a call for the Church to face its present and future in a spirit of discernment and mission as it responds to the growth of Hispanic/Latino communities in all regions of our country."[101]

One important purpose of the strategic document, and a valuable aspect, was to move LATINX ministry beyond being solely "equated to immigrant ministry" and begin to take seriously the presence of nonimmigrant LATINX people and communities in the United States that are second, third, and fourth generations away from immigration, if they were immigrants at all. The report was presented at the 2009 General Convention and was commended in resolution 2009-D038. Although this resolution was not adequately resourced, many of the findings of the report have informed the Latino/Hispanic Ministry Office's work and approach over the last decade. In a way typical of the Church, several items presented in the strategic plan were finally resourced in 2015 as part of General Convention Resolution 2015-A086.

According to Guillén, this strategic plan was the Latino/Hispanic Ministries Office's response to the Atlanta Manifesto.[102] The Atlanta Manifesto had gone to presiding bishop Griswold directly but did not go anywhere from there. As seen in the impetus for "ethnic ministries" or "hyphenated-ministry," this shift in focus toward demographics and marketing by itself is not what has been detrimental to the strengthening and deepening of ministry among Latinx people and communities, but the increasingly one-sided intense focus on demographics and marketing, as well as sociological understanding of immigration generations (such as Rev. Albert R. Rodríguez's transgenerational understanding of Latinx communities), has furthered the othering and self-othering of Latinx ministry from ministry itself. Positive contributions with some negative consequences. Meanwhile, the opportunity to ground and root this ministry in liberation theologies, including developing Latinx Anglican/Episcopal theologies, has become more and more remote.

Parallel to the Strategic Vision, in 2009, Rev. Juan M. C. Oliver published *Ripe Fields: The Promise and Challenge of Latino Ministry*. Oliver's book offers a different approach to ministry with and among Latinx people and communities. Along with the few works on liberation theologies in the Episcopal Church, Oliver's book should be required reading for all seminarians. Three characteristics of this book are worth mentioning. First, it is deeply Latinx and deeply Anglican/Episcopalian. Second, it builds on the vast body of knowledge and experience that Oliver has in the field of liturgy. Third, it addresses the myth that congregations associated with Latinx ministry are not able to become self-sufficient.[103] Oliver believes that the Episcopal Church should stop seeing Latinx communities as a "'mission field' for Anglos—or worse, as a new 'market base' that might save dying Anglo institutions," but rather as "potential partners in mission."[104]

Moreover, at Nuevo Amanecer in 2008 I was disappointed, in part, because of the frustrating tone focused on what "we need" from the Episcopal Church, replicating the long list of complaints that have been reproduced since the institutionalization of the ministry in the 1970s. In 2012, the tone of the conference was dramatically different. No longer was the emphasis on basic content or a litany of complaints, but on supporting the leadership of lay and ordained people involved in ministry to, with, and among Latinx people and communities across the Episcopal Church, as well as "a pep rally" on the gift Latinx people are for the Church and the gifts they bring to our congregations and our actions of ministry. The keynote address by Rev. Simón Bautista went far in making this change truly felt. This showed the fruits of decades-long efforts, a maturity, and a coming into ourselves that was beautiful to see, and which afforded to all those attending the opportunity to delve deeper into what it means to be Church and do Church in a Latinx manner, but not focused solely on how to survive as a Church by bringing Latinx people to our churches—the dual demographic panic: there are so many of them; if we don't get them in we are going to die/close.

Since 2008, there has been a Nuevo Amanecer conference every two years, and five Nuevos Horizontes conferences since 2013. Various courses and trainings and varied approaches and tools have also been organized throughout the Church, coordinated out of the Office of Latino/Hispanic Ministries. Some progress has been made, but all as a program of the Church, not as something that permeates its very fabric and truly fulfills its mission—for the whole Church. Many of these programs aim at various competencies: cultural, social media, community/congregational development.

Notwithstanding the institutional failures of the Episcopal Church with regards to LATINX people and communities, there have been significant advances in offering tools for ministries to, with, and among LATINX people and communities across the Church. There are now cultural competency courses, mission-developer conferences, more opportunities for those involved in these important ministries to meet, coaching and professional development opportunities. Notwithstanding, my observation is that these continue to be done without a theological grounding. Without being undergirded by an equal emphasis and investment in theological education, it will not gain the necessary rootedness for the Church into the second half of the twenty-first century.

The current mission of the Office of Latino/Hispanic Ministries of the Episcopal Church is:

> Latino/Hispanic Ministries yearns for a church that embodies the multiethnic, multilingual and multicultural context we live in today. Our vision is to make the Episcopal Church known to Latino/Hispanic communities that they may experience our church and embrace it as their spiritual home.
>
> We support dioceses and congregations by producing resources, developing networks, and providing opportunities for formation of lay and ordained leaders.[105]

As I hope is evident, one of the things that I argue in this book is that one of the ways we have lost our way in LATINX ministries is because we have been focused solely on resourcing the church and demographics, we have forgotten the theological grounding of ministry in general, and the theological grounding for this ministry in particular. Yet, I also believe that we are coming into a time in which Anglican/Episcopal theologies from LATINX perspectives are emerging, as well as LATINX theologies from Anglican/Episcopal perspectives. One example of this was a conference in 2018, sponsored by the Seminary of the Southwest in Austin, Texas. The conference was titled "Theologizing *Latinamente*: A Conference on Latino Cultures, Liturgies, and Ethics." It was a hopeful sign for the Church. Parallel to the important everyday work that is done in parishes, we need to continually develop theologies that are relevant to the work of ministry today, and for us today. We continue to have a very relevant starting point: thinking about the implications of liberation theologies for the Episcopal Church today. This work cannot continue to be neglected.

## Notes

1. Presiding Bishop John E. Hines was the diocesan bishop of the Diocese of Texas (coadjutor 1945; diocesan 1955) when he was elected presiding bishop in 1964.

2. Kenneth Kesselus, *John E. Hines: Granite on Fire* (Austin, TX: Episcopal Theological Seminary of the Southwest, 1995), 204.

3. John L. Kater Jr., "Experiment in Freedom: The Episcopal Church and the Black Power Movement," *Historical Magazine of the Protestant Episcopal Church*, Historical Prolegomenon to the Renewal of Mission: The Context of the Episcopal Church's Efforts at Outreach 1945–1975, 48, no. 1 (March 1979): 74. See also Robert E. Hood, *Social Teachings in the Episcopal Church* (Harrisburg, PA: Morehouse Publishing, 1990), 121–22. Hines visited the Bedford-Stuyvesant area of New York City with Mr. Leon Modeste in late summer 1967. John Booty, *The Episcopal Church in Crisis* (Cambridge, MA: Cowley Publications, 1988), 51; Gardiner H. Shattuck Jr., *Episcopalians and Race: Civil War to Civil Rights* (Lexington: University of Kentucky Press, 2000), 175–76.

4. Shattuck, *Episcopalians and Race*, 176–77.

5. Kater, "Experiment in Freedom," 74; see also Donald S. Armentrout and Robert Boak Slocum, *Documents of Witness: A History of the Episcopal Church, 1782–1985* (New York: Church Publishing, 2000), 508–10.

6. David L. Holmes, *A Brief History of the Episcopal Church* (Valley Forge, PA: Trinity Press International, 1993), 165. See also David L. Holmes, "Presiding Bishop John E. Hines and the General Convention Special Program," *Anglican and Episcopal History*, 61, no. 4 (December 1992): 393–417.

7. Holmes, *Brief History*, 166.

8. "A Declaration by Priests Who Are Negroes," The Church Awakens: African Americans and the Struggle for Justice, accessed March 3, 2019, *https://www.episcopalarchives.org/church-awakens/items/show/198*.

9. Kater, "Experiment," 78–79; Hood, *Social Teachings*, 122.

10. Hood, *Social Teachings*, 122.

11. Robert W. Prichard, *A History of the Episcopal Church*, rev. ed. (Harrisburg, PA: Morehouse Publishing, 1999), 263. The Rudyard Kipling reference is to Kipling's poem "The White Man's Burden: The United States and the Philippine Islands" (1899) published in *The New York Sun* (February 1, 1899): 6. A quick search of digitized United States newspapers in the Library of Congress yields hundreds of instances of this poem printed throughout the country in 1899 alone. Historic American Newspapers, accessed August 9, 2019, https://chroniclingamerica.loc.gov.

12. Holmes, "Presiding Bishop," 407.

13. Hood, *Social Teachings*, 123–24.

14. Shattuck, *Episcopalians and Race*, 202; ENS, "General Convention Special Program Receives Praise," May 21, 1970 [87–8].

15. Shattuck, *Episcopalians and Race*, 202–3.

16. Prichard, *History* (rev. ed.), 263.

17. Regarding UBE and the GCSP see Shattuck, *Episcopalians and Race*, 210.

18. I am grateful to Rev. Anthony Guillén for sharing this important information with me during a conversation in May 2019.

19. Isaías A. Rodríguez, *Historia del Ministerio Hispano en la Iglesia Episcopal: Logros, frustraciones y esperanzas* (Atlanta, GA: Sauters, Diocese of Atlanta, 2015), 34–35.

20. The name was changed at a meeting in 1977. ENS, "Hispanic Projects Receive Funding," July 14, 1977 [77241]. CNAH is the acronym in Spanish: *Comisión Nacional de Asuntos Hispanos*.

21. ENS, "Protestant Episcopal Church in the USA National Commission on Hispanic Affairs" (hereafter PECUSA NCHA), February 23, 1972 [72023]; see also "Executive Council Summary of Action," February 24, 1972 [72026].

22. ENS, "PECUSA NCHA" and "Executive Council Summary of Action."

23. Kater, "Experiment," 80; ENS, "Modeste to Produce Permanent Report on GCSP," December 13, 1973 [item 73266]. Modeste's report was never published. Hood, *Social Teachings*, 123–24.

24. ENS, "Executive Council Meets—A Summary," December 13, 1973 [73265]; Rodríguez, *Historia del Ministerio*, 36.

25. Hood, *Social Teachings*, 124.

26. Hood, *Social Teachings*, 125.

27. Shattuck, *Episcopalians and Race*, 211; Hood, *Social Teachings*, 124.

28. Kater, "Experiment," 81.

29. Lewis, *Yet With A Steady Beat*, 147; Harold T. Lewis, "By Schisms Rent Asunder? American Anglicanism on the Eve of the Millennium," in *A New Conversation: Essays on the Future of Theology and the Episcopal Church*, ed. Robert Boak Slocum (New York: Church Publishing, 1999), 5.

30. A gripping account of the ordination of the Philadelphia eleven is found in Darlene O'Dell, *The Story of the Philadelphia Eleven* (New York: Seabury Books, 2014). Title II, Canon 9 read "The Provision of these canons for the admission of Candidates, and for the ordination to the three Orders: Bishops, Priests and Deacons shall be equally applicable to men and women."

31. O'Dell, *Philadelphia Eleven*, 195.

32. O'Dell, *Philadelphia Eleven*, 196.

33. The Rt. Rev. José Antonio Ramos Orench, bishop of Costa Rica, was one of the four bishops that participated in the service of the Philadelphia ordinations. Even though Ramos was not one of the ordaining bishops, his influence was diminished and the impact on his career was real. Ramos wrote about these experiences in *Las María Dolores—Memorias y Reflexiones* (San José, Costa Rica: Editorial Nuestra Tierra, 2007).

34. *General Convention, Journal of the General Convention of . . . The Episcopal Church, Minneapolis 1976* (New York: General Convention, 1977), C-109.

35. ENS, "Changes in Hispanic Commission Staff Announced," August 8, 1973 [73192]; see also, Rodríguez, *Historia del Ministerio*, 35.

36. NOTE: I'm curious to imagine how LATINX Ministries from the Episcopal Church Center would have evolved if the leadership had remained in the hands of women and lay people.

37. ENS, "Hispanic Commission Plans for Mission," March 14, 1977 [77086].

38. ENS, "National Consultation on Hispanic Ministries Held," September 15, 1975 [75314].

39. ENS, "Meetings on Hispanic Ministries Held," October 31, 1975 [75382].

40. Rodríguez, *Historia del ministerio*, 37; ENS, "Hispanic Task Force Meets in Puerto Rico," March 26, 1976 [76105].

41. ENS, "Caribbean Seminary to Close," June 8, 1976 [76190].

42. Rodríguez, *Historia del ministerio*, 37.

43. In English, Armed Forces for Puerto Rican National Liberation.

44. Another presumed point of connection was a school in Chicago that had received funds from the NCHA. ENS, "Chicago Puerto Rican School Investigated," May 12, 1977 [77154]. The Rt. Rev. James W. Montgomery, bishop of Chicago, investigated the allegations and found them to be unfounded.

45. Arnold H. Lubasch, "Two Episcopal Aides Are Ordered to Testify in a Terrorism Case," *The New York Times*, February 6, 1977, 43. Accessed December 11, 2018. *https://www.nytimes.com/1977/02/06/archives/two-episcopal-aides-are-ordered-to-testify-in-a-terrorism-case.html*. William Claiborne, "Puerto Rican Group Claims Responsibility for N.Y. Blasts." *The Washington Post*, March 22, 1977, *https://*

www.washingtonpost.com/archive/politics/1977/03/22/puerto-rican-group-claims-responsibility-for-ny-blasts/96920f6d-11e5-4ad5-ba70-861efea952d6/; ENS, "Three Brothers Jailed in F.A.L.N. Inquiry," August 31, 1977 [77283]; "Former Consultant Jailed for Refusing to Testify," *The Living Church* 175 (September 25, 1977), 5. Luis (Commission member 1975; Consultant 1976), Julio (Commission member 1972–73) and Andrés Rosado, and Pedro Archuleta (Commission member 1972–73). The grand jury appeal for Archuleta is found in *https://books.google.com/books?id=6ACQ07B_QwUC&lpg=RA1-PA3&dq=maria%20cueto%20episcopal%20church&pg=PP1#v=onepage&q&f=false* (In the Matter of the Special February 1975 Grand Jury; United States Court of Appeals for the Seventh Circuit, 1977, No. 77-1885).

46. Present at a meeting in Puerto Rico in March 1976 were "Lydia López and Carlos Alberto Torres, members of the Theological Development Work Group of the National Commission on Hispanic Affairs; the Rev. Ricardo T. Potter, consultant to NCHA; and Maria T. Cueto, Luis Rosado, and Raisa Nemikin, NCHA staff." ENS, "Hispanic Task Force Meets"; ENS, "Church Center Cooperates in Bombing Investigation," February 17, 1977 [77058].

47. ENS, "Bishop Allin Puts Two Staff on Leave of Absence," March 14, 1977 [77094]. This sequence of events leaves some interesting gaps in the narrative. How is it that Rev. Arrunátegui is appointed so quickly, even before Cueto and Nemikin appeared before the grand jury or were put on unpaid leave? How is it that they were not placed on unpaid leave until March? A longer treatment of this case would have to pay attention to the subtext of the timeline of events. Further indication to me that Allin was still functioning out of a GCSP mindset.

48. ENS, "Maria Cueto Comes Home," June 5, 1986 [86125]. A resolution to show solidarity had been passed by General Convention in 1985: GC1985-D031: Affirm Solidarity with Maria Cueto and Other Prisoners.

49. ENS, "Fr. Arrunátegui to Be Hispanic Officer," January 6, 1977 [77007]. From the same article, "Fr. Arrunátegui was a Methodist pastor in Panama City before entering the Episcopal Seminary of the Caribbean in Puerto Rico in 1964. He was ordained deacon and priest in 1965 by the Rt. Rev. R. Hebert Gooden, at that time Bishop of Panama and the Canal Zone. . . . In addition to his training at the Puerto Rican seminary, Fr. Arrunátegui received degrees from the National University of Panama and Union Seminary of Matanzas, Cuba." In 1985 Arrunátegui was awarded a doctor of ministry degree from the Theological School of Drew University.

50. ENS, "Hispanic Commission Plans for Mission," March 14, 1977 [77086].

51. ENS, "Hispanic Conference to Be Held in Miami in September," May 19, 1977 [77170].

52. ENS, "Hispanic Delegates Set Directions," October 7, 1977 [77318].

53. "Hispanic Commission Approves Grants," 5; ENS, "Hispanic Projects Receive Funding."

54. ENS, "Hispanic Delegates Set Directions."; ENS, "Provincial Hispanic Ministry Expanded," June 29, 1978 [78183].

55. ENS, "Prayer Book Translation Is Well Advanced," November 9, 1978 [78317]; "Provisional Hymnal Published in Spanish," November 6, 1980 [80393]. This was a revision of the provisional hymnal of 1961.

56. ENS, "Hispanic Consultation Sets Education Goals," August 2, 1979 [79246]; see also "The Report of the Special Task Force of the National Commission on Hispanic Ministries: 'The Hispanic Challenge to the Episcopal Church: Opportunity for Mission in the 80's Opportunity for Mission in the 80's'" (New York: National Hispanic Office, Episcopal Church Center 1980), 103–5. The news article mentions a forthcoming report written by Nina Soto, then of the Diocese of Newark. If such a report exists, I have not seen it.

57. Rodríguez, *Historia del ministerio*, 38.

58. ENS, "Hispanics Envision Churchwide Report," January 31, 1980 [80032]; Rodríguez, *Historia del ministerio*, 42.

59. "The Report of the Special Task Force," 9, 125.

60. "The Report of the Special Task Force," 126–27.

61. ENS, "Hispanic Vocations to Be Lifted Up," August 28, 1980 [80289].

62. "Report of the 1981 Hispanic Theological Consultation" (New York: Office of Hispanic Ministry of the Episcopal Church Center, 1981).

63. "Report of the 1981 Hispanic Theological Consultation," n.p.

64. "Latin America in the 80s: A Challenge to Theology," Meeting in Organization of American States, Washington, DC, September 25–27, 1983 (New York: Office of Hispanic Ministry, Episcopal Church Center, 1983).

65. Marcos McGrath in "Latin America in the 80s," 23.

66. McGrath in "Latin America in the 80s," 23–24.

67. McGrath in "Latin America in the 80s," 26.

68. Justo L. González, *The Hispanic Ministry of the Episcopal Church in the Metropolitan Area of New York and Environs* (New York: Grants Board of Trinity Parish, 1985), 1.

69. Wilfredo Ramos Orench, "The Hispanic Ministry: A Challenging Future," address on April 15, 2005, at Virginia Theological Seminary for a National Gathering of Hispanic Seminarians for the Episcopal Church, ed. Daniel Caballero (New York: Office of Hispanic Ministry, Episcopal Church Center, 2005).

70. "A Time for Understanding: Colloquium on Central America," Conference, New Orleans, Louisiana, November 1–3, 1985 (New York: Office of Hispanic Ministry, Episcopal Church Center, 1985).

71. *Now Is the Time: Report of the National Hispanic Strategic Conference* (New York: Office of Hispanic Ministry, Episcopal Church Center, 1988), preface.

72. *Now Is the Time*, 2.

73. Ronald J. Salazar, *A Celebration of Diversity: Hispanic Ministry in the Episcopal Church. An Evaluation of the Current State of Hispanic Ministries in the Episcopal Church of the United States* (New York: Office of Hispanic Ministry, The Episcopal Church Center, 1988).

74. "Un Manifesto Hispano," in *Reflexiones Teológicas: Modelos de Ministerios, Revista Teológica de la Comisión Hispana de la Diócesis de Nueva York 2* no. 2 ( Jan.–Jun. 1989), 32.

75. "Un Manifesto," 32.

76. "Un Manifesto," 34.

77. "Un Manifesto," 36.

78. "Un Manifesto," 36–37.

79. "Un Manifesto," 37.

80. Wilfrido Ramos Orench, "Una visión del ministerio Hispano en la Diócesis Episcopal de Connecticut—Documento de trabajo," in *Reflexiones Teológicas*, 1–10. José Enrique Irizarry, "Charla dictada en la segunda conferencia anual de la Coalición de Hispanos Episcopales (CHE)," in *Reflexiones Teológicas*, 24–30.

81. "Our Hispanic Ministry I: Essays on Emerging Latin American Membership in the Episcopal Church"(New York: Office of Hispanic Ministry, Episcopal Church Center, 1989); "Our Hispanic Ministry II: How We Claim Ethnic Membership in the Episcopal Church" (New York: Office of Hispanic Ministry, Episcopal Church Center, 1991).

82. Albert R. Rodríguez, *Theological Education and Preparation for Hispanic Ministry: A Survey of Accredited Episcopal Seminaries in the United States* (New York: Office of Hispanic Ministry, Episcopal Church Center, 1990).

83. Herbert Arrunátegui, ed., *Hispanic Ministry: Opportunity for Mission*, 3rd ed. (New York: Office of Hispanic Ministry, Episcopal Church Center, 2001), 1. Original from 1998.

84. *Hispanic Ministry: Opportunity*, 1–2.

85. *Hispanic Ministry: Opportunity*, 5.

86. Rev. Herbert Arrunátegui is currently retired in Florida. I have never met Rev. Arrunátegui—my assessment is based on the review of an extensive written body of work written over a period of more than two decades.

87. González, "Hispanic Ministry," 1.

88. Lewis, *Yet With A Steady Beat*, 162–63.

89. "The phrase 'Decade of the Hispanic' was first used in an article about Latino appointees working in the Carter Administration published by *U.S. News & World Report* in 1978. Many Latinos working in Washington, D.C., at the time were quoted by the news magazine, but the final word went to a Cuban-American named Maria Elena Torano. 'The blacks had the decade of the '60s; women had the '70s. The '80s will be the decade for Hispanics,' she said. *U.S. News* used Torano's phrase to end the 1,500-word report, and even ran a picture of her, using 'The '80s will be the decade for Hispanics' as the caption underneath. *Times* librarians found 173 additional print-media citations of that phrase in the ensuing 11 years." Frank del Olmo, "Commentary: Latino 'Decade' Moves Into '90s," *Los Angeles Times*, December 14, 1989, *http://articles.latimes.com/1989-12-14/news/ti-1_1_latino-community*.

90. González, "Hispanic Ministry," 9.

91. Jonathan Vespa, David M. Armstrong, and Lauren Medina, "Demographic Turning Points for the United States: Population Projections for 2020 to 2060," March 2018, *https://www2. census.gov/library/publications/2018/demo/P25-1144.pdf*. Population estimate on January 1, 2019, is 328,231,337 people.

92. "The Atlanta Manifesto with Addendum and a Pastoral Letter," 3rd ed. (New York: Office of the Ministry, Episcopal Church Center, 2002). Bold choice given the Black Manifesto of 1969.

93. "The Atlanta Manifesto," 2.

94. "The Atlanta Manifesto," 3–9. Emphasis in original.

95. ENS, "Council Told Staff Changes Will Enhance 20/20 Movement," March 1, 2002 [2002-051].

96. Ramos Orench, "Hispanic Ministry," n.p. The bolden words are in the original document.

97. ENS, "Latino/Hispanic Missioner Appointed," September 20, 2005 [092005-1]. Rev. Caballero is retired in Wisconsin.

98. E-mail correspondence with Guillén on July 2, 2018.

99. There is no clear rule-of-thumb on how congregations are defined. This is especially true if these are defined by being economically self-sustaining, having parish status, or having a clergy person to support the congregation. Furthermore, it is not clear on how congregations in Province IX are counted.

100. My gratitude to Hugo Olaiz for reminding me of this in 2018; in a moment in which I needed to hear something hopeful about our Church.

101. "The Episcopal Church: Creating a Welcoming Presence: Inviting Latinos/Hispanics to Worship," (New York: Office of Hispanic Ministry, Episcopal Church Center, 2009), 1.

102. Anthony Guillén, e-mail to the author, July 2, 2018.

103. See Roland review of *Ripe Fields*.

104. Juan M. C. Oliver, *Ripe Fields: The Promise and Challenge of Latino Ministry* (New York: Church Publishing, 2009), 115; Juan Francisco Martínez, *The Story of Latino Protestants in the United States* (Grand Rapids, MI: William B. Eerdmans, 2018), 212.

105. "Latino/Hispanic Ministries," accessed July 12, 2019, *https://www.episcopalassetmap.org/networks/latinohispanic-ministries*.

# Chronology

| | |
|---|---|
| 1958 | Lambeth Statement on Latin America. |
| 1962–65 | Second Vatican Council. |
| 1963 | First Latin American Consultation (Cuernavaca, México). |
| 1964 | 61st General Convention (St. Louis, Missouri); creation of Province IX; election of Rt. Rev. John Hines as presiding bishop. |
| 1965 | Episcopal Church in Brazil becomes an autonomous Anglican province. |
| 1966 | Episcopal Church in Cuba becomes extraprovincial to Canterbury. |
| 1966 | The Anglican Communion and Latin America: consultation at Sao Paulo, Brazil (January 24–28, 1966). |
| 1967 | Episcopal Church in Costa Rica begins process of autonomy. |
| 1967 | 62nd General Convention (Seattle, Washington); creation of the General Convention Special Program (GCSP) |
| 1968 | CELAC Meeting—R.C. (Medellín, Colombia); initial outlines of liberation theologies. |
| 1968 | Third Latin American Consultation (Paraguay). |
| 1968 | Lambeth Conference: Resolution 64. |
| 1969 | Special General Convention (South Bend, Indiana). |

### 1970s

| | |
|---|---|
| 1970 | 63rd General Convention (Houston, Texas). |
| 1971–73 | Rev. Jorge Juan Rivera Torres named first LATINX staff officer of the Executive Council. |
| 1972 (Feb.) | National Commission on Hispanic Affairs charter approved by Executive Council. |
| 1973 | 64th General Convention (Louisville, Kentucky); establishment of LATINX "Desk"; GCSP placed under Mission Service and Strategy (MSS). |
| 1973 (Aug.) | Ms. Maria T. Cueto appointed as second LATINX officer. |
| 1974 | Rt. Rev. John Allin becomes presiding bishop. |
| 1974 | Philadelphia eleven ordinations. |
| 1974 (Jul.) | First meeting of MSS (Denver, Colorado). |
| 1974 (Sep.) | Mr. Nelson Canals appointed associate LATINX officer. |

| | |
|---|---|
| 1975 (Jan.) | Bombing of Fraunces Tavern in New York City. |
| 1975 (Apr.) | Hispanic Ministry Consultation in New York City. |
| 1975 (Sep.) | First National Consultation on Hispanic Ministries (Dallas, Texas). |
| 1975 (Oct.) | Meeting with Presiding Bishop Allin. |
| 1976 (Feb.) | Hispanic Charter changes proposed to Executive Council; meeting called by Allin and NCHA; First Annual Hispanic Ministries Conference (Houston, Texas). |
| 1976 (Mar.) | Theological Development Task Force Meeting in Puerto Rico. |
| 1976 | 65th General Convention (Minneapolis-St. Paul, Minnesota); approval of women's ordination. |
| 1976 (Sep.) | *Seminario del Caribe* closes; Comisión de Educación Teológica para América Latina y el Caribe (CETALC) is created. |
| 1976–77 | Grand Jury Subpoenas. |
| 1977 | Missionary Diocese of Costa Rica becomes extraprovincial. |
| 1977 (Jan.) | Rev. Herbert Arrunátegui appointed LATINX officer. |
| 1977 | NCHA becomes National Commission on Hispanic Ministries (NCHM). |
| 1977 (Sep.) | Second National Consultation on Hispanic Ministries (Miami, Florida). |
| 1977 | The *Instituto Pastoral Hispano* is founded by the Diocese of Connecticut. Transferred to GTS in 1980. |
| 1978 (Apr.) | Province VIII begins LATINX work. |
| 1978 | Second Annual Hispanic Ministries Conference (Los Angeles, California). |
| 1978 | Episcopal Church in Puerto Rico becomes extraprovincial (1978–2003). |
| 1979 | CELAC Meeting—R.C. (Puebla, México): further development of liberation theologies. |
| 1979 (Jun.) | Third Annual Hispanic Ministries Conference. |
| 1979 | The quarterly magazine *Avante* is published. |
| 1979 | 66th General Convention (Denver, CO); mandate to conduct survey of LATINX ministries. |
| 1979 (Nov.) | GC Survey Conducted; Rite II published in Spanish. |

## 1980s

| | |
|---|---|
| 1980 (Feb.) | GC Survey report completed; National Commission on Hispanic Ministries; "The Report of the Special Task Force of the National Commission on Hispanic Ministries: 'The Hispanic Challenge to the Episcopal Church: Opportunity for Mission in the 80's'" (New York). |

| | |
|---|---|
| 1980 | The first week of Advent designated as the "Week of Prayer and Concern for Hispanic Vocations." |
| 1980 | Provisional Hymnal (*Himnario Provicional*) in Spanish published. |
| 1980 | Official publication *CNMH* replaces *Avante*. |
| 1980 | Center for Hispanic Ministries for Province VII begins in Austin, Texas (housed at Episcopal Theological Seminary of the Southwest). |
| 1980 | Diocese of Chicago establishes Saint Augustine's University. |
| 1981 | Third National Consultation on Hispanic Ministries (Austin, Texas): "Hispanic Theological Consultation," March 23–26, 1981. |
| 1982 | 67th General Convention (New Orleans, Louisiana): *Libro de Oración Común* approved; establishment of the "Hispanic Scholarship Trust Fund." |
| 1983 (Sep.) | Conference "Latin America in the 80s: A Challenge to Theology." (Washington, DC). |
| 1984 | Fourth National Consultation on Hispanic Ministries (Pasadena, California). |
| 1985 | 68th General Convention (Anaheim, California); first time simultaneous interpretation is provided by volunteers; video called "*Presencia Hispana*" was offered. |
| 1985 | "The Episcopal Church and the Hispanic challenge: A Report on the State of Hispanic Ministries." |
| 1985 | Arrunátegui concludes a DMin with the thesis "Evaluation of the Development and Implementation of Hispanic Ministries Programs in the Episcopal Church and the Role of the National Hispanic Officer." |
| 1985 | Rev. Justo L. González, concludes report "The Hispanic Ministry of the Episcopal Church in the Metropolitan Area of New York and Environs: A Study Undertaken for the Trinity Grants Board." |
| 1985 (Nov.) | "A Time for Understanding: Colloquium on Central America." (New Orleans, Louisiana). |
| 1985 | Center for Lay Formation, *Casa Russack*, is founded (Los Angeles, California). |
| 1986 (Oct.) | Hispanic Heritage Bishops; Advisory Committee on Hispanic Ministries. |
| 1987 (Feb.) | First National *Encuentro* (Miami, Florida); theme: "Hispanic Ministry Toward the Twenty-First Century." "Comentarios sobre el encuentro de Miami." |

1987      Booklets issued titled "Nuestra Historia."

1987 (Nov.)      First Latin-American Anglican Congress (Panamá).

1988      69th General Convention (Detroit, Michigan); first time that bilingual booklets were offered.

1988 (Jan.)      Follow-up to Miami *Encuentro* (Princeton, New Jersey).

1988 (Feb.)      Follow-up to Miami *Encuentro* (Dallas, Texas).

1988 (Mar.)      Follow-up to Miami *Encuentro*, Duncan Center (Delray Beach, Florida); issuing of report, "Now Is the Time: Report of the National Hispanic Strategy Conference, March 9–11, 1988."

1988 (Jul.)      "Hispanic Manifesto" distributed at the General Convention in Detroit from June meeting in New York City that included the *Coalición Hispana Episcopal* (C.H.E.)

1988      "The Celebration of Diversity: Hispanic Ministry in the Episcopal Church." An Evaluation of the Current State of Hispanic Ministries in the Episcopal Church.

1988 (Dec.)      "Hispanic Ministries: Recruitment, Training and Deployment," Duncan Center (Delray Beach, Florida), December 8–9, 1988.

1988      Lambeth Conference; simultaneous interpretation used for the first time.

1988 (c.)      Rev. José Enrique Irizarry, ed. "The Hispanic Challenge to the Diocese of New York," A Working Paper Prepared by The Committee on Mission and Strategy of the Hispanic Commission of the Diocese of New York.

1989 (Mar.)      Second annual conference of the *Coalición Hispana Episcopal—* C.H.E. (Bridgeport, Connecticut).

1989      Publication *El Informador Episcopal* (The Episcopal Informant); provides news until 1999.

1989      "Our Hispanic Ministry I" report.

1989      First Encuentro de Seminaristas Hispanos—SSW (Austin, Texas); organized by Anthony Guillén, Juan M. C. Oliver, Wilfredo Benítez (funded by Council of Seminary Deans).

## 1990s

1990      Rev. Juan M. C. Oliver: first LATINX to receive Episcopal Church Foundation doctoral fellowship.

1990      Second Encuentro de Seminaristas Hispanos—SSW (Austin, Texas); organized by Anthony Guillén, Wilfredo Benítez, Candida Feliú-González (funded by Council of Seminary Deans).

1990      *Book of Occasional Services* is published in Spanish.

1990 (c.)       Forward Movement begins publishing the daily devotional *Día a Día*.
1990 (Oct.)     "Theological Education and Preparation for Hispanic Ministry:
                A Survey of Accredited Episcopal Seminaries in the United States."
1991            70th General Convention (Phoenix, Arizona).
1991            "Our Hispanic Ministry II" (essays on emerging Latin American
                membership in the Episcopal Church).
1991            Third Encuentro de Seminaristas Hispanos—SSW (Austin, Texas).
1992 (c.)       Forward Movement begins translating their pamphlets into
                Spanish.
1992 (Nov.)     Primer Congreso de Episcopales Latinos (Camp Allen, Texas);
                creation of *Organización Nacional Hispana de Episcopales* (ONHE).
1993 (Feb.)     Symposium on the theme of "The Challenges of the Past,
                The Challenges of the Future," February 25–27, 1993—CDSP
                (Berkeley, California).
1993 (Mar.)     Consultation on Spanish-Language Theological Education,
                March 9, 1993—CDSP (Berkeley, California).
1993 (Mar.)     "Ministry in a Culturally Diverse Church: Report of a Hispanic
                Consultation on Recruitment, Training, and Deployment,"
                March 13–14, 1993, Duncan Center (Delray Beach, Florida).
1994            71st General Convention (Indianapolis, Indiana).
1994 (c.)       Province IV organized and established a LATINX network.
1995            Episcopal Church in México becomes an autonomous province
                of the Anglican Communion.
1996 (Jun.)     Leadership conference, June 7–9, 1996 (Sewanee, Tennessee);
                creation of New Orleans Hispanic Coalition.
1997            72nd General Convention (Philadelphia, Pennsylvania).
1997 (Feb.)     First "Anglicanism and the Hispanic Experience" course;
                Bishops' conference on LATINX Anglicanism (Cocoyoc, Morelos,
                México); Report provided to the House of Bishops.
1998 (c.)       Forward Movement prints original pamphlets in Spanish.
                Written mostly by Rev. Isaías A. Rodríguez.
1998            "Strategies for Renewal in the Episcopal Church: Recruitment,
                Training, and Deployment for Effective Ministry in the Hispanic
                Communities." "Estrategias para una renovación en la Iglesia
                Episcopal." (Houston, Texas).
1998            Second "Anglicanism and the Hispanic Experience" course.
1998            "Hispanic Ministry: Opportunity for Mission" by Arrunátegui
                (reissued in 2001)

| | |
|---|---|
| 1998 | Iglesia Anglicana Región Central de América (IARCA) becomes a province of the Anglican Communion. |
| 1998 | *El Himnario* published. |
| 1998 (c.) | *Albricias* published. |
| 1999 | Arrunátegui retires after twenty-two years as LATINX officer. |
| 1999 | Rev. Daniel Caballero is named interim LATINX missioner— permanent in 2000. |
| 1999 | National Gathering of LATINX Seminarians—SSW (Austin, Texas). |

## 2000s

| | |
|---|---|
| 2000 | United States Decennial Census. |
| 2000 | 73rd General Convention (Denver, Colorado). |
| 2000 | Programa Latino en Teología Pastoral—GTS (New York, New York). |
| 2000 | National Gathering of LATINX Seminarians—CDSP (Berkeley, California). |
| 2000 | Jubilee Ministries Meeting, Camp Capers (San Antonio, Texas); idea of a "Nuevo Amanecer" conference. |
| 2001 | Quarterly publication *Caminos* from the Hispanic Ministries Office of the Episcopal Church published until 2007. |
| 2001 (Apr.) | "Atlanta Manifesto: The Wake-Up Call to Action"— (Atlanta, Georgia). |
| 2001 (Sep.) | Organizational meeting for the second national gathering named *Encuentro Nacional: Un Nuevo Amanecer* (Hartford, Connecticut). |
| 2001 | Rev. Carla E. Roland Guzmán: first Latina to receive Episcopal Church Foundation doctoral fellowship. |
| 2002 (May) | Second *Encuentro Nacional: Un Nuevo Amanecer:* "A New Dawn" (Los Angeles, California); "Nuevo Amanecer: Desafíos y Oportunidades." |
| 2002 (Jun.) | Executive Council passes a resolution that all communications from the Episcopal Church Center must be available in both English and Spanish. |
| 2002 | "The Atlanta Manifesto with 'Addendum' and a Pastoral Letter." 3rd ed. |
| 2002 | Dioceses of California and Utah use *Center for Anglican Leaning and Life* (CALL) for theological education and training in Spanish— CDSP (Berkeley, California). |
| 2002–03 | Homilies for the Common Lectionary (A, B, C) are published in Spanish. |

2003        74th General Convention (Minneapolis, Minnesota): consent
            to episcopal election of Rt. Rev. Gene Robinson.
2003 (Feb.)  Victor Ruiz, "Opportunity Knocks," article in *Episcopal Life*. 14,
            no. 2, 1, 6–9.
2004        Rev. Isaías A. Rodríguez published *History of the Catholic,
            Anglican, and Episcopal Church* in Spanish.
2005        Rt. Rev. Nedi Rivera, suffragan bishop, Diocese of Olympia.
2005        Rev. Isaías A. Rodríguez published *Popular Devotions by Hispanics:
            Brief Dictionary* in Spanish.
2005        Rev. Isaías A. Rodríguez's *Introduction to Worship: Liturgy as
            the Work of the People* in Spanish is added to the books of AETH
            (Asociación para la Educación Teológica Hispana).
2005 (Apr.)  "The Hispanic Ministry: A Challenging Future," Rt. Rev. Wilfrido
            Ramos Orench, April 15, 2005; National Gathering of Hispanic
            Seminarians—VTS (Alexandria, Virginia).
2005 (May)  Caballero retires.
2005 (Oct.)  Latin American Anglican Theological Congress "Globalization
            and Its Implications in Latin America: A Challenge to the Episcopal/
            Anglican Church" (Panamá City, Panamá).
2005 (Nov.)  Rev. Anthony Guillén appointed LATINX missioner; Guillén
            adds "Latino" to title and name of office. Now Office of Latino/
            Hispanic Ministries.
2006        Visión y Homenaje—VTS (Alexandria, Virginia).
2006        75th General Convention (Columbus, Ohio); first (almost daily)
            Spanish-language newspaper printed during the convention
            by the Office of Latino/Hispanic Ministries.
2006        Instituto de capacitación de clérigos (ICC) —VTS (Alexandria,
            Virginia).
2007        ICC and first Ándale (Academia de Líderes Episcopales:
            Quito, Equador).
2007 (Feb.)  Juntos Creceremos (Florida).
2008 (Jun.)  *Nuevo Amanecer* (Peachtree City, Georgia).
2009        Book by Oliver: *Ripe Fields: The Promise and Challenge
            of Latino Ministry*.
2009 (Feb.)  "The Episcopal Church: Creating a Welcoming Presence:
            Inviting Latinos/Hispanics to Worship." Planning Document.
2009        76th General Convention (Anaheim, California): "The
            Episcopal Church's Strategic Vision for Reaching Latinos/
            Hispanics" July 2009; GC2009-D038.

## 2010s

2010 (Aug.)   *Nuevo Amanecer*, Kanuga (Hendersonville, North Carolina).

2010 (Sep.)   Founding of "Coalición de Episcopales Latinos" in Arizona by Rev. Carmen Guerrero.

2012   77th General Convention (Indianapolis, Indiana).

2012 (Aug.)   *Nuevo Amanecer*, Kanuga (Hendersonville, North Carolina).

2013 (Aug.)   Mission Developer Training with ELCA (Chicago, Illinois).

2013 (Aug.)   First *Nuevos Horizontes*—SSW (Austin, Texas).

2014   Center for Theological Education for Latinos, Diocese of Atlanta.

2014 (Apr.)   First *New Camino* held in Diocese of Newark under the name "Convocation for a New Horizon."

2014 (Aug.)   *Nuevo Amanecer*, Kanuga (Hendersonville, North Carolina).

2014 (Nov.)   *New Camino* (first one held under this name) in Diocese of New York (offered on three different occasions by region: February and April 2015). "New Camino: Reimagining Latino/Hispanic Ministry in the Diocese of New York in the 21st Century"

2015 (May)   *New Camino* Diocese of Southern Virginia (Richmond, Virginia).

2015   78th General Convention (Salt Lake City, Utah); GC2015-A086.

2015   Forward Movement translates/adapts full-length books into Spanish and publishes the Living Discipleship Curriculum in Spanish.

2015 (Feb.)   Mission Developer Training (Denver, Colorado); first REDIL.

2015 (Aug.)   *Nuevos Horizontes*—SSW (Austin, Texas): "ConeXión with the New Latino Generation."

2015   Book by Rodríguez, *Historia del Ministerio Hispano en la Iglesia Episcopal: Logros, frustraciones y esperanzas.*

2015 (Dec.)   *New Camino* Diocese of Northern California.

2016 (May)   *New Camino* Diocese of Idaho.

2016 (Aug.)   *Nuevo Amanecer*, Kanuga (Hendersonville, North Carolina).

2017 (Jun.)   First Episcopal Latino Ministry Competency (ELMC) course—SSW (Austin, Texas).

2017 (Jul.)   *Nuevos Horizontes*, Camp Allen, Texas (Latino Ministry for the Next Generation).

2017 (Aug.)   First meeting of Latino diocesan missioners (Miami, Florida).

2017 (Oct.)   Second Episcopal Latino Ministry Competency course (Chicago, Illinois).

2018 (Apr.)   *New Camino* Diocese of San Joaquin.

2018 (May)   *New Camino* Diocese of San Diego.

2018 (Jun.)   Third Episcopal Latino Ministry Competency course—Bloy House (Los Angeles, California).

2018 (Jul.)   79th General Convention (Austin, Texas). Report: "Task Force for Latino/Hispanic Congregational Development and Sustainability."

2018 (Aug.)   Fourth Episcopal Latino Ministry Competency course (Sewanee, Tennessee).

2018 (Aug.)   *Nuevo Amanecer*, Kanuga (Hendersonville, North Carolina).

2018 (Oct.)   Theologizing *Latinamente* conference—SSW (Austin, Texas).

2019 (Jan.)   Fifth Episcopal Latino Ministry Competency course—VTS (Alexandria, Virginia).

2019 (Jul.)   *Nuevos Horizontes*: Community Development, A Tool for Community Engagement—SSW (Austin, Texas).

2019 (Jul.)   Episcopal Youth Event for IARCA and Province IX (Panamá).

# PART II

## UNMASKING AND (RE)FRAMING LATINX MINISTRIES

The overall purpose of part I was to sketch and (re)frame the history of the institutionalization of ministry to, with, and among LATINX people and communities, specifically over the last fifty years. I traced this process to the General Convention Special Program (1967) and the subsequent establishment of Ethnic Ministries in 1973. Furthermore, I placed this institutionalization into a broader history of race and racialization, as related to Anglicanism and the Episcopal Church, which is perpetuated by discourses, such as those of the "black legend," and the various ways minoritized communities are treated in the Episcopal Church and prevented from access to power and resources; communities controlled and contained by keeping these ministries as programs of the Church and LATINX people as hyphenated-Episcopalians.

The second part of this book moves toward unmasking discourses and myths that allow for the institution to keep ministry to, with, and among LATINX people and communities as a program of the Church. Some of these discourses were contextually introduced in part I, yet are now further analyzed in chapter 3, while adding a few other discourses about language and the vernacular. I title this chapter "Things Done and Left Undone." In chapter 4, I delve into the challenges related to leadership development and theological education, and argue that we will only strengthen the Church, and thus truly focus on fulfilment of the mission of the Church, if the necessary extravagant investment in theological education and leadership formation is accomplished. If this investment is not made, the future desired for the Church will never be attained. This investment will require an honest look at how theological education institutions have not truly dealt with racism and misogyny, and how this partly informs their decline. Finally, in chapter 5, I present some avenues forward that lift up gifts from Anglicanism and the Episcopal Church, and those from LATINX people and communities; these avenues, I hope, offer promise and possibility.

## More on Demographics

As presented in chapter 2, one aspect that pushes the Episcopal Church to engage in ministry to, with, and among LATINX people and communities is the demographic reality of LATINX communities in the United States. At an Episcopal LATINX gathering in Los Angeles in 2002, Rev. Justo L. González, said, "Where the country's population is growing is among its ethnic minorities . . . [consequently] the majority of historic American churches will continue to lose members if they do not include people from other cultures."[1]

This observation was not surprising; as we have already seen, González, a Methodist, had been telling the Episcopal Church the same thing since the 1980s; almost any report that has to do with ministry to, with, and among LATINX people and communities, whether written by an outsider or insider to the Church, mentions the demographics of LATINX communities. Nevertheless, the problem has never been the lack of recognition of this demographic reality, but an inability of the Church to fully engage in ministry to, with, and among LATINX people and communities without making them/us commodities. Demographics, in essence, have been reified as both an opportunity and a barrier.

Here Rev. Juan M. C. Oliver's observation in *Ripe Fields* (2009) is useful:

> There is a growing interest in Latino ministry in the Episcopal Church, partly the result of an increasing awareness of the accelerated growth of the Latino population in the United States. . . . What is the Episcopal Church planning to do to respond to this challenge in evangelism? So far, the answer is not clear. Despite strong statements by Latino bishops, such as the Atlanta Manifesto, and the good will of hundreds of clergy and laity across the nation, the Episcopal Church still does not have a national plan for the development of Latino ministry.[2]

Oliver's statement was true in 2009 and still holds true. Yet the Church not only does not have a plan, it also does not have a theological foundation to develop these ministries beyond being a program of the Church.

Although demographics is often mentioned, the reality is that our Church is smaller in 2020 than it was in 2000, both in raw numbers and as a percentage of the population.[3] In fact, from 2008 to 2018 Average Sunday Attendance decreased by 24.9 percent.[4] Yet the focus on demographics is more acute and misguided than ever. In fact, as recently as 2018, in a report to General Convention on 2015 Resolution A086, the "The Task Force for Latino/Hispanic Congregational Development and Sustainability" began the report by stating:

> The Episcopal Church has recognized the radically changing demographics that show that Latino/Hispanics are one of that fastest growing groups in the United States. The Church has also decided, as stated in the Strategic Vision for Reaching Latinos/Hispanics (2009), to strive to be "courageous, resourceful, passionate and enthusiastic in its response to these new circumstances." Moreover, in that same strategic vision document, the Church has stated that "We can grow vibrant and fruitful Churches by inviting the Latino/Hispanic community to a welcoming and inclusive environment, sharing our rich liturgy and implementing innovative and pertinent programs."[5]

Again, demographics cannot be the sole impetus and marketing cannot be the underlying approach. The understanding of both demographics and marketing must have a theological grounding, beginning with the gospel and the mission of the Church—"to restore all people to unity with God and each other in Christ." The mission of the Church, above all accomplished by the whole church, through prayer, worship, the proclamation of the gospel, and the promotion of justice, peace, and love.[6] What must be at the center is the people, not the institution. Otherwise, we are just any other voluntary organization with some LATINX people in our midst. Furthermore, the Church will not reset itself in God's direction without acknowledging and dealing with its continuing participation in and perpetuation of racism and misogyny. The same warning applies: dealing with racism cannot be solely driven by changing demographics. For example, in the 1994 pastoral letter from the House of Bishops on the sin of racism, demographics and race are explicitly connected.

> The lingering image of the Episcopal Church as essentially white and Anglo Saxon does not serve us well. We are affected by continuous shifts in the domestic population and by the constant arrival of new waves of immigrants.

The church's missionary strategy must take seriously the changing complex-
ion of its broadening constituency.[7]

Although well intentioned, the self-consciousness of the statement by the
Task Force for Latino/Hispanic Development and Sustainability is misguided.
It is still focused on the institution as it is and changing demographics saving it
while not changing the very racist and misogynist structures that are hindering
its growth.

Since the 1970s, although we have had some (unavoidable) success as a
denomination, we have also had a tendency to repeat the same mistakes over
and over—what Oliver describes as "recurring patterns."[8] In fact, the various
stories that frame Oliver's analysis (also supported by my own analysis),

> show both the ingrained obstacles that prevent the church from developing
> this increasingly crucial ministry in the United States and the opportunities
> before the church to engage in this ministry in a successful way across every
> aspect of its common life.[9]

Central to Oliver's statement is the reality that it must be "across every
aspect of its common life." Thus, the challenge of ministry to, with, and among
LATINX people and communities is that it is too often treated as a program
of the church, something discreet and encompassed, rather than as something
that permeates throughout. It is systematically and structurally separated. Put
differently, ministry to, with, and among LATINX people and communities is
made to be different than ministry. It is as if we continue to innovate, come
up with new approaches, learn more and more, yet still try to implement these
innovations in the same systems. Therefore, the call to dismantle the very institutional structures of the Episcopal Church that are hindering its fulfilling of
its mission and its success in becoming a more intercultural and polycentric
church must be heeded in order to truly bring the Church to a place where it
reflects the breadth of the reign of God: a new creation.

> So if anyone is in Christ, there is a new creation: everything old has passed
> away; see, everything has become new! All this is from God, who reconciled
> us to himself through Christ, and has given us a ministry of reconciliation;
> that is, in Christ God was reconciling the world to himself, not counting
> their trespasses against them, and entrusting the message of reconciliation to
> us. (2 Cor. 5:17–19)

What then are we called to dismantle? We must take apart anything
that creates or perpetuates an *us/them* dynamic, anything that sees as success

"acculturation" or "becoming like us," because it is fed by an *us/them* hyphenated-reality, rather than a *both/and* polycentric and intercultural possibility. Oliver calls this a failure to thrive, which is related to "the cultural isolation and naiveté of monocultural church leaders."[10] The *us/them* discourses are biases, in our church and in society, that must be acknowledged, disrupted, and discarded. These include, but are not limited to:[11]

- LATINX people and communities are immigrants/foreigners/undocumented and "Anglos" are citizens.
- LATINX people and communities are Roman Catholic and "Anglos" are Protestants (Episcopalian).
- LATINX people and communities are poor and thus are dependent "objects of ministry." "Anglos" are agents of ministry and of means.
- LATINX people are lazy; "Anglos" are workaholics.
- LATINX people are overemotional; "Anglos" repress feelings, the "frozen chosen."
- LATINX people are aggressive; "Anglos" are passive aggressive.
- LATINX people are uneducated and can't be good administrators or leaders; "Anglos" are efficient robots.
- LATINX people are solely Spanish speaking.
- Only LATINX people can be involved in LATINX Ministries, and not any other "ministry."
- LATINX people are monolithic.
- LATINX culture is *machista* (sexist/patriarchal); "Anglo" culture is egalitarian.

These are only some of the discourses. Unfortunately, many more exist. Awareness of the *us/them* biases is crucial in the tearing down and building back up in the knowledge that we have a role in a new creation. I yearn for and want the Episcopal Church to actively work toward building a new creation in Christ. This is prophetic work. This is transformative work. This is uncomfortable work. One of the first steps is the systematic relinquishing of power and resources, which begins to dismantle the very structures that prevent the Church from fulfilling its mission. In January 2019, Rt. Rev. Jennifer Baskerville-Burrows preached to this prophetic work. On the feast of St. Paul's Conversion, Baskerville preached about "our call to live a scandalous, dangerous, and transformative faith": a way of life that must dismantle and unmask our misguided "respectability politics."[12]

## The Scars of the General Convention Special Program

With the "sour feeling" or "after-effect" of the General Convention Special Program, as the Episcopal Church continued to wake up to the needs and numbers of LATINX people and communities, it approached this "mission field" as a program or project of the Church, never truly resourcing ministry to, with, and among LATINX people and communities appropriately, nor relinquishing and sharing power with those that have traditionally been excluded from its structures. Innovation is stifled when it is implemented in the same vessel that requires the innovation in the first place—the vessel being the institution, not the tradition. This, in part, explains why certain exciting and innovative ministries stay peripheral to the institution or function completely outside of it. Or, why centers of wealth in white-majority churches do not need the institution, and smaller entities are more connected to the institution for access to resources—that will still piecemeal be shared.

By keeping ministry to, with, and among LATINX people and communities as a program of the Church, the institution limits access to resources and power, thus failing to truly fulfill its mission of restoring all people to unity with God and one another in Christ. These discourses are limiting our ability to share the gospel in an Anglican/Episcopal way. It is my belief that anything that overtly or implicitly prevents the Church from fulfilling its mission amounts to sin.

The idea of "sin" is present in the celebration of the Holy Eucharist. In the *Gloria* we sing "you take away the sin of the world," which is also echoed in the *Agnus Dei* (Fraction); in the Confession of Sin, "we confess that we have sinned against you." In the Lord's Prayer we ask, "Forgive us our sins as we forgive those who sin against us." My preference is to say "sin" rather than "sins," since I see "sin" as anything that breaks our relationship with God and one another. Sin, then, is the "contra-mission." There may be an infinite number of ways in which this happens, but it is one "sin." Our mission of reconciliation to God and one another is imperative in our broken world; thus, seeking reconciliation is a way of building the reign of God. There are two sides to this sin: an individual one and a corporate one.

Whenever I meet with parents, guardians, and godparents for baptismal preparation, I go over the prayer book baptismal liturgy to place its aspects in a historical and theological context. As you may surmise, the language of each question of the Baptismal Covenant matters to me. I emphasize an aspect, that each question is not an "if, then" construction, that they are declarative statements of "what is" and "what should be." This means that we will fall into sin and we are called to see Christ in all—not some, respect all—not some, serve all—not some.[13]

In 2020, we may wonder if we are living in unprecedented polarizing times. It is a fair question. Yet as a church historian, I can see that all times have polarizing elements; this time is the one affecting us. Our task is to recognize the people, or groups of people, we have been hurt by, have enmity with, or do not care for.

Those are the ones that we must see Christ in, respect their dignity, and serve. This is one way Jesus invites us into deeper relationship with God and one another. The imperative of love is one of the most difficult imperatives to accomplish. Every time we renew our own baptismal promises we are confronted with the same questions, and we are held to account in our progress to fulfill these promises.

Our promises in baptism should make us uncomfortable. Lack of comfort is not a bad thing; it is what moves us forward as a Church and as a society. I'd rather be uncomfortable and moving than comfortable and stuck, even if the movement is failure at trying something radical together as a Church. Our continual call is to *metanoia*, to transformation—the transformation and conversion of ourselves and the world about us. We would do well to have a motto that says, "Uncomfortable for Christ." It may not be sexy, but it reminds us not to domesticate what it means to be disciples of Christ that are sent into the world to share the Good News.

Prophetic work requires discomfort. Our uncomfortable call is to seek ways to dismantle oppressive structures while at the same time bringing people along to the new possibilities and freedoms—the new creation. We are called to divest of oppressive structures while not alienating the people that have historically benefited from those structures. Another challenge is how do we dismantle structures while caring for those that may feel worried, or left behind? How do we talk about these things while keeping reconciliation at the center rather than have people retreat to their silos of comfort and belief and further alienating each other? These are not angsts solely of our moment in the United States, but issues for the Episcopal Church to actively engage in, ever humbled by the challenge they pose. How do we radically change the Church from the deeply rooted insidious structures and biases it has allowed to exist for centuries? The question is especially uncomfortable because it requires the sharing of power and resources, even the giving up of power and resources, and there may be some who do not want to participate in this.

More specifically, knowing that sin is a human condition: what does this sin look like for the institution? Here the work of Rev. Alberto L. García and Rev. John A. Nunes is helpful in a variety of ways. The Church must be able to identify structural sin, its own idols, as it evaluates itself. A way to identify this structural sin is to unmask the areas where the church has "turned to itself." García here uses the image of selfies and our current state of "self-absorption" and "self-importance."[14] Nunes shares a different image of "a group's fundamental identity [becoming] incurved."[15] For García and Nunes this structural, individual, and communal sin fundamentally distort *diakonia* (service) and *koinōnia* (community).

The prophetic and uncomfortable work the Episcopal Church and Episcopalians are called to is about the whole Church. Ministry to, with, and among Latinx people and communities is only one piece. The Episcopal Church over the next decade must choose to radically move away from its current ministerial focus on hyphenated-ministries, the "feel-good" ministries, the *us/them* ministries; stop avoiding the hard conversations; and boldly and prophetically transform the structures that keep the Church functioning from a fundamentally racist, biased, and *whiteness* point of view. (Whiteness being what is normative.) The transformation and conversion toward a Church that is intercultural, representative of our communities, and embracing of intersectional and polycentric identities will take place when the Church is focused on its mission, not on its own sustainability, self-perpetuation, or maintenance. A Church not focused on such a mission will continue to fail at being welcoming, inclusive, solidaric, and a place of belonging. In other words, will the Church stop dealing with the symptoms of things and desire deeply to delve into dismantling the root causes of our sin? Believing that we are above racism and xenophobia, or not talking and doing something about it will not make it go away.

In the *New York Times Magazine* of November 2, 2016, Trevor Noah, host of *The Daily Show* on Comedy Central, was asked about the current divisions in the United States. Noah responded:

> America is the place that always seems to treat the symptoms and not the cause. In South Africa, we're very good at trying to go for the cause of racism. One thing that really never happened here, which is strange to me, was a period where white America had to reconcile with what it had done to black Americans.[16]

Rev. Harold T. Lewis characterized the issue in a similar vein, "The Church has been most successful, therefore, in treating the most prevalent symptoms of the disorder in question, and not the disorder itself."[17]

# Notes

1. As quoted in Victor Ruiz, "Opportunity Knocks," *Episcopal Life* 14, no. 2 (February 2003): 1, 6.

2. Juan M. C. Oliver, *Ripe Fields: The Promise and Challenge of Latino Ministry* (New York: Church Publishing, 2009), 1–2.

3. From 2008 to 2018 the membership in the Episcopal Church decreased by 17.5%. Most of that decrease comes from domestic dioceses. Over the same decade the dioceses that saw growth were Haiti, Tennessee, Arkansas, Navajo Missions, Taiwan, Colombia, Ecuador-Litoral, Venezuela. From 2017 to 2018 there were twenty-four dioceses that saw increases or no-change: Haiti, Rochester, NW Pennsylvania (no-change), Pittsburgh, Alabama, Central Gulf Coast, Lexington, South Carolina, Tennessee, Western North Carolina, Indianapolis, Colorado, Iowa, Wyoming, Arkansas, Texas, Western Missouri, Western Kansas, Navajo Missions, Colombia, Dominican Republic, Ecuador-Litoral, Venezuela (no change). Note that this is good news for Pittsburgh and South Carolina as they are rebounding from their respective splits. The new numbers that include 2018 were released on September 12, 2019. Episcopal Church, "Baptized Members by Province and Diocese, 2008–2018," Accessed September 30, 2019. *https://www.episcopalchurch.org/files/2._baptized_members_by_province_and_diocese_2008-2018.pdf.*

4. From 2008 to 2018 Average Sunday Attendance (ASA) increased in Taiwan, Colombia, Ecuador-Litoral, Venezuela. From 2017 to 2018 ASA increased in Haiti, Fort Worth, Northwest Texas, Navajo Missions, Colombia, Dominican Republic, Puerto Rico, Venezuela (no-change). Episcopal Church, "Average Sunday Attendance by Province and Diocese, 2008–2018." Accessed September 30, 2019. *https://www.episcopalchurch.org/files/updated_3._average_sunday_attendance_by_province_and_diocese_2008-2018.pdf.*

5. The Task Force for Latino/Hispanic Congregational Development and Sustainability 2018 General Convention report, *https://extranet.generalconvention.org/staff/files/download/21185.*

6. BCP, 855.

7. ENS, "Bishops Release Letter on Sin of Racism, Urge Reading in Parishes on May 15," April 21, 1994 [94080]; "House of Bishops Pastoral Letter on Sin of Racism, March 1994," April 21, 1994. [94090].

8. Oliver, *Ripe Fields*, 3.

9. Oliver, *Ripe Fields*, 4.

10. Oliver, *Ripe Fields*, 21, 22.

11. Some of these come from Oliver, *Ripe Fields*, 10.

12. Jennifer Baskerville-Burrows, sermon at the closing Eucharist of the 2019 Forma Conference in Christ Church Cathedral, Indianapolis, Indiana, Feast of Saint Paul's Conversion, January 25, 2019.

13. The baptismal liturgy begins on page 299 of the English-language Book of Common Prayer. The Baptismal Covenant begins on page 304.

14. Alberto L. García and John A. Nunes, *Wittenberg Meets the World: Reimagining the Reformation at the Margins* (Grand Rapids, MI: William B. Eerdmans Publishing, 2017), 79.

15. García and Nunes, *Wittenberg*, 110, 144.

16. Ana Marie Cox, "Trevor Noah Wasn't Expecting Liberal Hatred," *New York Times Magazine*, November 2, 2016, *https://www.nytimes.com/2016/11/06/magazine/trevor-noah-wasnt-expecting-liberal-hatred.html.*

17. Harold T. Lewis, *Yet With A Steady Beat: The African American Struggle for Recognition in the Episcopal Church* (Valley Forge, PA: Trinity Press International, 1996), 164.

# CHAPTER 3

# Challenges

## Things Done and Left Undone

### Unmasking Hyphenated-Ministry: LATINX Ministry Is Ministry

If we are to dismantle the structures that are hindering our Church from fulfilling its mission, we not only need to know our history—to not repeat it, and the discourses that maintain it—but we also need to understand what needs to be dismantled. In the introduction, I defined hyphenated-ministry as reified specialized ministries, where the hyphenated is no longer a descriptor and is detached from the most basic understandings of ministry. In other words, ministry becomes secondary. Hyphenated-ministries are, by definition, dependent on the institution, and do not ruffle the institution or make waves.

The phrase "ministry to, with, and among LATINX people and communities" begins with ministry, rather than ends with it, and better describes the various ways ministry is defined with respect to LATINX people and communities. This phrase also roughly coincides with the shifts in this specific institutionalized work. The oldest LATINX ministry actions are ministry to, not with.

Creating diverse and polycentric congregations requires uncomfortable work. It is easier to have monolithic congregations, and, perhaps, it is human nature to gravitate toward that which is known and comfortable, especially on Sunday morning when many would rather be comfortable; however, comfortable is not the same as comforted. Many of our majority-culture churches mirror the communities around them; other churches that have remained reflective of that prior majority culture are in communities that are differently composed and have a diversity that the congregation does not reflect.

How then do we grapple with changing demographics? How do we create more diverse and polycentric congregations, or congregations that at least reflect their communities? This change is messy, and many are trying to meet the challenge. What is the role of congregations that indeed reflect their communities and are not diverse racially or economically? The message sometimes comes across as "if there are not LATINX persons in your congregation you are not doing things right." And they may ask themselves, "do we need to import diversity that is not present in our congregation?" Sandra Maria Van Opstal offers an answer to these questions: "Congregational worship should reflect the diversity of God's people, even if a local congregation is not diverse."[1] Yes, this is about demographics, but not survival; it is about fulfilling the mission of the Church in our little idiosyncratic corners of the world, including the people in our communities and parishes, while at the same time being reflective more broadly of the diversity of the reign of God.

One way to grapple with changing demographics is to meet the needs of those in our midst. Most Episcopalians feel good and comfortable with helping the *other*, but struggle with having *others* in their midst. Since we are a majority-white Church, most ministry to, with, and among LATINX people and communities is often ministry *to*, rather than *with* or *among*. Even when we welcome *others* in our congregations, we are content that they remain in the pew, and do not need for them to feel included or develop a sense of belonging. In fact, we want those that are already in our congregations to become more like *us*. The "us" is considered normative. A consequence of this "us mentality" is it renders invisible the LATINX people and other people of color already in our majority-culture congregations.

Perhaps a story will illustrate this erasure. I feel very much loved by the congregation I serve. They love me so much that they might even inadvertently erase parts of me. In 2016, with the coverage of discriminatory bathroom legislation aimed at transgender people, I shared with the vestry about my own experiences over twenty-five years in being challenged for entering women's bathrooms, given that I am gender nonconforming. They were incredulous. Since they knew me, they could not understand or *see* how I presented out in the world. They recognized the hardship for others but could not see it for those closest to them. This is a type of exceptionalism and erasure.

"Ministry to" assumes that the only thing we have to give is "aid." "Ministry to" erases those already in our congregations, or exceptionalizes them as those "others" who don't materially need something from "us"; therefore, they are one step removed from them. Added to this is our limited imagination in how to make our congregations more polycentric and diverse. With these mindsets, many Episcopalians are likely to feel more comfortable with companion relationships and specifically designated LATINX congregations, rather than worshipping with or among "non-erased" LATINX people. Can we dare to change the vernacular of our worship? Furthermore, without radical changes of the institution, if these LATINX-defined congregations do not have equal footing in the diocese, these are still examples of "ministry to." These congregations, in essence, are still dependent and are viewed as less than other congregations—mere programs of the Church.

It is easier for many Episcopal churches to work from what Rev. Juan Francisco Martínez calls a "deficiency perspective," or seeing LATINX people and communities as materially needing from the Church, or "lacking" in numerous ways.[2] These congregations prefer to work from an "outreach" perspective. This is also seen in educational assumptions and the supposed challenges in "leadership development" or the need for separate programs. "Ministry to," "social services," or "outreach" are not inherently bad, except when they are based on ontological and epistemological assumptions about who offers and who receives, or how they keep the same power structures in place. "Ministry to" should not be considered evangelism. There is a difference between sharing the Good News and doing "good." Majority-culture, white, progressive Christians don't want to hear this; "social ministries" as Martínez describes are their "conscience palliative."[3] They end up going "just far enough," but maintain the structures of power and oppression.

There is, however, one problem with merely offering programs to people who are in need. When they come to the Church and accept our services, we tend to feel good because we have helped them. That is not enough.[4] "Ministry to" tends to be paternalistic and creates dependency but does not raise leadership among those being ministered to. It is "for the community, something envisioned, developed, and supported from outside."[5] In fact, there are "Anglos" that would rather fund something external than to work with or among the same communities.[6]

It is also about power and resources. Ministering "to" retains power structures and control over resources, so that the institution remains unchallenged. It guarantees the status quo: individual people may benefit from the largess of those in power, yet by maintaining the "to," they are in fact guaranteeing that the power relationship remains the same. Oliver writes:

> It is no wonder that we, who have found out that the world has room for many ways of being, are considered best at being ministered *to*, even *managed*, for monocultural members of the dominant culture are sensitive enough to feel that we "others" are permitted to act out our world, we may well construct and express a different world from theirs with a different order of power and meaning. Naturally, this is profoundly threatening to them.[7]

Oliver continues by noting that "Latinos who are *doing* rather than *receiving* ministry are a dangerous lot."[8] Focused ministry "to" guarantees that even ministry "with" and "among" also remain as hyphenated-ministry. Ministry with and among *others* requires that we value building a multicultural, intersectional, and polycentric reflection of the reign of God over our individual comfort in less diverse or monocultural settings. It also requires majority-LATINX congregations to also be mission-minded in their own communities and parishes.

## Selling Indulgences

Rev. Alberto L. García and Rev. John A.Nunes offer a different and more damming way to look at this "ministry to" reality in the Church. They argue that the motivations are akin to the selling of indulgences. In its most basic way, ministering to LATINX persons and communities is for the self-interest of the majority-culture Church and not out of an interest in true *diakonia* or building *koinōnia*. I'll let their words speak for themselves.

> The most practiced modus operandi for outreach to Hispanics in North America (and for that matter in Latin America) sounds like the selling or buying of indulgences. . . . [In other words, the] investment in ministries among the people in the margins is usually envisioned as a way of "selling indulgences." The number one reason that the US Latino population is being addressed is to build our own churches or membership. There is the tendency to serve others for our own sake rather than to walk with them in their need.[9]

When I read this I immediately thought of all those who purchased indulgences for the building of St. Peter's in Rome. Of course this is a correct point of reference, we want to build our many St. Peter's. García and Nunes continue with an explanation of how this looks in a parish: "Many leaders and parishioners within congregations view their church as theirs because they bought it with their offerings. Outreach is envisioned to find ways that outsiders can contribute to preserve their status quo."[10]

This idea of indulgences does not end with the preservation and perpetuation of the congregation—the institution—but also extends to "ministry at the margins" to the mission-field, where ministry, defined by García as *diakonia*, "is envisioned as one for the sake of us rather than walking with others in the margins." Therefore it remains as a "doing for them. . . . those poor people what they cannot do for themselves."[11] To be clear this means that by sharing their largess they believe they have the power to effect their own salvation. Tragically, this also means that we do not actually "want to pay the cost of carrying our own cross by walking [with those at the margins] in life and death."[12]

"Ministry to" can never be truly *diakonia* if it continues to be "turned to itself." Again, García and Nunes offer the following images: "standing with and not merely for the least"; "not a *diakonia* for others" which is really self-serving, "but rather a *diakonia* with others."[13] They understand the biblical story to show the apostles's witness of a "*diakonia* in light of the cries from the margins"; as well as the story of the early church's witness "not a *diakonia* of selling indulgences but rather a *diakonia* of openness, risk, and vulnerability by walking with others."[14] Finally, in order for *diakonia* to not be self-serving, it must be always interconnected to *koinonia*. In their words,

> *service* apart from *life together* tends toward patronizing acts of charity that create dependency, that do not honor an individual's or community's capacity, and that do not lead to sustainable development. Or, conversely, *life together* apart from the sense of responsible *service* tends toward a crisis of stewardship, blind to the opportunity to aggregate intentionally goods and services so that they meay be extended to those in need.[15]

## The Deficiency Model

I love Puerto Rican rice and beans. There are many family stories about me eating rice and beans. One is about me asking Doña Paquita, the school cafeteria supervisor, to give my mom the recipe for how they made rice. I believe I was in kindergarten. For most of my schooling, I ate rice and beans with some sort of variation of a protein and vegetables every day. In Puerto Rico, in public school, school lunch was free. In middle school, I was in Amarillo, Texas. The food was very different, and I had to pay for lunch. As an adult, I realized the difference between the two systems and the presumptions behind them.

In Puerto Rico, because the continental United States considered us poor and in need, we all qualified for free lunches. We were also measured and weighed regularly, we were lined up and vaccinated, and dental clinics came on a yearly basis. This was our normal. To my knowledge, we did not experience this as negative or stigmatizing, perhaps because none of us was specifically singled out. Yet from the point of view of the federal government and other organizations, we were thought of as being in need and less-than: "automatically qualifying." There is much that could be examined in this story. What I want to focus on is the difference in point of view. What is normative? Why?

The assumptions about economic means often extend to assumptions about capacities. Similar assumptions are made about children and youth in the continental United States who receive free and reduced-price lunches, but those factors should not determine the overall future and possibilities for any person. People in my graduating class are PhDs, MBAs, and MDs, they have earned bachelor's degrees, and are licensed engineers, lawyers, CPAs, mechanics, and artists. They defy the idea that nothing good comes from Nazareth—I mean Puerto Rico.[16]

Puerto Rico's economic growth is often measured by comparing similar indices with the state of Mississippi, the economically poorest state in the United States. Puerto Rico's median and per capita incomes are less than half of those of Mississippi. In recent years the gap has increased. The poverty rate in Puerto Rico is over 45 percent. Much can be written on the reasons Puerto Rico's economy continues to stagnate. One of the root causes is that Puerto Rico is a colony of the United States and is treated as such.

Three examples of how Puerto Ricans are treated as second-class citizens should make the point: first, the response by the federal government in the aftermath of hurricanes Irma and Maria in 2017; second, the fact that Puerto Rico's economic growth is dependent on decisions made by a Fiscal Control Board appointed by the United States Congress; and, third, the fact that the federal government can do what it chooses with Puerto Rico, yet Puerto Ricans living on the island cannot vote for the president of the United States, nor have a voting member in Congress. All these things continue to foment a culture of dependency and stagnation and project Puerto Rico as "less-than" or deficient. If this is clearly colonial, then the Church also has a history of colonialism and acts from the perspective of that history.

These colonial assumptions also permeate United States culture and inform denominational understandings related to the "deficiency model" of ministry to, with, and among LATINX people and communities, which "focuses on what Latinos supposedly cannot do,"[17] or "the needs of the Latino community and how to respond to them."[18] LATINX people and communities have many resources and bring much to the table.

The deficiency model is fueled by the long-standing discourses of the "black legend" and I believe that there are ways in which this perception still holds sway in the twenty-first century and in the Episcopal Church. The deficiency model in the Episcopal Church looks like a "special ministry" or hyphenated-ministry. In congregations it looks like "ministries to" or outreach. The institutional structure of Ethnic Ministries fundamentally works from a deficiency model—from scarcity. This is a fundamental reason why I believe "Ethnic Ministries" should not be a *program* of the Church. The various ethnic ministries are faced with decisions on what money to request from the Church to maintain the structure that allows it to do some ministry, but never allows it to do the extent of work that is actually needed. So long as it is a program or project of the Church, the "solution" to the challenge will never be properly and prophetically resourced.

Thus, as I have shown, Ethnic Ministries function as a project of the Church, historically hindered by their own institutionalization, inadequate resourcing, and the perpetuation of the very structures they have tried to ameliorate. Note the disconnect. By creating a structure to bring awareness of certain communities, the Church has, in effect, kept those communities subjugated and *other*. My case is supported by the fact that there is no "White Desk." The whole Church is primarily for whites; projects of the Church are for *others*. This is also corroborated by the long-standing treatment of black Episcopalians by the Church. The institutional Church feels just fine making "policy decisions" for those that fall under "Ethnic Ministries."[19]

*Special* or hyphenated-ministries become reified objects (thingified). Rather than "ministry" defining the work or action, that which is *special* or *hyphenated* becomes the determiner; it is no longer ministry, but something else or *other*. The depth at which this reification functions is part of the DNA (epistemic foundation) of the Episcopal Church as an institution. Even people of good will and good intentions believe the perpetuated narratives that keep these people and communities as "objects" of the Church's ministry, rather than "agents" of ministry living out their baptismal promises and fulfilling the mission of the Church. The truth is, however, that LATINX ministry *is ministry is ministry is ministry.*

In sharing with colleagues about the idea for this book I asked, "What would you find helpful in such a book?" They mentioned, among other things, wanting to know what is specific or different about LATINX ministry and how to do this ministry without knowing Spanish? I asked in return, if we call LATINX ministry just ministry, what are the questions and how do we answer them? From a LATINX ministry perspective, the answers are to find out what these people need and see how a parish can meet those needs—and, perhaps, find a Spanish-speaker to do the outreach. If it is seen as ministry, the starting point may well be different—perhaps related to prayer, worship, Bible study, and sacraments: the difference between a programmatic approach and a missional approach; and not mission as equated to outreach.

Showing solidarity with oppressed communities and seeking their liberation is one way to fulfill the mission of the Church. Solidarity is sacramental—the outward and visible sign of inclusion. In other words, we are called to show that we all have a stake in each other's liberation. Reconciling people to one another is important; it is a requirement in prophetically proclaiming justice and peace and alleviating the spiritual and material suffering of people and communities. In this sense solidarity fits with García and Nunes's sense of *diakonia* discussed above.

There are several (interrelated) ways in which this understanding of ministry emerged. Around the turn of the twentieth century, before the rise of specialized ministries, there was a response to real needs, especially in growing urban centers and changing economic systems—a living into the social gospel. That social gospel evolved into a narrower outlook of solidarity with the poor and those suffering from the ravages of racism.

In most progressive intentions, the institutionalization of programs perpetuate the very structures that they thought were being changed. For example, the emancipation movement that deeply divided our Church along a North-South matrix presented the promise and intention for the liberation of all those enslaved and all who had historically been kept down in this society based on the color of their skin. We know that many of our churches, in both North and South, benefited from slave labor. We know that many of our churches were worshipping communities that sat segregated in the same buildings. We also know that the idea of emancipation was not necessarily extended to the emancipation of the Church itself. And we know that we fall short from the imperative of our Baptismal Covenant to "respect the dignity of every human being." Yet the legacies of slavery and racism are so deeply embedded in the institutions and structures of the Episcopal Church that over one hundred and fifty years later the Church continues to participate in the sin of racism by its ongoing inability to truly share power and resources.

Specialized ministries, rather than broadening the reach of churches, "created congregations composed of members of a single economic or racial group."[20] To be clear, the rise of "special ministries" emerged as a response to real needs and the desire to ameliorate them. Yet in their institutionalization, they have also served to *other* certain communities from the "mainstream" of the Episcopal Church; while making their difference ontological.

The inability to share power and resources is paternalistic and creates systems of dependence. In his 1998 report, Rev. Herbert Arrunátegui said, "From the very beginning, Hispanic ministry in the United States has been surrounded by ambivalence, insecurity, paternalism, and misunderstandings."[21] Rather than creating truly emancipatory systems to give people agency in their own liberation and ways to live out their own Baptismal Covenant, programs or projects were created that would make side A (generally white) feel good for helping side B. Rather than all being agents, certain groups were objectified and commodified for the benefit of those understood as "normative."

## Hyphenated-Americans: Hyphenated-Episcopalians

You cannot right a wrong without dismantling the structures that allowed for the wrong to exist in the first place. The existence of Ethnic Ministries inherently creates a difference between Episcopalians and hyphenated-Episcopalians. In the same way that LATINX people can, at best, only be hyphenated-Americans in our current cultural climate, they can also never be Episcopalian enough. Several things are at work here, including the failure to understand that Anglicanism can accommodate a breadth of expressions, as expressed in Article 34, rather than one normative white and colonial Church—albeit one that was itself an adaptation of the English Church in a new context. LATINX people and communities cannot be fully Episcopalian because they are not *white* ("Anglo") enough; thus, the need for hyphenated-ministry.

As long as there continue to be hyphenated-ministries based on indelible identities, the future of the Church is precarious. Hyphenated-ministry ensures that ministry to, with, and among LATINX people and communities remains "other"; the "mainstream" can feel good that it exists, but does not have to change anything to deal with the legacies of the discourses of the "black legend" that it continues to perpetuate, or open themselves up to share power, or dismantle the legacies of racism and misogyny. Another curious consequence of the hyphenated-Episcopalian is that it also erases all LATINX people who have been long-standing Episcopalians in congregations that are not specifically designated as LATINX, many of whom are bilingual and understand multiculturalism.[22] This challenge is so pervasive that even within LATINX communities, LATINX persons that attend majority-culture churches are also exceptionalized and excluded from being LATINX within the Church.

In January 2019, I spoke about the problems with hyphenated-ministry at a conference, and I was asked to clarify the problem with qualifying the type of ministry. It is a fair question, and it is my hope that folks will realize that the problem is the reification of what comes before the hyphen, thus detaching it from what it was meant to describe in the first place. When LATINX is dissociated from ministry, there is a problem because the ministry of majority-white culture is normative and the LATINX descriptor makes it *other*.

The existence of hyphenated-Americans and hyphenated-Episcopalians is also related to the perceived failure or capacity of LATINX people to be fully American or fully Episcopalian. This, in turn, is related to the long-standing expectation that when LATINX people have become Protestants they were on the road to assimilation, acculturation, and becoming good citizens. This is an inherent hierarchy between Anglo and LATINX, Protestant and Roman

Catholic. We can believe that this is isolated or in the past, but it continues in the Church today. This deficiency understanding is long-standing. Martínez provides an example from the nineteenth century:

> Latinos were seen as people with many needs and the Protestants of major-ity culture had the responsibility to supply those needs. These people needed the gospel, but they also needed to learn US customs, the English language, hygiene, and technological advances. The Protestant missionaries and churches saw their mission among Latinos as their responsibility both as good Christians and as good US citizens.[23]

Since the nineteenth century there has been a connection between Protes-tantism and assimilation, evangelization, and Americanization.[24] The ideal of assimilation also presumes that LATINX ministry is temporary because in sub-sequent generations LATINX people will be integrated into majority churches. This perpetuates the idea that the LATINX community is transitory and will "assimilate and disappear as a distinctive community or lose interest in having their own church[es]."[25]

As with any other community, LATINX people have a variety of attach-ments to their own ethnic identities. LATINX people also have varying connec-tions to majority culture. Furthermore, LATINX people have varied experiences and expressions in their religious lives. The difference in ascertaining whether something is good or not among LATINX people lies in evaluating the coercive nature of the goal, the access to power and resources, and the ability to fulfill one's dreams. For most of the populations, hopes and aspirations, as well as ave-nues of realization fall along various points in these paradigms.

## Power and Resources

Since colonial times, the religious history of the United States has generally been characterized by ethnic-specific churches. Moving toward diversity is not merely allowing or adapting to the increased diversity of the United States, or letting this diversity affect our churches and denomination as if by osmosis but allowing the very nature of our congregations and denomination to change. This change requires the sharing of power and resources and the surrendering of control.

The type of resource and power sharing that is required is one that dis-mantles the structures rather than create a veneer of power and resource sharing and inclusion. Without dismantling structures, the efforts to be more inclu-sive are short-sighted and superficial. It is unexpectedly masking, in the guise of transparency and progress, that the Church regularly changes the names of different initiatives, committees, and departments, and on occasion even revamps canons. Things certainly sound/read differently than fifty or one hundred years ago. But, isn't it in reality like changing Macy's holiday windows from one year to another? They may look different, but are they? These are just different colorful masks covering the same structures.

Because of the mere nature of the institution, change takes a long time. It is not enough for the Church to simply benefit from the passage of time and the changes in demographics. Institutions have ways of settling back into the same exclusionary structures unless those structures are consciously dismantled. Slow movement hides the continued control, management, containment, and restraint of particular communities.

In October 1992, there was a hate-filled homophobic incident at Cornell just before a Coming Out Day celebration. Sidewalk chalking about the event were defaced with comments like "1-800-DIE-HOMO." The incident led to my coming out publicly and getting involved in LGBTQ activism there. Over the following year, the student assembly made demands of the administration through the LGBT Coalition and met with the president of the university, Frank H. T. Rhodes. Rhodes assigned Vice President Larry Palmer to meet and negotiate with LGBTQ leaders. Vice President Palmer, a black man, was often the person that had to deal with issues related to minoritized groups on campus.

I mention this last detail because putting a black person in charge of a minoritized issue absolves the institution from any failure. If *they*—the minoritized—cannot come to an agreement, then *we* (the institution) are not responsible. The institution absolves itself from the failures, but eagerly takes credit for the successes. Two of the demands made of the administration were a LGBTQ housing unit and a resource center. A resource center under the umbrella of the dean of students opened in 1994. A designated residence hall opened twenty-five years later.[26] This power dynamic allowed the institution to move at its own pace and keep its power structures intact.

Analogously, the Episcopal Church, having Ethnic Ministries and keeping ministry to, with, and among LATINX people and communities as a program of the Church guarantees that ministry to, with, and among LATINX people will remain restrained by the power structures and the lack of sharing in resources. The success of ministry to, with, and among LATINX people and communities reflects positively upon the denomination; its failures fall on LATINX people and communities. This holds true for all ethnic ministries of the Episcopal Church.

In order to justify the lack of sharing of power and resources, the Episcopal Church can go back to the challenges posed by the General Convention Special Program or the alleged connections between the Hispanic Commission and the FALN. Those in power can indicate the need to control resources to avoid the pitfalls encountered earlier. Add the biases that "those people" do not have the education, leadership, or plain-old-sense to use these resources well, and the institution continues to be able to absolve itself. It pats itself on the back because it funds these programs but absolves itself from succeeding. Ethnic Ministries provide a façade of power sharing, all the while creating structures of dependency or at least codependency.[27]

Why is it a problem that ministry to, with, and among LATINX people and communities is treated as a program? One reason has to do with the inherent challenges when programs are institutionalized. Another reason comes from the challenges of the way religious institutions and denominations function. We know that our churches, dioceses, and denominational structures cost money to run. We also know that we must be ever mindful to balance the resource costs of the institution with the resource costs of accomplishing the mission of the institution—its purpose for existing. Institutionalization of a program sets up a dependency upon the umbrella institution and part of its resources are then used for the institution itself. It is an intricate dance between knowing what is needed and asking for what may be given or asking what is needed and not getting the resources to accomplish it. At the church I serve I worry about paying the bills and I know that the upkeep of the facility enables the broader work of the congregation. Sometimes, though, it feels like it is only about paying the bills. A fundamental difference between working from a perspective of abundance or one of scarcity.

## Budgets Say a Lot about Institutional Priorities

One of the ways to show how the structure of an institution impacts the sharing of power and resources is by looking at the allocation of funds. When I began serving at the Church of Saint Matthew and Saint Timothy, I worked with the new rector Rev. Frank Russ. I was hired as the Hispanic assistant. Russ was a great mentor and involved me in the administration of the church, especially because I had a background in operations and management. I did not think of myself as the priest to some parishioners and not to others. I felt that I was a priest to the whole congregation, whether English- or Spanish-speaking. Soon, it became clear that the budget needed restructuring because it divided items between "Hispanic" and those without descriptor. There was "outreach" and "Hispanic outreach," for example. The restructuring of the item codes was accomplished in the next budget cycle.

In the Diocese of New York, a similar issue presented itself. The budget included a line item for Hispanic Ministry. The funds, around $400,000, were a lump sum of money for salaries and programs. At the time, the diocese also had a separate Congregational Support Plan (CSP). Clergy in churches under the CSP, which included some LATINX clergy, had three-year contracts, but the reality was that clergy covered under the Hispanic Ministry line item were technically under one-year contracts renewed with the convention approval of the budget. (A note—women and people of color are more often in part-time or termed positions.)

It was unclear what amount of the funds was for programming. Turns out that the programming portion was about 20 percent or around $80,000; the Hispanic Commission of the diocese distributed monies to congregations who made specific applications. When the bishop and others were made aware of this, the line item was subdivided for more transparency. Yet the reality remained that Hispanic Ministry was seen as a program, similar to university chaplaincies.

In the Episcopal Church, budgets are approved at the triennial General Convention. Here is a bird's eye view of the four most recent triennial budgets of the Episcopal Church, which is no easy task, given that each triennial budget does not use the same template and analogous items can be found in different areas. My point is that budgets can say a lot about the priorities of an institution. Furthermore, the request of funds happens through various General Convention resolutions and are allocated through Executive Council, so numbers may not exactly match what happens during a triennium, or what was requested as part of a resolution. Another set of challenges is defining what should be categorized under "Ethnic Ministries" and what is specifically appropriated for "LATINX Ministries." I have made the decision to not include block grants. It is my belief that grants, in the case of the Episcopal Church, are used by the grantees for ministry, but it is not ministry of the larger institution by transitivity.

The General Convention of 2009 approved a triennial budget for 2010–2012 of $141,271,984 million dollars.[28] This budget did not reflect the yet-to-be realized impact of the Great Recession. The budget report indicates that 62 percent of the budget was for programming. For the triennium, Ethnic Ministries accounted for 3 percent of the budget.

| Ethnic Ministries | 2010–2012 |
| --- | --- |
| Asian | $349,470 |
| Black | $349,470 |
| Indigenous | $595,200 categorized under racial justice |
| Latinx | $649,470 includes $300,000 for D038 |
| Multicultural | $141,960 (does not exist after this triennium) |
| People with disabilities | $111,020 (does not exist after this triennium) |
| Staff | $2,047,838 (I estimate $290,000 for Indigenous Ministries included elsewhere) |
| TOTAL | $4,244,428 (3 percent of the total budget) |

The Strategic Vision, introduced in chapter 2, was presented at this General Convention. Resolution 2009 D038 called for a budget of over $3.5 million dollars.[29]

> *Resolved*, That the General Convention request the Joint Standing Committee on Program, Budget and Finance to consider a budget allocation of $3,565,000 for the implementation of this resolution regarding Strategic Vision for the 2010–2012 triennium; and that this budget is composed of the following elements:

> Funding for 46 new congregations at $40,000 each over the triennium: 1,840,000
>
> Providing resources to 100 existing congregations          1,000,000
>
> Lay Leadership Development          200,000
>
> Tools and Training, Marketing Resources          450,000
>
> Evaluation          75,000
>
> Total          $3,565,000

Looking at this resolution in 2019, here are a few observations. My hope would be that the $40,000 funding for new congregations would have been offered as a one-time sum to each, in order to make a durable impact that could be built upon. Otherwise, the request for the funding of forty-six new congregations would have been at an average of $13,333 each per year, which would have made it more difficult to realistically make a sustainable effect. For the basic operation of a congregation, a one-time $40,000 investment could only work if there are other significant funds, or if this congregation is not saddled with any significant clergy or building costs (salaries and benefits, rent, utilities, insurance, etc.). In other words, buildings and clergy are costly; thus, the model of base communities, or even that of the house church, which are focused on laypeople and their leadership, are realistic models for congregations that have only a piecemeal or paltry investment. Similarly, the support of existing congregations would also have to have been as lump sums in order to be impactful, since receiving $10,000 is very different than receiving $3,333 for three years.

All the above is conjecture given that only $300,000 was allocated to this resolution. Putting aside my reservations about what kind of impact these funds can actually make and about the Strategic Vision and its marketing approach, isn't it disingenuous to even concur with a resolution knowing the funding envisioned was never going to be granted? I wonder, also, whether many of those who voted in favor of the resolution know how underfunded it was? It is difficult to be prophetic and proactive when you have no control over the allocation of funds. It would be better to boldly invest in something that might fail, rather than to tokenize something that will never succeed. Yet the perception was about all the funds *they* get.

Earlier I quoted Rev. Robert W. Prichard regarding the rise of special ministries in the Episcopal Church and the assessment that this trend continues to this day. Prichard elaborates in a footnote, "The special ministry is still alive in the Episcopal Church of the twenty-first century. More than ten percent of the 2012–15 adopted by the General Convention of 2012 was, for example, devoted to Ethnic Ministries."[30]

The General Convention of 2012 approved a triennial budget for 2013–2015 of $111,546,000 million dollars.[31] This budget reflected the impact of the 2008–2009 recession (a 21 percent reduction). The budget was divided into several large sections. Five of those sections were the "Five Marks of Mission." Separate from the "Five Marks" was Ethnic Ministries with an allocation of $6,172,181. The fact that it is separate shows that the Five Marks of Mission are for the whole Church—*us*—and Ethnic Ministry monies for *them*. The $6.2 million dollars included a $2,025,000 block grant for historically Black Episcopal colleges and universities.[32] At times these grants were not included under Ethnic Ministries. Therefore, Ethnic Ministries in fact accounted for 3.18 percent of the budget, not the "more than ten percent" indicated by Prichard.

| Ethnic Ministries | 2013–2015 |
|---|---|
| Asian | $302,500 |
| Black | $302,500 |
| Indigenous | $534,000 now categorized under Ethnic Ministries |
| Latinx | $330,000 |
| Staff | $2,080,981 |
| TOTAL | $3,549,981 (3.18 percent of the total budget) |
| New Community | $197,000 (3.36 percent) |
| New Congregations | $2,000,000 *not solely for Ethnic Ministries congregations |

As I think further about Prichard's footnote, I ask, "Is 10 percent too much or too little?" The footnote requires clarification. Does Prichard arrive at the 10 percent number by including block grants to Province II, VI, VIII, and IX? Do grants amount to ministry?

The General Convention of 2015 approved a triennial budget for 2016–2018 of $125,012,531 million dollars.[33] This budget was divided similarly to the previous one with the priorities related to the "Five Marks of Mission." Ethnic Ministries was separate from the "Five Marks" with an allocation of $6,425,727, which included a $2,045,000 million block grant for historically Black Episcopal colleges and universities. Therefore, Ethnic Ministries in fact accounted for 3.43 percent of the budget, or 3.5 when the New Community monies are added or 4.38 percent with the Evangelism Initiatives.

| Ethnic Ministries | 2016–2018 |
|---|---|
| Asian | $420,000 |
| Black | $518,000 |
| Indigenous | $576,000 |
| Latinx | $520,000 |
| Staff | $2,256,727 (includes some funding for a second Latinx Missioner) |
| TOTAL | $4,290,727 (3.43 percent of the total budget) |
| New Community | $90,000 (added to the above then 3.5 percent of the total budget) |
| New Congregations | $3,000,000 + $2,823,226 *not solely for Ethnic Ministries congregations |
| Evangelism Initiatives | $1,100,000 from the above, as part of resolutions D005 and A086. (4.4 percent) |

Although the budget structure changed for the 2019–2021 triennium, the numbers are not much different. The new triennial budget was approximately $133.9 million dollars.[34] The format of the budget changed given the new conceptualization of the "Jesus Movement."[35]

| Ethnic Ministries | 2019–2021 |
|---|---|
| Asian | $330,000 |
| Black | $360,000 |
| Indigenous | $325,000 |
| Latinx | $458,000 |
| Staff | $2,951,844 (this includes the second LATINX Missioner and $333,000 for a second Indigenous Missioner) |
| TOTAL | $4,424,844 (3.3 percent of the total budget) |
| New Community | $395,000 (each of the ministries was allocated $98,750 for this collaborative work)—added to total above this is 3.6 percent |
| New Congregations | $3,000,000 *not solely for Ethnic Ministries congregations |

One of the difficulties in comparing these four triennial budgets is that some initiatives come in, others drop out, and there are differences in the allocation of funds. It is possible, though, to state some observations.

1. Ethnic Ministries generally account for 3 to 3.5 percent of the budget.

2. The programming coming out of Ethnic Ministries accounts for 1.4 to 1.55 percent of the budget. Because of the A086 amendment to the 2016–2018 budget, this percentage increased by 0.88 to 2.5 percent (with the added $1.1 million). The lowest programming amount is in the current triennium, even with the expanded "New Community" collaborations.

3. The 2019–2021 budget slightly exceeds inflation from the previous triennium. The same is true for "Ethnic Ministries."

   a. Without accounting for the one-time evangelism initiative, when Ethnic Ministries is analyzed by staff and program, there is a net effect of $394,000 less for programming in this new triennium.

   b. The increase in the current total is solely attributed to the two new staff positions.

4. The ground lost in the budget on account of the Great Recession will never be recovered. If we were to adjust the 2010–2012 budget for inflation to

2018 it would go from $141.3 million to $166.2 million. The 2019–2021 budget is $133.9 million.

5. Furthermore, some of the added funds are in effect grants, not programs coming out of the Episcopal Church as a whole. They are distributed amongst dioceses, programs, and churches that work well within the institutional structures, staying then within, and without challenging the structures of the Church.

With this brief outline, I hope you can get but a glimmer of what these budget numbers say about the Episcopal Church's commitment to LATINX ministries, let alone a commitment to LATINX people and communities. At the very least, the amount of lip service given to LATINX demographics has not translated into the priorities of the Church, let alone the budget. I suspect that if I was to dig even deeper into all areas of the budget, I would find other ways in which the Church is not focused on its mission, but instead on the perpetuation of the institution. The fact that the budget numbers for 2019–2021 barely keep up with inflation is telling. If we compare where we were in 2009 in adjusted numbers to the present, the Ethnic Ministries program budget is more than $700,000 less.

The Episcopal Church must embark on a discernment process of identifying the structural issues that are preventing the fulfillment of the mission of the Church. These structural changes may be canonical, administrative, and programmatic. The foundations and structures of the very systems need to be transformed, challenged, and dismantled.[36] This observation is not new, the "Theological Consultation" report of 1981 implored that

> The Episcopal Church must reexamine its own structures to eradicate areas of injustice against minorities and against Spanish-speaking people in particular. We allow racism and sexism to exist in the Church. We allow unfair financial support for Hispanic congregations and unjust representation in decision-making bodies of the Church. We tolerate the presence of superficial hospitality and deprecating attitudes towards Hispanics. Therefore, we urge action to confront structural injustice wherever it exists.[37]

Almost forty years later, we are still chasing a different way of thinking about the deficiencies in the resourcing of ministry to, with, and among LATINX people and communities that considers the way the institution has historically allocated personnel and funds.

In the previously cited 1985 report, González wrote about the difficulties in successful LATINX ministries that emerge from congregations that have experienced "white-flight."

What is in fact often taking place when plans are being made for such a Hispanic ministry and congregation is that the needs of the church are made to determine the needs of the people, and the existence of facilities and the need to upkeep them is allowed to determine the nature of the program.[38]

A different way to think about this is putting a clergyperson in a position because the position is open—and that person needs a job—or starting something in a location because the facilities/buildings are there. Either of these without doing any background work as to whether that is the right job or the right location.

## Unmasking Comfort—Ministry Models

Although identity or classification are not ontological/essential categories, the reality is that the Episcopal Church is 86.6 percent white (of non-Hispanic origin).[39] That is "whiter" than the rest of the United States. With that in mind, what does it mean to love one another as God has loved us? What does it mean to create a welcoming environment in our churches as we claim in "the Episcopal Church Welcomes You"? How do we create a Church where everyone has a sense of belonging and from which we go out into the world and live into our Baptismal Covenant?

I often preach that not only is keeping Jesus's love commandment very difficult, but that it does not mean that we are friends with everyone, or that love equals being nice—enabling or passive aggressive; we also hold each other accountable. In doing so, we are showing our love. I also preach and teach that the questions in our Baptismal Covenant are not conditional statements. We are called to respect the dignity of every human being, to seek and serve Christ in all people—not just of those whom we love or who respect us, but every human being. Achieving love of neighbor is among the most difficult things we can accomplish as followers of Christ.

The words of the hymn "For Everyone Born"[40] by Shirley Erena Murray are powerful. The hymn text was inspired by the words of the 1948 United Nations Human Rights Declaration. Whenever I listen to it or sing it, I am deeply moved. I imagine that for everyone born there will be a place at the table, and that includes me. Yet Murray presents a very uncomfortable image of what "everyone born" truly means.

For just and unjust, a place at the table,
abuser, abused, with need to forgive,
in anger, in hurt, a mindset of mercy,
for just and unjust, a new way to live.

This is the crux of the matter: until we can accept those whom we hate and those who hate us, no one truly has a place at the table. Even in writing this, what I want to write is "those whom we dislike and those who hate us," so that it is softer and reduces the reality of our sinfulness. We have to work hard at not absolving ourselves of the love imperative. Love, forgiveness, and reconciliation are aspects of the same commandment. Hate requires some aspect of judgement. It is difficult to judge someone whose story you have truly heard.

In January of 2018, I attended a national conference. During one of the panels, I felt my circles of inclusion expanding, creating a place for more people at my table. The people on the panel were some of the most marginalized people in our society and they spoke of their resilience and survival. I began my sermon the following Sunday by talking about a woman who had immigrated to the United States and suffered violence and hate, yet now provided shelter for dozens of people every night and employed a number of other marginalized people. She was feeding the hungry, sating the thirsty, clothing the naked, housing the homeless, employing the poor.

You may ask why I would be stretched by her story. She was a Latinx trans woman who had survived through sex work. Hearing her story and her playfulness around sex work was uncomfortable for me, but my desire for comfort did not override the love I felt and the love I know Jesus felt for her and the other panelists that day.

Welcome and belonging are values of the Episcopal Church. Achieving them is inherently not comfortable. If church is not a place where welcome and belonging matter more than feeling comfortable, we need to listen to the gospel in a new way. The way of the Cross is not comfortable; speaking truth to power is not comfortable; loving those we judge as sinners (or less than) is not comfortable. All these actions are part of being followers of Jesus. I wish we had congregations in which we were continually stretched, all the while being strengthened by a sense of welcome and belonging. One of our mottoes or values should be "Uncomfortable for Jesus." Or, perhaps, "Putting Aside Comfort for the Sake of the Gospel." The 1981 report of the Theological Consultation states:

> At the same time, we view ourselves and our future with fear and trembling, knowing that every culture needs self-criticism and the transforming power of the Gospel. We believe that the presence of Hispanics is a God-given opportunity for traditional Anglo-Episcopal congregations to escape a dangerous self-centeredness and complacency and to encounter a more fully authentic life and valid ministry in the name of the Risen Lord.

## Unmasking the Demographics: Who Are We Talking about When We Talk about LATINX People and Communities?

According to the United States Decennial Census, in 2010, LATINX people accounted for 16.3 percent of the total population of the United States, or over fifty million people. The LATINX population in the United States was 63 percent of Mexican descent, 9.2 percent of Puerto Rican descent, 7.9 percent of Central American descent, 5.5 percent South American, 3.5 percent of Cuban descent, 2.8 percent of Dominican descent, and 8.1 percent not identifying by some "national" heritage.[41] The United States Census Bureau's 2018 estimate of the United States' total population is more than 327 million. Of these 18.1 percent are categorized as LATINX—more than 59 million.[42] Though I could spend many pages on descriptive demographics about LATINX people and communities, the only relevant point is that LATINX people and communities are part of the United States, are underrepresented in the Episcopal Church, and have something to add to our congregations. Our congregations are a place where LATINX people can have a deep sense of belonging.

I am a numbers person, yet census figures and other quantitative data do not really get at who we are as people or communities. Furthermore, when I see these numbers, they speak to me in a way that is different from how they might be interpreted by any reader of this book. My understanding of these numbers is also shaped by my experiences. Getting at the complexity of LATINX identity is difficult and beyond the scope of this book. Thus, it is important for every reader to both grasp the numbers and understand their own specific context and limitations. Yet, statistics should not be used to essentialize and homogenize people and communities.

Since going to college in New York state I have always found the question "Where are you from?" to be curious, in part because often I answer Puerto Rico, but only to find out that they were asking, "Where did you live before moving to school?"—something not necessarily connected to identity or heritage. For me, the answer to both was Puerto Rico. At a recent meeting, I was asked the question and answered, "I'm from Puerto Rico; I live in New York City." Although New York is where I have lived the longest, I still answer that I am from Puerto Rico, which is where I grew up. I also know that when I answer Puerto Rico that people will presume I was born in Puerto Rico, which they think is not possible since I don't "look Puerto Rican." I lived on the island and then moved to New York for college, with a brief interlude in Amarillo, Texas, which means I moved from a majority context to a minoritized environment. These are just a few ways I have experienced the complexity of LATINX identity in the United States.

Although I was born in Texas, I identify as Puerto Rican because it is the culture in which I was formed and where I did most of my primary and secondary education. It is the side of my extended family with whom I have my closest relationships and experiences. Although there are things with which I can identify and experience with my father and his family, they did not form me in the same way. I can't say that I equally like Puerto Rican rice and beans and southern-fried steak with mashed potatoes, gravy, and green beans; Puerto Rican rice and beans will always win.

My experience with being labeled with a pan-category—"Hispanic" then "Latino/a"—began when I moved to the continental United States for college, which coincided with the rise of various claims of pan-identities that later coalesced under "identity politics." Being labeled with the pan-categories Latino/a, Hispanic, and LATINX is a way to create a homogenized conglomerate of very different groups of people from dozens of national backgrounds. These pan-categories also try to group a collective of ethnic backgrounds that then are placed alongside racial categories such as white, black, Asian, and Indigenous, when in fact LATINX people can be both LATINX and any one or combination of the other racial categories and polycentric identities.

One of the reasons for an identity based on "national background" has to do with differing migration histories, or no migration at all. The ancestors of many people of Mexican descent did not cross a border, the border crossed them. There have been various waves of Puerto Rican migration. The majority of Puerto Ricans are not island born, but all Puerto Ricans are citizens. Political turmoil and U.S. military involvement may contextualize the migration patterns of Cubans and Dominicans. Civil war and violence may inform the migration pattern of Central Americans. All these places also have different population sizes. The answer of who LATINX people are is further complicated by whether the question is answered from within LATINX communities or from outside. Most LATINX people tend to identify first by national background, then, perhaps, by pan-categories. A further complication is that LATINX people are minoritized within the United States context and have varied relationships to the majority culture.

(LATINX) people have complex polycentric identities. I will borrow some useful descriptions offered by Martínez. In the United States, the conglomerate of LATINX people is the largest minoritized group. It continues to grow and diversify. Because LATINX people come from many national backgrounds, they also come from many cultural backgrounds, thus LATINX communities are inherently multicultural. Although some connection to Spanish is true for many, there are LATINX people that have more of a connection to English and others to Portuguese.[43] Sixty-five percent of LATINX people in the United States are U.S. born.[44] A similar percentage is English-language dominant.

As mentioned before, all the reports from the middle of the 1980s (Arrunátegui, González, Diocese of New York) make mention of the dual foci of population and poverty. Demographic information was partially the impetus for ministry to, with, and among LATINX people and communities since the 1960s and 70s; things changed at the turn of the millennium. For the Episcopal Church, the census of 2000 created what I term "a demographic panic." Yet at the turn of the millennium, it was as though no one could have predicted the rise in the number of LATINX people and communities living in the United States.

Almost any article or book that has to do with LATINX ministry will mention demographics—it has become a trope. In the book *Walking with the People: Latino Ministry in the United States*, Martínez begins, "During the first decade of the 21st Century Latinos became the largest minority group in the United States."[45] The discourse of demographics is absolutely ingrained in church and society, and as such it is often founded on an underlying fear. This fear or panic must be acknowledged and understood for it to be overcome as a barrier in developing meaningful ministries with and among LATINX people and communities, as well as becoming centers of welcoming and belonging in our already existing congregations. Furthermore, the underlying fear must be challenged in order to address the scapegoating being experienced by LATINX persons in the United States of today.

What is clear to me is that the approach toward LATINX people and communities cannot be about survival. So far it has proven to not mitigate the numeric decline of the Church. In 2014 LATINX people were 3.6 percent of the Episcopal Church;[46] up 0.1 percent from 2010. LATINX Episcopalians are less than 1 percent of the total LATINX population of the United States.[47] In other words, if the Church has not grown from the majority population, how does it expect to grow from a relatively small constitutive minority? Furthermore, could we honestly say that if the diversity of the Episcopal Church mirrored that of the country (16 to 18 percent) that it would be numerically larger than it is today?

There is something structural to be addressed when the Church cannot keep up with population growth, even if they remain the same as a percentage of the population. It used to be said that membership in the Episcopal Church remained steady in proportion to the population, about 2 percent; that is no longer true and has not been for a while. In 2011 there were 1,923,046 active baptized members in the Episcopal Church, a 17 percent decrease in 10 years.[48] In 2016 this number is 1,745,156, an additional 9 percent decline.[49] The 2017 fact sheet of the Episcopal Church based on parochial reports indicates that there are a little over 1.7 million active Episcopalians; in 2018 there was another 2 percent decline to under 1.7 million.[50] Of those about 35,000 are LATINX.[51] In short, the demographic increase or decrease of the Episcopal Church cannot be on the shoulders of LATINX people.

From 2007 to 2014, Pew Research identified an overall 3.4 percent decrease in the number of people identifying with mainline Protestant traditions.[52] During the same period, the percentage of people of color in mainline Protestant churches increased from 9 to 14 percent.[53] This increase does not hold true for the Episcopal Church. Notwithstanding the demographics, the growth envisioned by the General Convention of 2000 of doubling in twenty years (the 20/20 Vision) was not realized. The demographic panic that led to a marketing approach to appeal to LATINX people and communities will never work because marketing is not about getting to know people, about building relationships, nor about fulfilling the mission of the church. Marketing is about selling something and we don't even know what we are selling.

Trends in membership cut across denominations: For example, the share of adults belonging to mainline churches dropped from 18.1 percent in 2007 to 14.7 percent in 2014. This is similar to the drop seen among U.S. Catholics, whose share of the population declined from 23.9 percent to 20.8 percent during the same seven-year period.[54] The mainline tradition's share of the Protestant population has declined along with its share of the overall population. Today, 32 percent of Protestants identify with denominations in the mainline tradition, down from 35 percent in 2007. Evangelicals now constitute a clear majority of all Protestants in the United States, with their share of the Protestant population having risen from 51 percent in 2007 to 55 percent in 2014.

It is my sense that the message and theology that the Episcopal Church has to offer LATINX people and communities is different from the evangelical/born-again churches that are growing. Therefore, we must focus on who we are and what we offer, rather than trying to be something else or substitute for something else. The sheer force of the demographic numbers of LATINX people and communities will not by osmosis save or change the Episcopal Church; the subheading of a recent article in *The Atlantic*—"Demography Is Not Destiny"—makes this point.[55]

## Immigrants

Puerto Ricans living on the island are second-class citizens, as clearly evidenced by the Federal response to the devastation caused by hurricanes Irma and Maria. Regularly, decisions are made for Puerto Ricans living on the island by people they do not have the right to vote for. On the other hand, citizenship has also afforded many Puerto Ricans easy travel to and from the continental United States. The territorial and citizenship relationship also inform the variable understanding, or advocacy and solidarity, Puerto Ricans at times may have with the plight of undocumented people from other Latin American countries.

Another often-held notion is that all LATINX people are immigrants—especially recent immigrants. This is related to the belief, as seen above, that LATINX people are mostly monolingual Spanish speakers. LATINX people and communities are continually treated as foreign in the United States context, or as an "eternal first generation."[56] Yet, the 2016 United States Census Bureau estimates indicate that 64.9 percent of LATINX people in the U.S. are native born and 77.1 percent are citizens.[57] These discourses are insidious.

In 1998 there was a gathering in Mexico of bishops from the Episcopal Church called "Anglican and the Hispanic Experience." Rt. Rev. Sergio Carranza-Gomez, bishop of Mexico, said, "People were praying and writing books here more than 100 years before the first church was built in Virginia." Carranza argued that it is vital to the success of any Hispanic ministry to break the stereotype of the "illiterate immigrant."[58]

In the first three hundred years of colonial dependency, following the Spanish Conquest, indigenous peoples were considered "objects of evangelization, not as subjects of a shared Gospel," said Dr. Alicia Puente, professor at the University of Mexico and a vice president for the Center for Historical Studies of the Church in Central America. She expressed concerns that the same colonial spirit toward Hispanics is present today and warned that "theology without history is absurd." Although this does not absolve the Church, by often identifying by ancestral/family national background, LATINX people sometimes contribute to a sense of "outsideness," or sometimes reinforce the myth that LATINX people are only immigrants.[59]

## Roman Catholicism

I am a cradle Episcopalian. My parents were married at the Episcopal Cathedral of Saint John the Baptist in San Juan in 1967. My mother grew up knowing about the Episcopal Church. My dad grew up with Lutheran roots from western Pennsylvania and Iowa. Many in our family in Puerto Rico were Roman Catholic, but growing up I knew Mormons, Baptists, Lutherans, Presbyterians, Episcopalians, some Pentecostals, and Muslims, among others. I was aware of the institutional power of the Roman Catholic Church, but I did not assume that everyone was Catholic. I'm not sure that I knew all the differences between the Episcopal Church and a Roman Catholic one, but I felt they were different. In college, I chose the Episcopal Church.

As with so many things, perspective matters. If you look at something directly in front of you, you may not see the smaller object behind it, much like the difference between full and partial eclipses. Once you change perspective, different information comes into the picture. As I have lived most of my adult life in the continental United States, the assumption tends to be that I am an Episcopalian because of my father, and that I must have grown up as a Roman Catholic in Puerto Rico. Yet I have always identified as an Episcopalian, even though I did my first communion in the Roman Catholic Church, as my cousins did. The reasons for that were not the reasons assumed by those that declare that I must have grown up in the Roman Catholic tradition. This assumption is more about discourses concerning LATINX people than the reality of our lives.

In fact, Puerto Ricans, both on the Island and in New York, were some of the earliest participants and leaders in Pentecostal congregations. According to the Pew Research Center, in 2014, 56 percent of people in Puerto Rico identified as Roman Catholic, 33 percent as Protestant, 8 percent unaffiliated, and 2 percent as other.[60] This also means that less than half of the people living in Puerto Rico are active Roman Catholics.

The identification of LATINX people and communities as Roman Catholics, because of a historical connection, which only continues for some, has been a de facto excuse for the Episcopal Church not to minister with and among LATINX people and communities. It is one explanation why Latin America was not open to evangelization to the Anglican Communion until 1958, or the Episcopal Church's limited presence in the Southwest of the United States in comparison with other Protestant denominations in the second half of the nineteenth century, and the continued lagging by our denomination into the twenty-first century.

Yes, many LATINX people identify as Roman Catholic; that does not mean that all LATINX people are Roman Catholic. LATINX people are identified as Roman Catholic because they are seen as coming from "Spanish-origin," one of the most insidious discourses of the "black legend."[61] This has two effects. First, we do not reach out to these people or communities because we think they are already part of a different faith community. Second, Episcopal churches compromise on their Catholic and Protestant heritage by relying on a Roman Catholic veneer to attract LATINX people to their churches. Believing that all LATINX people are Catholic has led some Episcopal churches in the United States to appear Roman Catholic. Curiously enough, in Latin America Episcopal churches often move toward more "evangelical" or "Protestant" in order to clearly separate themselves from anything Roman Catholic.[62] To be clear, I do not equate a "Roman Catholic veneer" with "Anglo-Catholicism." Anglo-Catholicism, -evangelicalism, or -Protestantism, or broad church can ALL be expressions in the Episcopal Church. The same is true of conservative or evangelical Episcopal churches that mirror the conservative religious and denominational context around them.

Some churches should reflect on how many people attend their Episcopal church and think it is "no different than a Roman Catholic church," or don't even know that they are not in a Roman Catholic church. Pew data from 2013 indicates that in the United States 55 percent of LATINX people identify as Roman Catholic, 22 percent as Protestant (broadly—5 percent mainline), 18 percent as unaffiliated, and 5 percent other.[63] Unaffiliated can also be seen as "nones."

Literacy of our tradition, theology, and ecclesiology is less than it should be. Given the overall changes in the demographics of Episcopalians over the past half a century, in addition to a rigorous Christian formation, we should be embarking in serious Anglican/Episcopal formation. Oliver recognizes that "Latino members of the congregation must be Episcopalians who are able to participate in parish life as members equal to our Anglo brothers and sisters in the church."[64]

Believing that all LATINX people are Roman Catholic, or have been, not only limits our ministry with and among LATINX people and communities, but also brings with it assumptions about their inability to pledge and or take leadership roles. This is also a justice and power issue. The Episcopal branch of the Jesus Movement may not be the expression that appeals to all people, but how will people know if they do not have access to the Episcopal Church at all? I believe that this "confusion" between Roman Catholicism and the Episcopal Church is one that needs to be addressed. Furthermore, we need to stop calling ourselves "Catholic-lite."

## Communion

Growing up, coffee hour at the Episcopal Cathedral of St. John the Baptist in Puerto Rico happened in the school cafeteria and in the courtyard. I have memories of running around in that courtyard. One of those memories, probably influenced by photographs, is my sister Rosalind in a white dress posing behind a cake in the shape of the *Agnus Dei*—appropriate because it is a symbol associated with John the Baptist and also part of the coat of arms of Puerto Rico. This is the same courtyard where the processions to both of my ordinations gathered. I have a memory, also enshrined in a photograph, of my cousins Carlos and Natja and me, also dressed in white, in the parking area of St. Luke's Roman Catholic Church in the community called Húcares in a sector of San Juan called Cupey. If you did not know that these two churches were of different denominations, you could think that both were the same type of celebrations, just different family members.

My sister was celebrating her confirmation and concurrent admission to Holy Communion.[65] For my cousins and me, it was our first communion. Looking back, the differences were unknown or seemed inconsequential or unimportant.

They became an issue when I began exploring the ordination process in Puerto Rico because we mistakenly remembered the two things as having been the same, when in fact I had not been confirmed in the Episcopal Church yet.

This confusion came to the fore during a conversation with Bishop Álvarez. Álvarez, confirmed me on the next scheduled visitation at the chapel in the Episcopal hospital in Guayama, Puerto Rico. My sister, who thought she had had her first communion, while in college in Canyon, Texas, was again confirmed, this time in the Diocese of North West Texas, while at winter church camp, and attending St. Peter's Episcopal Church. I share this story because it has been insightful for me in my ministry and as I experience many parents wanting to do things with their kids as they remember them from when they were kids or teenagers. In the Episcopal Church, many born before the mid-1970s may remember having to wait to receive communion.

## Admission to Communion: An Excursus

Ruth A. Meyers in *Continuing the Reformation: Re-Visioning Baptism in the Episcopal Church* provides an invaluable look at how we came to see baptism as full initiation to and open communion for all the baptized, including children. "Baptism is full Christian initiation. [And,] Confirmation is a mature acceptance and ratification of the baptismal promises."[66]

Until the 1970s, culminating with the 1979 Book of Common Prayer, confirmation was technically what afforded admission to communion in the Episcopal Church. Although variously enforced, the increased availability of confirmation had made it normative from the nineteenth century forward.[67] As non-Episcopalians received communion in the Episcopal Church with increasing frequency, it highlighted the anomaly of excluding baptized but unconfirmed Episcopalians.[68]

The issues of children and admission to communion, baptism as full initiation, and the place of confirmation continued to be debated throughout the 1970s and even into the 1980s. In 1985, at an international Anglican liturgical consultation, it was recommended that "since baptism is the sacramental sign of full incorporation into the church, all baptized people be admitted to communion."[69] Keeping in mind that the change was more fully implemented with the 1979 prayer book, as reflected in the rubric and canonical change, in the time when my sister was first confirmed it was not a settled question. Given this little bit of history about communion and confirmation and the Episcopal Church, it should be evident that there are, in fact, some significant differences with Roman Catholicism.

## The Similar Ways—Yet Not—My Sister and I Were Admitted to Communion or Confirmed

We cannot assume that lifelong Episcopalians know that baptized children are welcome to receive communion. The issue of children and communion is not a resolved matter in the congregation I serve. This is related to both the fact that grandparents or other elders are adamant about waiting until a first communion, whether they had one in this very congregation, or they are more familiar with Roman Catholic practice. In a congregation where there are lifelong Episcopalians who remember waiting to be admitted into Holy Communion and former Roman Catholics who had their first communion and are now parents, the question of communion seems to be a reasonable one. Yet underlying the question is also the fact that we, as a Church, have not done the best job in differentiating ourselves from Roman Catholic churches or educating our congregations about important differences and changes between the two in sacramental theology—and for that matter, ecclesiology, liturgy, etc.

In my time at the Church of Saint Matthew and Saint Timothy, I have baptized close to one hundred people. This means that I have had scores of baptismal preparation classes and have shared about admission to communion at each one. Yet tradition and grandparents are strong forces that are often hard to overcome. If I cannot break that family wall, I at least tell them that on the day of their baptism, I expect the child to have communion.

There are some crucial pieces to this. First, who understands the mystery of the Eucharist? The answer is no one. We do as God taught us, yet we cannot presume to understand the mystery. Therefore, there is not an arbitrary moment in which children are going to grasp something that none of us will ever fully be able to. Second, there are other ways to teach about care, concern, and proper behavior in church, such as worship, Sunday school, and by modeling correct behavior. Yet if we say that we are worried that children do not know what they are doing, aren't we actually saying that we are protecting God? I believe God can protect Godself, and that thinking we can protect God from a dropped wafer, for example, seems a type of idolatry of our own capacities. Finally, if participating of the holy meal is, in a most basic sense, about being included and fed, then, no matter the age, or capacity to articulate this, persons of all ages know what that feels like.

Someday, I hope that we have a Church in which participation in communion is so normal that people do not experience exclusion at the altar. Yet, it will have to be up to everyone to believe this as well. Adults need to learn that they are not the gatekeepers to communion. Adults also need to find ways to not exclude themselves from communion. Going back to that mystery thing, I believe that communion is life-giving in ways that we cannot ever explain. As a matter of fact, it is my thought that the life-giving nature of communion beckons us to the Table precisely when we feel distress or distance from God. It is a balm that brings us back into community and relationship with God. This is not a message that folks receive in the Roman Catholic Church; and a gift we have to offer. It saddens me every time someone removes themselves from communion, from this grace, especially when you can see that they need it so much.

The members of the church I serve often attend other churches and denominations. There are dozens of churches within a short walk from our church. Moving in and out of traditions is not unheard of, especially if different family members belong to different churches. In my family's case, this fluidity contributed to the "first communion" confusion. Yet we must find a way in which this is not the case; and the only way to do that is by being clear in our own tradition. At times, if not often, we allow things in one church to look like they are elsewhere to keep everyone happy. In other words, we do not always do enough to explain the difference and why we do not have first communion. Having knowledge and confidence of our tradition in fact enables us to have better appreciation of other ones.

## Should We Offer First Communion Classes?

I believe not. Some of the reasons I have expressed above, yet, in my context, I specifically dislike it, although I do so at the request of parents as a pastoral matter but reiterating that it is not required in the Episcopal Church. Also, many of these parents opt for a "short-term" class instead of committing to Christian formation, which is a lifelong journey. I know this is full of judgment, but it is evidenced by the fact that they are not regular churchgoers and they are doing this at abuela's church. As I've mentioned, I offer, as a pastoral response, some sort of "communion preparation" for children whose parents or grandparents ask. Unfortunately, this is contrary to what I advocate, because it reinforces that we offer these classes because "we've always offered these classes."

What is it that we are not communicating well that is specific to the Episcopal tradition? What about the open table? What about the canonical requirement for only the baptized to receive communion? People in the pews will not understand that people may be in different places on these questions.[70]

Challenges abound: does calling it "communion preparation" change the understanding? What about this for the unchurched? And ultimately understanding what this is about? I believe that the reason we continue to allow for an emphasis on a time for "communion" has to do with control. This would then seem to be a structural issue for the Church to continue grappling with. One thing I know is that in LATINX contexts in particular, doing this because the Roman Catholics do it is wrong and condescending.

A 1977 statement summed up the problems with communion preparation classes:

> It warned against the adoption of 'certain artificial norms,' such as the arbitrary setting of a fixed age for 'First Communion'; the introduction of children to the Sacrament in a context that separates them from their own families; and the temptation to form 'First Communion classes' on the model of Confirmation classes.[71]

## Is the Spanish Language a Barrier or an Excuse?

According to the Pew Research Center's analysis of 2015 data, "More than 37 million Latinos in the U.S. speak Spanish at home, making it the country's most common non-English language."[72] The United States is ranked, by population, in the top five Spanish-speaking countries in the world. Nevertheless, the share of LATINX people speaking Spanish at home has declined 5 percent in ten years to 73 percent. As with all averages, this 73 percent number is not the same in all regions: in Denver only 57 percent speak Spanish at home; in Miami the rate is 90 percent.[73] With the decline in the share of people speaking Spanish at home, the corollary naturally is that the share of LATINX people speaking English at home is increasing. Yet these numbers say nothing about LATINX people speaking English outside the home in the United States.

According to the 2017 *American Community Survey*, 28 percent (over 15 million) of LATINX people spoke only English; to these can be added another 54.6 percent (over 29 million) who speak English "well" or "very well" for a total of 82.6 percent of LATINX people. Monolingual Spanish-speakers are 5.7 percent (just over 3 million).[74] This means that another 11 percent have some command of English yet are Spanish-dominant. This is an assertion that many LATINX people are English-speaking. It is not an assertion that all our worship should be in English. What is does mean, however, is that in addition to Spanish-language worship, we can also change the way worship in English is expressed to speak more fully to the LATINX vernacular expression.

I am fully bilingual. I can read, write, and speak both English and Spanish. This is an accident of my context growing up, who my parents are, and my educational opportunities. As an adult I have, to my dismay, discovered that I am terrible at learning to speak other languages. Twenty years ago, I took two years (four semesters of five days a week) of Arabic and I cannot speak it nor understand it, and I probably can't read much of it anymore. It terrifies me to even say, "Good day," "God willing," or "Thanks" in Arabic, even though these phrases readily pop up in my head when I enter bodegas in New York City where Arabic-speaking people work.[75] I mention this because I understand more than one language, and do not comprehend others at all. When I'm asked about Spanish-language competency and I answer, "It is not about language," I am not minimizing how difficult it is to speak a new language. I am challenging the assumptions being made when language (like demographics) is the driving impetus.

With Spanish and English, I have been able to travel easily in English- and Spanish-speaking countries: Spain, the United Kingdom, Venezuela, Honduras, and even manage in Brazil, for example. In part because of my fluency I was hired to work at my current parish. As a fully bilingual person, I can have conversations with everyone in the congregation. Yet this does not mean that I have gifts in LATINX ministry, or that I speak the vernacular of everyone in the congregation I serve. These are not the gifts I bring to my ministry; I have other gifts. Similarly, I have the experience of being in many contexts (where English and Spanish are spoken) that are not my own comfort or expression.

In the summer of 1992, as an Episcopalian doing a short-term mission with the Presbyterian Church (USA), I lived in Venezuela in a town south of Caracas called Ocumare del Tuy. Within hours of being with my host family, I recognized that my Puerto Rican Spanish was not going to get me very far. Thank God that there was a member of the local congregation that knew how to translate between Venezuelan and Puerto Rican Spanish. I've mentioned how much I like rice and beans. In Puerto Rico beans are *habichuelas*, but that means green beans in Venezuela; *caraotas* are the Puerto Rican *habichuelas*. Green beans in Puerto Rico are *habichuelas tiernas* (tender beans). Similar were bananas: *guineos* in Puerto Rico and *cambur* in Venezuela. It is in the quotidian that language varies the most; the more something is attached to the land, the more localized the language. At least with food I could point at things; other differences led to different misunderstandings. One day I was ready to get picked up, but I waited quite a long time because they said *ahora*, which I understood as now. In Puerto Rico *ahora* is now and *ahorita* is later; in Venezuela it is the opposite. We had a good laugh. And this is between just two regional types of Spanish. Imagine then, in the United States where Spanish-speaking people have many different national heritages, backgrounds, accents, and connections to the Spanish language. It is not about speaking one language or another. It goes well beyond words.

The day of my first sermon in Spanish at the congregation I serve, I said that I would "go all in" with them in the work that we are called to do. The word I used was *zumbar* and there was great confusion. In a congregation of many Ecuadorians, Dominicans, Colombians, Puerto Ricans, and others, I used this term in a way that is used only in Puerto Rico and Venezuela. One of the Puerto Rican parishioners interpreted to the rest of the congregation and we all had a good laugh. I felt very similarly when I was studying in English—I knew the language, but not the vernacular.

This happens in English-language contexts all the time. For example, there are five Episcopal Churches in the Upper West Side of Manhattan: evangelical, Anglo-Catholic, more "broad church," and bilingual (English/Spanish). All five churches offer worship in English in different vernaculars or expressions. Why is it that the congregation I serve is a specialized ministry and the others are not?

One of the most common questions I am asked regarding LATINX ministry is the proficiency needed in the Spanish language to embark in these ministries. The fact that I include this challenge as the last in this chapter is intentional. I do not believe that language proficiency should be a starting point in conversations about ministry with and among LATINX people and communities. The humblest answer is that if proficiency is the key, then my current ministry should be doing really well; which is not the case. The bluntest answer is that it is not about language, especially if language is used as an *a priori* barrier to ministry with and among LATINX people and communities. In this case, frequently Spanish-language aptitude is a made-up barrier used by people, often in leadership, who cannot wrap their heads arounds this ministry and feel impotent, so they create an excuse to not embark on it. We need leadership that is bilingual, multi(bi) cultural, and polycentric that can work in multigenerational settings where there may be various levels of monolingualism (English and Spanish) and bilingualism (English and Spanish)—whether the ear, the eye, and the mouth.[76] But the Church needs this, not just congregations for LATINX people and communities.

## The Vernacular

One of the issues taught about the sixteenth-century European reformations is the rise in the use of the vernacular. If Merriam-Webster is correct, "vernacular" is anachronistic since the term was first used in the seventeenth century. Putting that aside, the printing press and the rise in use of the vernacular were important and can be one lens through which to understand the European reformations. The vernacular, though, is not solely about spoken and written words that reflect *lo cotidiano* or everyday use of language or expression. Scripture and liturgy were now accessible to more people.

In looking at the definition of "vernacular," we should not limit it to language, but to understand the breadth of what can be included. One meaning of vernacular is "the mode of expression of a group or class," or "any medium or mode of expression that reflects popular taste or indigenous styles."[77] Although we think we use the vernacular in church, in fact, generally we do not. We have a sense that if it sounds "old" that it is dignified and appropriately separated from the profane. We don't use the vernacular because we think it is *less*. In other words, one of the challenges in expanding our understanding of the vernacular is that as a church of the "upper classes" we look down upon the vernacular.

In thinking about this definition, there is much to analyze with respect to the Episcopal Church. The Church of England has worshipped in English since the sixteenth century. The Episcopal Church inherited this tradition. But what exactly did the Episcopal Church inherit? The Episcopal Church inherited more that the words of the prayer book; it inherited an ethos. We quickly made that specific ethos static—we reified it. The Episcopal Church has not changed its vernacular. Even the language of the 1979 prayer book, though written in the vernacular when first issued, is no longer in the vernacular. Therefore, all Episcopalians have a vernacular. The challenge is not to normalize one vernacular over others.

The Episcopal Church is a church of empire; it is a Church that needs to be decolonized. One way to decolonize the Episcopal Church is to make sure to hold it accountable for using the vernacular of the local community in a parish. The simplest way to do this is to know the local vernacular. In some places the local vernacular may indeed match that which is reflected in our prayer books and worship. In other areas the local vernacular challenges the very premise that our tradition is in the vernacular any longer.

## Notes

1. Sandra Maria Van Opstal, *The Next Worship: Glorifying God in a Diverse World* (Downers Grove, IL: InterVarsity Press, 2016), 14.
2. Juan Francisco Martínez, *Walking with the People: Latino Ministry in the United States* (Eugene, OR: Wipf & Stock, 2016), xii, 19, 37.
3. Juan Francisco Martínez, *The Story of Latino Protestants in the United States* (Grand Rapids, MI: William B. Eerdmans, 2018), 94. Walter D. Mignolo and Catherine E. Walsh, *On Decoloniality: Concepts, Analytics, Praxis* (Durham, NC: Duke University Press, 2018) use the following phrase "well intending and conscientious whites," 81.
4. "Opportunities for Growth," in *Strategies for Renewal in the Episcopal Church: Recruitment, Training, and Deployment for Effective Ministry in the Hispanic Communities* (New York: Office of Hispanic Ministry, Episcopal Church Center, 1998), 20.
5. Martínez, *Story*, 102.
6. Martínez, *Story*, 117.
7. Juan M. C. Oliver, *Ripe Fields: The Promise and Challenge of Latino Ministry* (New York: Church Publishing, 2009), 15.
8. Oliver, *Ripe Fields*, 16.

9. Alberto L. García and John A. Nunes, *Wittenberg Meets the World: Reimagining the Reformation at the Margins* (Grand Rapids, MI: William B. Eerdmans, 2017), 92. See also, 84.

10. García and Nunes, *Wittenberg*, 93.

11. García and Nunes, *Wittenberg*, 93.

12. García and Nunes, *Wittenberg*, 94.

13. García and Nunes, *Wittenberg*, 85, 90, 98, 160.

14. García and Nunes, *Wittenberg*, 99, 100.

15. García and Nunes, *Wittenberg*, 103.

16. John 1:46.

17. Martínez, *Walking*, xii.

18. Martínez, *Walking*, 37.

19. See a similar description in García and Nunes, *Wittenberg*, 6.

20. Robert W. Pritchard, *A History of the Episcopal Church*, rev. ed. (Harrisburg, PA: Morehouse Publishing, 1999), 180.

21. Herbert Arrunátegui, ed., *Hispanic Ministry: Opportunity for Mission*, 3rd ed. (New York: Office of Hispanic Ministry, Episcopal Church Center, 2001), 8.

22. Martínez, *Story*, 10.

23. Martínez, *Walking*, 19.

24. Martínez, *Story*, 6, 34, 39, 94, 96, 99, 105, 118, 144, 158, 159; Juan Francisco Martínez, *Sea la luz: The Making of Mexican Protestantism in the American Southwest, 1829–1900* (Denton: University of North Texas, 2006), 15, 21, 44–46, 49; *Los Protestantes: An Introduction to Latino Protestantism in the United States* (Santa Barbara, CA: Praeger, 2011), 2, 26.

25. Martínez, *Walking*, 28.

26. Yuichiro Kakutani and Meredith Liu, "Cornell to Establish LGBTQ Program House 25 Years After Initial Proposal," *Cornell Daily Sun* March 1, 2018. Accessed September 30, 2019. https://cornellsun.com/2018/03/01/cornell-to-establish-lgbtq-program-house-25-years-after-initial-proposal/. Angela Li, "Loving House Grand Opening 'A Victory,' But 'Not the End of the Story,'" *Cornell Daily Sun* September 15, 2019, accessed September 30, 2019, https://cornellsun.com/2019/09/15/loving-house-grand-opening-a-victory-but-not-the-end-of-the-story/. Accessed September 30, 2019.

27. Martínez, *Walking*, 73.

28. General Convention, *Journal of the General Convention of . . . The Episcopal Church, Anaheim, 2009* (New York: General Convention, 2009), 885–ff. Reference is made to line Items: 220, 221, 310–17, 400, July 15, 2009, report of The Joint Standing Committee on Program, Budget and Finance.

29. General Convention, *Journal . . . Anaheim*, 181–82.

30. Prichard, *A History* (rev. ed.), chapter 8, FN34, the note references "See Joint Standing Committee on Program, Budget and Finance, 'Budget 2013–2015: The Episcopal Church,' July 10, 2012." Prichard does not indicate how he arrives at "more than ten percent."

31. Adopted Budget: 2013–2015: The Episcopal Church, July 10, 2012, report of The Joint Standing Committee on Program, Budget and Finance. Line items 27, 168–78.

32. Budget: 2013–2015: The Episcopal Church, July 10, 2012, report of The Joint Standing Committee on Program, Budget and Finance, https://extranet.generalconvention.org/staff/files/download/5890.pdf. The analysis of the numbers is illustrative. A separate conversation could happen regarding the role of block grants in the fulfilling of the mission of the church and the role of block grants in the transformation of congregations in the continental United States. One of my reasons for separating them is that the monies are used for "ministry" by those that receive the funds; the Episcopal Church is not doing "ministry" by giving those grants, the recipients are.

33. Adopted Budget: 2016–2018: The Episcopal Church, June 20, 2015, report of The Joint Standing Committee on Program, Budget and Finance. Line items 28, 168–78.

34. Adopted Budget: 2019–2021: The Episcopal Church, July 12, 2018, report of The Joint Standing Committee on Program, Budget and Finance. Line items 40, 50, 103–54.

35. Adopted Budget: 2019–2021, accessed January 31, 2019, https://www.episcopalchurch.org/files/documents/2019_-_2021_adopted_budget_clean_0.pdf. The analysis of the 2019–2021 numbers are calculated with the same assumptions behind my analysis of the 2013–2015 budget.

36. Gustavo Gutiérrez, *Teología de la liberación: Perspectivas. Con una nueva introducción, "Mirar Lejos"* (Lima, Perú: Centro de Estudios y Publicaciones, 1991), 201.

37. "Report of the 1981 Hispanic Theological Consultation" (New York: Office of Hispanic Ministry, Episcopal Church Center, 1981).

38. Justo L. González, *The Hispanic Ministry of the Episcopal Church in the Metropolitan Area of New York and Environs* (New York: Grants Board of Trinity Parish, 1985), 10.

39. This means that "technically" speaking, one of my sisters and my dad are included in white; my other sister, mom, and me are LATINX. The Episcopal Church Overview: Findings from the 2014 Survey of Episcopal Congregations, The Episcopal Church, accessed August 1, 2018, *https://www.episcopalchurch.org/files/episcopal_congregations_overview_2014.pdf.*

40. *For Everyone Born.* Words: Shirley Erena Murray. Words © 1998 Hope Publishing Company, Carol Stream, IL 60188, *www.hopepublishing.com.* All rights reserved. Used by permission.

41. Sharon R. Ennis, Menarys Ríos-Vargas, and Nora G. Albert, *The Hispanic Population: 2010 Census Briefs.* Issued May 2011. *https://www.census.gov/prod/cen2010/briefs/c2010br-04.pdf.*

42. U. S. Census Bureau, Quick Facts: United States "Race and Hispanic Origin," accessed February 7, 2019, *https://www.census.gov/quickfacts/fact/table/US/PST045218.* The population estimate as of January 1, 2019, was 328,231,337.

43. Martínez, *Walking*, 2.

44. Martínez, *Story*, 4, 141, 156, 158.

45. Martínez, *Walking*, ix.

46. Episcopal Congregations Overview 2014.

47. Religious Landscape Study, Pew Research Center, accessed August 1, 2018, *http://www.pewforum.org/religious-landscape-study/racial-and-ethnic-composition/latino/.*

48. Episcopal Church, "Episcopal Church Domestic Facts Trends: 2007–2011," accessed August 1, 2018, *https://www.episcopalchurch.org/files/domestic_fast_facts_trends_2007-2011.pdf.*

49. Episcopal Church, "Episcopal Church Domestic Facts: 2016: Based on Parochial Report Data," accessed August 1, 2018, *https://extranet.generalconvention.org/staff/files/download/19543.*

50. Episcopal Church, "Episcopal Church Domestic Facts: 2017: Based on Parochial Report Data" accessed January 2, 2019, *https://www.episcopalchurch.org/files/1._episcopal_domestic_fast_facts_and_fast_facts_trends_2013-2017.pdf.*; Episcopal Church, "Episcopal Church Domestic Facts: 2018," accessed September 30, 2019, *https://www.episcopalchurch.org/files/updated_2018_fast_facts.pdf.*

51. Religious Landscape Study: Members of the Episcopal Church, Pew Research Center," accessed January 2, 2019, *http://www.pewforum.org/religious-landscape-study/religious-denomination/episcopal-church/.*

52. "America's Changing Religious Landscape," Pew Research Center, May 12, 2015, 4. *http://assets.pewresearch.org/wp-content/uploads/sites/11/2015/05/RLS-08-26-full-report.pdf.*

53. Ibid., 4.

54. Ibid., 20.

55. Joan C. Williams, "The Democrats' White-People Problem: Donald Trump Likes to Pit Elite and Non-Elite White People Against Each Other. Why Do White Liberals Play into His Trap?" Politics Section in *The Atlantic* December 2018 Issue.

56. Juan Francisco Martínez, *Walk with the People: Latino Ministry in the United States* (Nashville, TN: Abingdon Press, 2008), 26; *Walking*, 12; *Sea la luz*, 4, 17, 79, 130.

57. "The Hispanic Population in the United States: 2016," United States Census Bureau, accessed December 4, 2018, *https://www.census.gov/data/tables/2016/demo/hispanic-origin/2016-cps.html.*

58. ENS, "Mexican Meeting Offers Episcopal Bishops and Staff a Hispanic Experience," March 19, 1998 [98-2118].

59. Martínez, *Walking*, 3.

60. Pew Research Center, "Religion in Latin America: Widespread Change in a Historically Catholic Region," November 13, 2014, 14, *https://www.pewforum.org/2014/11/13/religion-in-latin-america/.*

61. Curiously people already involved in this ministry overwhelmingly do not agree with this discourse. "A Celebration of Diversity: Hispanic Ministry in the Episcopal Church. An Evaluation of the Current State of Hispanic Ministries in the Episcopal Church of the United States" (New York: Office of Hispanic Ministry, The Episcopal Church Center, 1988), 23, 82.

62. Martínez, *Story*, 130: "Also, working alongside Catholics raised questions about whether they should draw people out of Catholicism into Protestant churches. Some historic Protestant churches attempted to address this issue by establishing more 'Catholic'-friendly practices, such as including Catholic saints and virgins. While Anglicans in Latin America have historically focused on the fact that they are Protestants, many Episcopalians in the United States that wanted to reach out to Latinos focused on a 'Catholic' worship style."

63. Pew Research Center, "The Shifting Religious Identity of Latinos in the United States: Nearly One-in-Four Latinos are Former Roman Catholics," May 7, 2014, 5, *https://www.pewforum.org/2014/05/07/the-shifting-religious-identity-of-latinos-in-the-united-states/*; Martínez, *Story*, 6.

64. Oliver, *Ripe Fields*, 68.

65. The Episcopal Church in Puerto Rico had recently become extra-provincial (1978–2003). In our memory, this must have been around 1980 or 1981, so my sister was 12 or 13.

66. Ruth A. Meyers, *Continuing the Reformation: Re-Visioning Baptism in the Episcopal Church* (New York: Church Publishing, 1997), 100.

67. Meyers, *Continuing the Reformation*, 87.

68. Meyers, *Continuing the Reformation*, 92. Intercommunion admission to communion was approved at the 1967 General Convention—Meyers, *Continuing the Reformation*, 101.

69. Meyers, *Continuing the Reformation*, 269.

70. Canon I.17.7: No unbaptized person shall be eligible to receive Holy Communion in this Church. Given the limited depth of Christian/Anglican formation across our church, I believe that an open table would exacerbate this. Although communion is about being included and being fed, those are the initial invitation to a deeper lifelong exploration, which I believe is for the baptized. Some of this may seem contradictory to the above, but I will have to elaborate elsewhere!

71. ENS, "Liturgical Commission Issues 'First Communion' Statement," November 9, 1977 [77368].

72. Jens Manuel Krogstad and Mark Hugo López, "Use of Spanish Declines among Latinos in Major U.S. Metros," Pew Research Center, October 31, 2017, *http://www.pewresearch.org/fact-tank/2017/10/31/use-of-spanish-declines-among-latinos-in-major-u-s-metros/*.

73. Krogstad and López, "Use of Spanish Declines."

74. U. S. Census Bureau, American Community Survey 2017, Table B16006: Language spoken at home by ability to speak English for the population 5 years and over (Hispanic or Latino), *https://factfinder.census.gov/faces/tableservices/jsf/pages/productview.xhtml?src=bkmk*.

75. Sabah al-kheir, In shā'a llāh, shukran.

76. Transgenerational is about generations since immigration that may coexist in families and congregations. This is a concept evaluated and expanded upon by Albert R. Rodríguez.

77. Merriam-Webster.com, s.v. "vernacular," accessed February 1, 2019, *https://www.merriam-webster.com/dictionary/vernacular*; Dictionary.com., s.v., "vernacular," February 1, 2019, *https://www.dictionary.com/browse/vernacular*.

# CHAPTER 4

# An Epistemic Challenge

n this book so far, I have focused on the history of the institutionalization of ministry to, with, and among LATINX people and communities as a
program of the Episcopal Church—a hyphenated-ministry—and how this
institutionalization guarantees that the power and resources of the Church
remain in the hands of an elite that benefits from the status quo, thus maintaining structures that are inherently racist and misogynist. All of this institutionalization is propped up by a series of discourses, structures, and presuppositions
that hinder the Episcopal Church in these ministries. These latter ones include
views of deficiency of LATINX people and communities, treatment of certain
people as hyphenated-Americans or hyphenated-Episcopalians, the structural
problems in sharing of power and resources, especially as exemplified in the
budgets of the Church, the problem with comfort in church, the conceptions
of LATINX people as immigrants, Spanish-speaking, and Roman Catholic, the
challenge of a Roman Catholic veneer, the crutch of the Spanish language as
a barrier to these ministries, and a lack of understanding across the Church of
what it means to worship in the vernacular. All these things show the myriad of
ways that hinder the Church in the fulfillment of its mission (#BCP855).

Yet none of what I have just summarized matters if the epistemological assumptions of the Episcopal Church are not fundamentally challenged,
debunked, and delinked from the Euro-U.S.-centric rhetoric of modernity; the
terms of the conversation need to radically change. In fact, postmodernity—or
post-anything—does not accomplish the task, since these function from the same
foundation. In other words, the Episcopal Church needs to delink from the "epistemic and hermeneutical principles upon which religions, science, and philosophy
were built."[1] And this decolonial epistemology begins as it is enunciated in Christian and theological formation in congregations and seminaries. This chapter
addresses these issues. Theology as developed in the West and imposed universally
as totalizing knowledge is a key component of the narratives of modernity.

Many know that for over two decades I have advocated for LATINX people and communities in the Church, and for most of the last three decades, I
have advocated for LGBTQ+ rights. Fewer people know that for decades I
have also been having conversations about theological education with anyone

who would listen. Sometimes, this has been framed specifically around LAT-INX seminarians, but I have always had the conviction that it is not solely about LATINX people—it is about the whole Church. Rev. Juan M. C. Oliver notes that we have failed in forming Christians, let alone in forming Episcopalians. This leads me to the assertion that in addition to the institutional inertia of the Episcopal Church, the biggest challenge confronted by the Church is not secularism, nor the cost of theological education, nor the "presenting symptom" of homosexuality; instead, it is an unrecognized epistemological quagmire, from all sides of the theological spectrum.

Increasingly, Episcopalians are not consciously and fully engaged with scripture, tradition, or reason, or generally approach these from Anglican/Episcopal points of view. In my estimation this has been the case for at least the last four decades and has contributed to the decline in theological education in the Episcopal Church. I am beginning to theorize, based on my research, experience, and observation, that we have become a more anti-intellectual Church than we even know, let alone care to admit.

Archbishop Thomas Cranmer had a vision for Anglicans that the fundamental Christian formation tool, including biblical literacy, would be the Book of Common Prayer: the regular reading of scripture in a three-year cycle and the regular reading of psalms, as well as the various scripture passages that imbue the various Daily Offices and Eucharistic celebrations. Bible study becomes familiar because the language of the prayer book is biblical. The challenge then is that Episcopalians don't know this gem, nor many other Anglican prayer books for that matter,[2] and thus, do not have an entry point into scripture or the Episcopal Church. Things become disconnected, or as I prefer to denote—dissociated.

I am a priest and church historian. Although this volume is an institutional history of ministry to, with, and among LATINX people and communities, writing this book has been about advocacy and justice, outside of my specific sixteenth-century academic interests—although the analysis of discourses is. In 2011 I wrote, as part of Oliver's book review, that further follow-ups were needed. Well, God is funny and here we are. My hope would be to enable others to expand this history. This book challenges parts of the foundational epistemologies of the Episcopal Church.

## My Epistemic Background

I attended school in Puerto Rico from kindergarten through six grade and ninth through twelfth. Seventh and eighth grades were in Amarillo, Texas. The change in middle school created some gaps in my knowledge base, especially in history and language courses. I took a class on Texas history and missed one on Puerto Rican history. I attended the science and math section of my high school and the engineering school at Cornell. Although I took as many courses in other fields as I could, until seminary I did not have an extensive humanities background.

I visited the Church Divinity School of the Pacific (CDSP) in 1994 and decided to apply there for my seminary studies. I chose to apply to CDSP in part because it was part of the Graduate Theological Union (GTU), and I could study in an environment that was not solely Episcopalian. I began my studies in the fall of 1997 and finished with two master's degrees in May 2001; I made great strides in the humanities! My theological education and formation at CDSP were great. I had the privilege of studying under Dr. Margaret Miles, Rev. J. Rebecca Lyman, Rev. Don Compier, Rev. Louis Weil, Rev. John L. Kater, Rev. Linda Clader, Rev. William Countryman, Dr. Donn Morgan, and Rev. Jay Johnson, among others. All these people have contributed greatly to the Episcopal Church in their fields and beyond, yet all primarily within a US-Eurocentric epistemological orientation. In my third course on history and theology, which covered the modern period, I learned about modernity and postmodernity. In the summer of 1999, I participated in the Hispanic Summer Program (HSP) and studied under Dr. Ada María Isasi-Díaz and Rev. Paul Barton and met Rev. Justo L. González.

After seminary I began my very long doctoral journey, first in the history department of the University of Texas at Austin (medieval and early modern church history focus), and then in a joint program in religious studies and theology between Hartford Seminary and the University of Exeter (focused on trans-Atlantic early modern church history). During my doctoral studies I read broadly in English, Spanish, and some French. At Harford, I began studying a variety of methodological approaches to religious studies including postcolonial ones; these were very important as the first stepping-stones in the development of my dissertation, and the beginnings of delinking from what I've learned. What Catherine E. Walsh and Walter D. Mignolo call "learn to unlearn to relearn."[3]

Yet all of this still puts me clearly in educational systems that primarily follow U.S.-Eurocentric and Western pedagogical models. With few exceptions, from individual faculty, anything that I have read that breaks through these models has been through my own research and by becoming aware of other scholarship in conversations with LATINX scholars, especially my Hispanic Theological Initiative (HTI) *familia*. The middle-school move, engineering studies, being educated in U.S.-Eurocentric systems, and my own reading and research all inform the knowledge base that I have and how I approach reading, writing, and learning. This is combined to my familial, cultural, sociopolitical knowledge absorbed from all my experiences outside of educational institutions: knowledge by being.

Even with all my experiences and education, I am keenly aware of the gaps, even that there are gaps I'm not aware of. Yet some of the gaps exist solely because of a value system that creates a hierarchy of knowledge and by extension of cultures. I haven't read William Shakespeare, nor does it interest me, but I have read Miguel Ángel Asturias.[4] Not knowing Shakespeare in the United States can be considered a deficit; but how many in the United States know Asturias, or Luis Rafael Sánchez, or Ana Lydia Vega?[5]

In the summer of 2017, all the St. Matthew and St. Timothy's office space was moved. This move was an opportunity to get rid of stuff, in my case lots of paper from the last decades, photocopies of books and articles, and cull through records no longer needed for the parish. I was able to consolidate all my written academic work into one box: essays, master's thesis, final papers, and dissertation. Thumbing through this work was illuminating. I came to some realizations: I have been quite consistent in what I have chosen to write about and the questions that I tend to ask of texts, and relatedly, that my method of approaching texts and reading them, including treating them as artifacts, can be traced to my AP Spanish literature class in high school taught by Ms. Janet Rodríguez. In all the literary, history or textual courses I've taken over the decades, I have never learned more about reading texts than I did with Rodríguez. I wrote my final paper for Rodríguez's class on the Guatemalan Asturias' *El Señor Presidente,* a writer that influenced the Latin American Literature Boom of the 1960s and 1970s.

Nowadays, I teach the second course in the church history sequence at General Theological Seminary, which covers from the fifteenth century to the present. Teaching this course is challenging; what used to be a three-course sequence is now two courses. Moreover, I don't only want to teach what I was taught, but I want to deconstruct it and add to it. I have aimed to add a global perspective, with a center beyond Europe and the north Atlantic, a nonwhite perspective, and bringing suspicion to the narratives as they are presented. I have been taught and trained in Western systems. I have to actively make a choice to present knowledge in a different way and from additional sources than those that have been considered normative in the Church. And believe me, my students were challenged by this approach. My students had to contend with my own approach and biases, and contest them as well.

The chapter before you is the most ambitious in this book, and at times even contradicts what I have presented thus far—this is in fact the challenge of the insidious rhetoric of modernity. I name and elaborate on these contradictions. Without hyperbole, this is the most important topic in this book—epistemology. Here I present, to the best of my ability, a brief sketch of decoloniality, and try to connect a decolonial praxis to the task ahead—delinking from the coloniality of knowledge and being[6] in terms of Christian and theological formation at all levels of the Church. As will be evident, I focus on theological formation in seminaries, yet I believe that the epistemic changes need to occur across all levels of the Church. I will let others develop a praxis for formation for all ages outside of seminaries. As I have mentioned earlier, innovation in the same system does not innovate. Here I will attempt to name and unmask some of the general narratives around the decline experienced by Episcopal seminaries. As the Church will not change without a fundamental change in its structures, theological education and formation that do not change the underlying framework of knowledge will not fundamentally change either. Finally, in this chapter, parallel to dealing with the epistemic challenge, I provide some examples of some immediate changes that can be done by seminaries and the Church. Changes that need to be intentional, sustainable, ongoing, and impactful.

## Decoloniality

In defining decoloniality, my conversation partners are Catherine Walsh and Walter Mignolo and I use, and adapt to our topic, their 2018 book *On Decoloniality: Concepts, Analytics, and Praxis*. Decoloniality comes from the concept of modernity/coloniality. "Coloniality . . . is the 'underlying structure' of Western Civilization and Eurocentrism."[7] Coloniality is the darker side of modernity; the other side of the story.[8] Coloniality codifies difference; difference that constructs a racialized, classed, gendered, heteronormativized order. We saw part of the codification of this difference in the discourses of the "black legend," as exemplified in missionary endeavors in Latinx communities. For example, in the nineteenth century, as I introduced in chapter 1, evangelization was as much about Americanization and civilizing *those* people, as it was about the gospel. This is epistemological and supported by colonial difference. The rhetoric of modernity made us believe that Indigenous people as non-European people needed universal religion and secular sciences and philosophy to become civilized and developed, that is, modern.[9]

Decoloniality is ways of thinking, knowing, being, and doing. The decolonial seeks to delink, disrupt, and transgress the narrative of modernity, which through colonial difference has been used for centuries to exploit, dehumanize, oppress, dispossess, and exploit racialized groups of people. Upon these bodies the ideals of neoliberalism and globalization have been constructed and perpetuated.

We must ask: Who has the power to name? Who gets to produce knowledge, act, theorize? How does the Church codify difference by commodifying minoritized groups into programs of the Church? How does the Church recover the memory and knowledge of people of color and women it has silenced, subjugated, and excluded?

## Language Matters

Recently, I submitted an article for peer review and received positive and challenging feedback; in the end, the article was not accepted for publication. The peer-review process is daunting, albeit important, and I believe that at times can be a matter of underlying epistemological battles. As is evident in this book, language choices matter to me, and as you can see in the brief introduction of decoloniality, others also make specific language choices, and these are intentional and meant to disrupt. Yet one of my peer reviewers just did not like this disruption. The feedback read as follows:

> Aside from content, the author should also avoid excessive italics, bold, and parenthetical words. They are distracting and take away from their purpose of giving emphasis, which should be used sparingly in the paper, if at all.
>
> The author should avoid nominalizing verbs, adjectives, and adverbs and verbalizing nouns (e.g., vulnerabilization, somatization, racialization, problematization, conceptualization, racialize, minoritize). These habits fill writing with jargon and impede clarity. I get that the concept "nominalization" is internal to the argument, but it too can convey jargon when overused.[10]

My article needs improvement, and perhaps it is more than one article, I do not contest this. Yet my choices were seen with suspicion since it deviated from an established hegemonic norm that I disrupt in my writing. I would argue that it is disruption not obfuscation. I had to defend my choices in a recently published article, and even in the publication of this book.

My typeset and language choices are intentional, and these may include the choice to use -ity or -ion or -ism as suffixes. Briefly -ity changes adjectives to nouns, and -ion and -ism constructs nouns from verbs—all these are types of nominalization. Moreover, there are distinctions between these, and they are also important. "Minority" versus "minoritize," for example, is a choice between describing ontologically or indelibly a group of people or describing what is done to a group of people as a process of colonial differentiation. Thus, the choice of colonialism and decolonization is different from coloniality and decoloniality. Colonialism is a historical process that even if decolonization happens—as was the case for Spanish and British colonies at different points in time—coloniality remains. Decolonization does not require the disruption of the narratives of modernity which are built upon coloniality.

Given these distinctions, which are not just nuance, any -ity, -ion, -ism, etc. also cannot be understood as stable terms for all times and places, or even in this text. This is not about relativity of terms, but about the hierarchy of which terms are privileged and used. For example, there are some fairly common terms that I use that are problematic. These include "multiculturalism," "intercultural," and "intersectional." These become problematic when they are functionalized (co-opted) by the existing hegemonic systems to maintain the system, rather than disrupt its structures. Walsh/Mignolo describe these terms in the following way: "Multiculturalism was introduced . . . as a component part of the logic of neoliberalism and its project to pacify resistance, fragment movements, and bring the excluded into global capitalism's all-consuming framework and structure."[11]

Multiculturalism is functional and still lives within a structure of "cultural superiority and benign and condescending hospitality"[12] and this is furthered by programs, even programs of the Church. Mignolo/Walsh also challenge me in the use of "intersectionality"—a term I even use in a group that meets at the church I serve—because it is predicated on racial and sexual colonial differences.[13]

In a similar way Rev. Alberto L. García and Rev. John A. Nunes warn about the challenge with the underlying and unexplored dimensions of the idea of diversity. Diversity as an *us/them* becomes ontological difference. "Lovers of diversity" may in fact contribute to the "misrepresentation and misrecognition" of minoritized communities, an "ontological escapism." They caution "those seeking intentionally to create inclusion, those overly valuing diversity [on the risk] of their tendency to define the 'other' according to a category, as an essential type, in such a way that forecloses the possibility of knowing authentically the other, because they are now encapsulated within an ontological and definitional framework that erects finite barriers preventing them from being fully and truly known."[14]

This may in fact be one of the most challenging aspects of the issue for folks that consider themselves progressives and cannot easily see their own participation in the maintenance of the oppressive structures of the institution.

## Modernity and the Black Legend

I have argued that there are a series of discourses that are replicated by the Episcopal Church, and these are part of the so-called "black legend." Unfortunately, dismantling these discourses will not, on its own, change the institution. This is because those discourses are part of a much broader colonial matrix of power that has been established since the sixteenth century, and of which the Church as an institution has contributed to and benefited from. Therefore, in order to change the institution, we have to delink the Episcopal Church from its current epistemological foundations. This is done through a decolonial praxis and I believe that this can be a LATINX epistemic and theological contribution to emergent Anglican/Episcopal liberative theologizing.

The epistemological system that the Church continues to function under is based on the logic of modernity, a logic that is Western and Eurocentric and constructs society around totalizing and universal ideas of progress, development, modernization, eurocentrism, science, economic progress, political democracy, and reason. All these are also components of today's neoliberalism and globalization.[15] This system also survives by the "racialized, classed, gendered, heteronormativized, and Western-Euro-U.S.-centric systems of power, knowledge, being, civilization, and life that such horizon has constructed and perpetuated."[16]

In the church history class I teach, we spend a significant time on nineteenth-century liberalism and the related narratives that still inform church and society. My students are surprised by this and how the rhetoric of liberalism and modernity still permeates, albeit communicated differently, today. The nineteenth-century discourses are replicated, only the words have changed. Walsh and Mignolo summarize it this way: "Development replaced progress and modernization replaced civilizing mission."[17] The "black legend" is but one piece.

## Narratives: The Decline of Seminaries and Historical Models of LATINX Formation

I started seminary over two decades ago. Over fifty people in all certificate and degree programs were in my entering class. A class of that size is nowadays atypical for most Episcopal seminaries. Since I graduated, the Graduate Theological Union (GTU) has changed drastically, the real estate footprint of the Church Divinity School of the Pacific (CDSP) has changed, and most individual seminaries or centers on holy hill are now affiliated in some way with larger institutions.[18] We have all heard that seminaries are struggling financially and took a very real hit during the 2008–2009 recession, are facing crumbling infrastructure, enrollment has decreased, in part, because of affordability and the inability of students to attend full-time residential seminary, and so on. I would propose that, although facts, these could all be considered symptoms, rather than the root of the problems. Seminaries are trying to reinvent themselves and are variously succeeding. Yet, I believe we are looking at the challenges incorrectly.

I put forward the hypothesis that the fundamental problem for seminaries today—also for the Church—is an epistemic one. And this problem has existed for decades. I would even say that the onset of the decline coincides with the increased enrollment and proportion of women and people of color in seminaries, however dismal racially/ethnically this may be, without seminaries doing anything to change the underlying epistemic structure that served a different constituency—white men. Racism and sexism as the integral components of heteropatriarchy are systems that are needed to prop up the rhetoric of modernity, and now neoliberalism and globalization. The real vestiges of the rhetoric of modernity ensure that racism and sexism will continue to plague our theological institutions. Seminaries did nothing to change the Western and Euro-U.S. Centric epistemic foundation, because there was no incentive to change, given that the related power structure remained. In other words, if seminaries remain unchanged epistemically, then other institutions of the Church are not threatened and there is no need to share power and resources.

A decolonial epistemology would move beyond universality to pluriversality, and allow other epistemic sources—ancestral knowledge, collective memory, experience—to be included. For example, in our case, the Episcopal Church and Episcopal seminaries must allow for LATINX people to act, produce knowledge, and construct theory; in short, to be agents of their own liberation rather than objects of the Church's largess. Just as ethnic ministries are programs of the Church—controlled and managed—seminaries will not overcome their epistemic challenge solely by hiring scholars and enrolling students from minoritized communities. Mignolo and Walsh describe this in the following manner:

> While Indigenous scholars, students, and leaders have made substantial inroads in some disciplines of the academy in terms of curriculum and programming, we have been less successful in gaining the academic's recognition of indigenous knowledge systems and intelligence on their own merits.[19]

Several things come to mind with this assertion. First, that it is not enough to hire scholars that have been underrepresented historically, have them teach a course or two, and count this as an epistemic change. Second, the addition of a pluriversality of epistemologies should extend to the whole institution, across subjects, and infiltrate all aspects of the life of the institution.

Given that the underlying challenge is epistemic, not demographics, not financial—whether seminary finances or the cost of attending seminary—we have to dismantle many presuppositions, including:

- A mere increase in their presence as LATINX seminarians will not save theological education in the United States. LATINX Episcopalians are too small of a percentage of the Church to make the impact that seminaries imagine.

- LATINX students should be able to attend seminary, as do other (non-LATINX) students, without the expectation that they will focus on ministry to, with, and among LATINX people and communities. This essentializes or reduces LATINX people to an ethnicity.[20]

- As with other demographics, some can afford the time and cost of residential seminary and others cannot. The financial ability cuts across all ethnic and racial groups. There are LATINX people who can afford the time and cost of full-time seminary.

- Full-time residential seminary is important, and we should aim for this type of formation—alongside part-time, night and weekend classes, long-distance and online courses, and Anglican certificate programs to expand the knowledge base of those that have master's degrees in other fields. Without an epistemic change, any innovation will not yield results.

- Additional models of education and formation must be as rigorous, if not even more, than full-time residential programs. Otherwise, we will not have qualified leadership preparing Christians and Episcopalians. In other words, depth in Christian formation—biblical, theological, ethical, liturgical, etc.—in our congregations is fundamental in the raising up of leaders for ordained ministry. In turn, the depth in and quality of theological education of leaders in the Church will then inform the level of Christian formation of the laity in congregations in leadership in the Church. It is a cycle. Furthermore, Oliver recognizes that "Latino members of the congregation must be Episcopalians who are able to participate in parish life as members equal to our Anglo brothers and sisters in the church."[21]

- All aspects of seminary education should include LATINX voices, as well as other voices historically silenced in curricula. This is part of the epistemic challenge.

- The fact that there are not more LATINX clergy in the Episcopal Church is not because there aren't enough LATINX people to go to seminary. The institution benefits and structurally limits LATINX leadership.

- Clergy trained in Roman Catholic seminaries need an additional Anglican foundation and a shift in mentality. This is necessary and not automatic.

- Seminary is not only for ordained leadership.[22]

We need the breadth of formation opportunities and backgrounds in seminaries; this as part of a needed pluriversality of epistemologies, not as a hierarchy or as an either/or proposition. As briefly introduced in chapter 2, in 1988 there was a consultation on "Recruitment, Training and Deployment."

Rev. Herbert Arrunátegui lifted up the need for Latinx people to have "complete inclusion in the life of the Church." The consensus was that more "money and resources" need to be devoted "if Hispanic educational leadership in the Church is to emerge."[23] Bishop Anselmo Carral said:

> The future of the mission and ministry of the Episcopal Church among the Hispanic community of the United States depends to a large extent on the effectiveness and intentionality of the recruitment of Hispanic-American leaders, focused not only on postulants for the priesthood but also for the lay ministry. This task will be incomplete without the training that could enable these leaders to respond properly to the spiritual and social needs of the Hispanic community they will be called to serve.[24]

Similarly, the Rt. Rev. Gordon T. Charlton was emphatic that "there should be no hint of shortcuts in the curriculum for any of our ordinands, no possibility that they could perceive themselves or be regarded by others as second-class."[25]

At this consultation a series of models for theological education were presented. The Very Rev. William Pregnall, then dean of the Church Divinity School of the Pacific, wrote of the need to prepare seminarians for "cross-cultural ministry," and also suggested the need to "develop more specialized programs, operate jointly with other types of institutes, and build supportive networks for seminarians."[26] All these things are very important, yet, related to my analysis here, I would argue that instead of "specialized programs" there is a greater need to enculturate different views into the overall curriculum. Every class should have something from the point of view of Latinx people and communities, as well as other sources historically silenced.

The model of collaboration with other institutions is still relevant alongside the pluriversification of models of training. It is important to point out the challenge with the ideas of "cross-cultural ministry" and "specialized programs" since these function as part of a matrix of difference, or what I earlier explained as a dissociation or separation of Latinx from ministry. In 2020, part of this model continues through courses titled "cultural competency." To be clear, competencies are needed; my point is that "competencies" are not something extra, for certain interested people, but an integral part of the whole.

Another perspective came from the Very Rev. Durstan McDonald, then dean of the Episcopal Theological Seminary of the Southwest, who argued for educating bishops, commissions on ministry, and other diocesan stakeholders on valuing "minorities who do not fit the European-American model." McDonald argued that the seminary model for formation was only one model and that alternative models should not "merely imitate seminaries." McDonald was also a proponent of the need for a "critical mass" of students, "Seminaries which are able to should specialize in Hispanic ministry, and incoming candidates should be referred to the seminary that is most likely to provide members of their cultural group with the type of training they need."[27]

I agree with the value of a "critical mass," but that is because white students have generally had a critical mass in seminary, and women generally do as well. Yet, the critical mass of people of color without a structural change does not accomplish much. Furthermore, a critical mass can only be accomplished with great investment and intentionality. Also, this model of critical mass puts the burden on seminaries that are amid a large number of LATINX people and communities, absolves others, all the while basing decisions on demographics and not on the mission of the Church.

Another collaborative program was presented by the Very Rev. James Fenhagen, then dean of the General Theological Seminary. Acknowledging failures in creating a welcoming environment, Fenhagen mentioned the decision to partner and strengthen relationships with the New York Theological Seminary (NYTS) and the Instituto Pastoral Hispano (IPH). These partnerships were important in creating "a more hospitable place."[28] Noting that hospitality maintains an *us-them* dynamic and does not change the fundamental structure of the institution, there are specific and acceptable norms of hospitality.

Rev. Maria Aris-Paul provided a very different view of theological formation, one still connected to the community and meeting seminarians where they were: "We must go to heal where it is hurting and acknowledge the pain that our Hispanic communities are having at this time"—relevant formation. While offering excellent formation, the IPH worked with an understanding that "all of our students continue to work in their communities and churches while they pursue their theological education," and a focus on a different pedagogical style, that of Paolo Freire, which brought "together academic studies and practical experiences."[29] Given that I'm using elements of base communities and liberation theology, I am partisan to this approach, but do not like that it is separate from "regular" seminary, because it inherently maintains a hierarchy of knowledge and creates a second-class group of clergy.

The last approach presented was that of Rev. Alonzo Pruitt, arguing that "we become more fully ourselves when we share this love with people who are not from our own communities." Pruitt presented all the ways we could learn from the experiences of the Church with respect to recruitment of black clergy and the important place of the Union of Black Episcopalians (UBE). Pruitt reminded us also that recruitment was not something that was ever completed:

"Recruitment is not in a separate department but is woven into the thread of everything we do."[30] I believe that some external, yet related organization such as UBE for LATINX Episcopalians would be an incredible asset. We have much to learn. There have been attempts at associations, but these have not been sustained or made inroads.

Looking at these approaches, I would like to point out something that is still limiting us today. All these seminary deans based their observations on structural issues and how to "add" something to the structure or make it parallel. None of the seminary deans proposed structural changes to theological education at seminaries, or the "traditional" MDiv. On the other hand, we have examples of efforts that have effected great change that could lead seminary structures to transform and to speak to new realities.

## Not Enough Clergy—The Prophetic Challenge to Seminaries

Since one of my contentions is that since this is an epistemic problem, it is a myth that there are not enough potential LATINX students. Yes, there are dwindling enrollments; yet this is not about dwindling potential. As I have said, LATINX ministry is ministry is ministry. Moreover, the challenges with dwindling numbers of seminarians and theological education in the Episcopal Church are not particularly different for LATINX students. The reports on the many consultations and *encuentros* held in the Episcopal Church about LATINX Ministries reference the lack of clergy, the need for alternative models of theological education, and the over-reliance on clergy from Province IX and elsewhere in Latin America. The present challenge would remain even if more clergy from Latin America came to the United States and were trained in the Anglican/Episcopal ethos because of the challenge presented by the multi(bi) cultural, transcultural, and differently polycentric environment in the United States, even within LATINX communities and majority-LATINX congregations.

All these observations are true, and I would argue also that this repeated list of challenges reflects the institutional structures that keep these ministries as stunted programs of the Church. If a list of challenges remains the same over too long of a period of time, repeating of the list is in fact a trope that only aids in the prevention of progress, maintaining the status quo, something that benefits the institution—in this case keeping LATINX people and communities in the Episcopal Church limited and under control.

No matter how many times the issue of the number of clergy has been mentioned, it has never been intentionally and systematically addressed. In 1980, around the time of the first survey of ministry to, with, and among LATINX people was done, Arrunátegui noted, "There are only 35 priests of Hispanic heritage in the eight domestic provinces of the Church and the need is urgent for well-trained, dedicated people who want to serve Christ and his Church through the Hispanic community."[31]

In 2019 during a three-month absence from the congregation I serve, there was only one person who could cover me, and at that for only three Sundays; this is worse than five years ago and much worse than ten years ago. A related myth is about the capacity of LATINX people. Oliver, in *Ripe Fields*, argues that LATINX people are capable of rigorous academic work at the graduate level, and asserts that "as long as the standard for Anglos is the Master of Divinity degree," it should also be the standard for LATINX peoples. Oliver puts this issue into a broader context and shows that "the tendency to undervalue rigorous formation is not limited to Latino theological education."[32]

An oft-repeated challenge faced by the Episcopal Church is the shortage of clergy. Two popular explanations are the cost of traditional theological education and the time and requirements of an MDiv degree. Yet what LATINX people are usually offered is alternative theological preparation, which usually leads to a second-class status. In the case of people called to LATINX ministries, a popular misconception and tendency is to think that non-LATINX people cannot do this ministry or that most LATINX people do not have the academic background needed to enroll in a master's level program. Another issue is the over-reliance on clergy with Roman theological/seminary preparation that have not essentially made an Anglican shift.

One of the problems with thinking about theological education in the Episcopal Church is that it requires a long-term vision along with continual adjustment and implementation. It is an ever-evolving thirty-to-forty-year plan. In an idealistic way, imagine a person coming of age in an Episcopal church in the early 1990s, starting the ordination discernment process in 1994, attending seminary in 1997, graduating in 2000, and beginning to serve solo in a congregation around 2003—about a decade. Imagine also a young person, very active in the Church, taking a confirmation class with this priest in 2005 (at age 13), graduating from high school in 2010, and from college around 2014—another decade.

With some luck this young person remained connected to and engaged with the Episcopal Church through some sort of campus ministry and, in their early twenties, even began the discernment process for ordained ministry. They attend seminary at twenty-seven, are ordained at thirty, and are leading a congregation soon after, where they begin to influence those getting ready for confirmation. Another decade went by—mid 2020s. Every day in which we are not engaged in the long-term vision for theological education is a day that extends that cycle. Using my example, which is meant to solely be illustrative and thought provoking, we can understand we don't have time to waste.

To add complexity, if the Episcopal Church compromises the rigorous expectations for theological training for future clergy, we then are putting those clergy into leadership positions for which they are ill-equipped to be the inspiration for their congregations and the future ordained leaders. And not only ill-equipped for inspiration, but also for forming Christians in this Episcopal branch that will be committed to our tradition and want to invest in its future, and will use different epistemic assumptions.

When there was an intentional MDiv program at General Theological Seminary, it primarily served New Jersey, New York, and Connecticut. Whether through the IPH or the Programa de Teología Pastoral, the Diocese of New York ordained LATINX people on a regular basis; a half dozen are still in active ministry. Since the *Programa* closed in 2008, and the ordination of Rev. Luis Gómez, the Diocese of New York has not ordained a LATINX person to the priesthood. The diocese has one of the longest histories of ministry with and among LATINX people and communities. It has seen its LATINX-identified congregations decrease in the last decade, rather than living into their growth potential. A few other areas in the United States have seen growth. There is so much that we are doing wrong. How are we missing the mark? Are we selling our identity short by relying on former Roman Catholic priests, usually now married, and having congregations that people do not see as any different than the local Catholic parish? What level of sustained investment, intentionality, and commitment is the Church and seminaries willing to do? When the solutions to challenges are properly resourced and the time is committed, long-lasting positive effects can happen.

## Case Study: Theological Education in Puerto Rico— The Long View

After the United States invaded Puerto Rico, the Anglican churches already in the island came under the jurisdiction of the Episcopal Church. Puerto Rico was designated a missionary district, and, as such, bishops were elected and appointed by the House of Bishops. In the early decades, the clergy was mostly English-speaking. In 1924, four local clergy from the Iglesia de Jesús were ordained for the Episcopal Church.[33] During the long episcopate of the Rt. Rev. Charles B. Colmore (1913–1947), the second appointed bishop, came the first local ordinations of Puerto Ricans: the three Villafañe brothers. Colmore believed there should be a "national presbyterate." In 1931, there were nine Puerto Rican priests, plus Bishop Ferrando.[34] By 1944, there were six-teen Puerto Rican clergy. Among the sixteen was Rev. Francisco Reus Froylán, ordained in 1942, who became the first Puerto Rican bishop appointed by the House of Bishops. Reus Froylán, like his father, had received his seminary train-ing at *DuBose Memorial Church Training School* in Monteagle, Tennessee.[35]

In 1944, although already having called for a coadjutor, Colmore recog-nized that the non–Puerto Rican clergy earned significantly higher wages. The bishop wanted to see improvement in the support for "our local clergy by their own people and by the National Council; therefore, being able to attract youth of the highest intellectual preparation."[36] Colmore understood the need for Spanish-speaking native clergy that could do the necessary missionary work, but also knew that could not happen if the work of the local clergy was not equally valued,[37] and also understood the difference between missionary work by English-speakers, who were in essence chaplains, and the local work with Puerto Ricans. Colmore outlined a plan for local theological education that would later be termed the "Puerto Rican Plan."[38] Colmore was optimistic about the future of the Episcopal Church in Puerto Rico: "I trust in a prosperous future for the Church in this Missionary District, culminating in a Puerto Rican Church self-sufficient from its own people, teaching them the benefits and blessings of the true faith and Catholic practice." The Episcopal Church in Puerto Rico would become self-sufficient toward the end of the 1970s—thirty-five years later.

The third bishop appointed for Puerto Rico was Rt. Rev. Charles F. Boyn-ton (coadjutor 1944, diocesan 1948–1950; later suffragan of New York). It was also Boynton's view that there should be an indigenous clergy and that their formation should also happen in Puerto Rico. In 1949 Boynton outlined a sim-ilar "Puerto Rican Plan" and prefaced it by stating:

> It is not prudent to send native postulants and candidates to the United States to complete their studies. It is very expensive, and it limits the num-ber of postulants that a missionary bishop may accept. But more important, it separates and distances the native postulant from their island, people and culture, causing great difficulties in their readjustment when they return to Puerto Rico.[39]

Boynton, like Colmore, proposed a plan that identified vocations while still in high school and accompanied them through at least two years of univer-sity study. They were given additional formation as postulants and candidates while pursuing another two years of university studies, then two years of sem-inary (following the model from Seabury-Western Seminary), required exams (modeled by a plan developed by bishops Mize of Kansas and Matheus of New

Jersey), ordination to the diaconate with a supervised year-long appointment to a rural parish (Castañer), and, once ordained, an appointment to an urban parish as an assistant or as priest-in-charge of a rural congregation.[40]

The documentary evidence does not indicate the success or failure of the two "Puerto Rican Plans" for theological training of local clergy. With Boynton's relatively short diocesan episcopate, it would have been impossible to fully implement the plan. Yet the local formation must have yielded some fruit, since in 1950 there was a call for the election of a Puerto Rican bishop and the suggestion to the House of Bishops that it be the Rev. Canon Arístedes Villafañe, ordained since 1925. Nevertheless, the next bishop for the missionary district was Rev. A. Ervine Swift. Swift's immediate assessment of the church in Puerto Rico was of a laity not rooted in or loyal to the Episcopal Church and led by former Roman Catholic clergy "without adequate Anglican preparation."[41]

> Although truly consecrated men, it cannot be denied that their training or preparation had been inadequate, and the church is suffering the consequences. I prefer to raise a Puerto Rican presbyterate instead of having too many from the continent, but I insist in the best possible preparation and seminary work in the United States.[42]

In Swift's estimation that meant a shortage for five to seven years, but it was worth it since they were preparing for the next thirty-five years.[43] Quickly, Swift identified four young men, enrolled several of them in the Episcopal high school in Trujillo Alto to study in English, then starting in 1955, three attended college in Wisconsin, the other in San Germán, Puerto Rico. The four then attended four different seminaries in the United States from 1959 to 1962. On the eve of the founding of the Episcopal Seminary of the Caribbean, there were sixteen Puerto Ricans studying in seminaries in the United States.[44]

In 1961 the Caribbean seminary opened in Puerto Rico. It remained open until 1976. In 1963, the first three students graduated; over fifteen years, more than seventy were trained.[45] The education offered at the seminary was on par with any seminary in the continental United States. A perusal of professors and graduates shows bishops and renowned priests throughout the Church.[46] Swift's practice of sending postulants to study at U.S. seminaries also guaranteed a depth of Anglican identity and training for its clergy that infused every level of the church in Puerto Rico.

After the Anglican Caribbean seminary closed, some postulants took advantage of the degrees offered at the local *Seminario Evangélico de Puerto Rico* (SEPR), probably in part through the encouragement of Rev. Wade Eaton, PhD, an Episcopal priest and Old Testament faculty member at the seminary since the 1960s.[47] It is my understanding that one of the last Episcopalians to get an MDiv through the evangelical seminary was Rev. Emilia Morales in 1998 (ordained June 1991, sixth woman in Puerto Rico); Rev. Joaquin Rabell graduated from SEPR in 1978. Less than a handful of Episcopalians have enrolled in SEPR in the last twenty years.[48]

With few exceptions the remaining people who have been ordained in the last thirty years have been trained in either the local diocesan seminary San Pedro y San Pablo or through the Roman Catholic seminary process. Of the four final candidates in the 2016 diocesan Episcopal election process, one attended an Episcopal seminary; the other three were trained in Roman Catholic seminaries. That one was me, and I was not elected. I firmly believe that, in part, the future of the church in Puerto Rico is dependent on the depth of theological training and Anglican/Episcopal formation of the leadership of the Church.

The closing of the seminary of the Caribbean in 1976 has had repercussions even into 2020. A trust fund—Commission for the Theological Education of Latin America and the Caribbean—was created by Executive Council.[49] About $350,000 dollars are distributed annually with no diocese receiving more than $10,000 each year. What can $10,000 really accomplish? This guarantees a program status—a commodification of LATINX people and communities.

As seen above, in the documentary evidence, the concern for theological formation of local Episcopal clergy in Puerto Rico has existed since the early years of the twentieth century. Even today, some of the leadership in Puerto Rico, and elsewhere in the United States, can trace their heritage to some of the first Puerto Rican clergy who were ordained—Villafañe, Rivera, Reus, Ramos Orench, Álvarez, Vilar—all with multiple generations of clergy, including six bishops. Yet Swift's observation regarding theological formation and Anglican grounding and the decision to send seminarians to the United States changed and formed the church in Puerto Rico for decades after his pronouncement in 1951.

Although my Episcopal roots are in Puerto Rico, my leadership in the Church on the island has been limited. However, I was mentored by many of those who were seminarians or grew up in the Church in the 1950s and 1960s—and this is not solely a generational phenomenon. According to the "recruitment" report of 1988 discussed earlier, in the mid-1980s there was a surplus of clergy in Puerto Rico.[50] This was a direct result of the intentionality and investment that Swift implemented and the existence of the local accredited Anglican seminary. Some of them served in churches in the continental United States. For reference, those were the years I was in high school; I was directly impacted by the decisions made in 1951. Now, almost seventy years later (two 35-year cycles), I am writing this book.

In the summer of 2000, the faculty for my clinical pastoral education included Rev. José (Cheo) Vilar (Yale) and Rev. Jorge Juan Rivera Torres (GTS), along with Rev. Emilia Morales (SEPR) and Rev. Manuel C. Olmo. In 1998, as I prepared for the English-language service at the Cathedral of St. John the Baptist in San Juan—and for years afterwards—I regularly ran into Rev. Miguel (Mickey) Vilar and Rev. Wade Eaton (CDSP) in the sacristy.

This generation of priests and those that were directly affected by them had a great influence in my ordained life. Many of them were contemporaries of my mother. As I mentioned, Bishop Tony Ramos married my parents in 1967, a year before becoming bishop of Costa Rica. And I grew up in a time in which the realization of a church led by Puerto Ricans had been achieved in the episcopates of Reus Froylán and Álvarez, and well after the ordination of women. This generation formed me and, in their final years of ordained ministry, mentored me into a life in ministry.

I don't want to say that what happened in Puerto Rico was better or needs to be replicated. What I want to focus on is the fact that intentional focus and rigorous theological education grounded in our Anglican/Episcopal tradition has great ripple effects. On the other hand, when that rigorous Anglican/Episcopal formation does not exist, there are no ripples. I don't want to romanticize the past, but it is illustrative of where we are in the present. Or, put differently, in the Diocese of New York, what is the correlation between not lifting up vocations in LATINX communities, not offering theological education that is truly open to LATINX students, and the fact that LATINX folks have not been ordained to the priesthood in over a decade?

## 2019: General Theological Seminary's Distinguished Alumni Award

In May of 2019, GTS awarded Rev. Jorge Juan Rivera Torres the Distinguished Alumni Award. GTS recognized Rivera for work as the first LATINX missioner for the Episcopal Church (1971), as historiographer of the Episcopal Church in Puerto Rico with three published books, and close to sixty years of ordained ministry. Rivera was a member of the CPE faculty when I did my internship in 2000—little did I know then that I would be there when the alumni honor was awarded. It was a historic moment for GTS and for the Church. I'm not sure Swift could have articulated a vision of the ramifications of a decision on theological education in 1951 seventy years later, but Rivera was one of the postulants who went off to college in 1955 and seminary in 1959, graduating and being ordained in 1962. Swift's decision still has small ripples today; those ripples will soon completely dissipate; isn't it time to make sure that there are ripples going forward?

The leadership that the Church needs in 2050 is already growing up in our society, in high school, and some even in our Episcopal churches. The leadership of the church in 2050 may very well be the ones taking confirmation classes in 2019. That means that the formation my nephew Evan received at St. Mark's in San Antonio, Texas, leading up to his confirmation in April 2019 was of the utmost importance for the future of the Church.

The issue of education is not unique to the Episcopal Church. Once in a conversation with my sister Rosalind about education in Texas, the scenario came up that Texas may experience a shortage in native skilled workers in twenty years. What made so much sense to me was her reminding me that even beginning to prepare pre-kindergartners right now meant that they were already behind. If clergy are generally starting their ministries in their thirties, these future clergy are in middle school now.

Given my hypothetical scenario of the thirty-year cycle, imagine how many vocations have been lifted that have been informed either by a limited Episcopal ethos or by a masked Roman Catholic ethos given the particular type of training they receive? Or worse yet, how many vocations have we failed to lift? The deficient vocations can be remedied; the not lifted are lost.

## A Starting Point

Over the past two decades I have spoken to many seminary deans and presidents, as well as bishops, about crafting theological education that includes a significant number of LATINX students. I have also argued that this is not solely about LATINX seminarians and leaders. Sustained, intentional, properly resourced theological education will have long-lasting repercussions for the whole Church and the fulfillment of its mission. One piece is LATINX. I propose, in broad strokes, that a starting point will require a $5 to 7-million-dollar investment, while establishing the ways in which it will become part of the fabric of seminaries and the Church:

- Years 1 and 2: Intentional recruitment
- Year 3: Enroll 6 LATINX students; 2 MDiv, 2 MA, 2 certificate. Two graduates.
- Year 4: Enroll 4–6 MDiv students and 2–4 MA students, and 2 certificate. Four graduates.
- Year 5: Enroll 4–6 MDiv students; 2–4 MA students; 2–4 Anglican certificate students. Ten graduates.

- Year 6: Enroll 4–6 MDiv students; 2–4 MA students; 2–4 Anglican certificate students. Ten graduates.
- Year 7: Last year of fully funded program: enroll 4–6 MDiv students; 2–4 MA students; 2–4 Anglican certificate students. Ten graduates.
- Year 8: Reduced funding: same enrollment.
- Year 9: reduced funding: same enrollment.
- Year 10: no funding (self-sustaining): same enrollment
- After ten years there are approximately sixty additional LATINX leaders in the church. This is not the end of a program, but the beginning of a transformed Church.

I am not attached to this specific plan, nor do I personally have the resources. My hope is that someone or a group reads this book and is inspired and able to get the ball rolling.

## Leadership Development

The epistemological challenge brought forth by the insidiousness of modernity extends as well to how we measure the *other* in terms of capacity and worthiness. We don't even know all of the ways in which we have universalized an Episcopal culture that privileges a certain expression over any other.[51] This is ultimately about respecting the dignity of every human being and acknowledging their truth and potential as being a gift to the Church, as others historically without challenge have shared their own gifts. A fundamental aspect of this epistemological challenge is whether we can envision all of the ways that those currently at the margins can evangelize us? This also means, whether we can imagine all of the ways in which those at the margins can teach us? Moreover, can we dare to expect to live into our baptismal life while being led by those on the borderlands? In short, are we willing to enter into community with those whom may radically change and transform us?

As many laypeople and clergy have done, I have taken the Myers-Briggs personality inventory. I am an INTJ—Introvert, Intuitive, Thinking, Judgmental. Yet, as a church leader, I found the DISC typology (high DC) to be more helpful in my interactions with other church leaders, staff, and parishioners. It is my sense that the church needs people with all types of personalities or management styles. Alongside these tools, I believe that the discernment of spiritual gifts is as important.[52] All of this is parallel to theological training and gaining competencies in specific areas needed for professional work in the Church.

Everyone has gifts and leadership qualities. Part of the challenge in leadership development and theological education is that leadership and seminary training are defined in a "Eurocentric" and *white* manner, thus identifying only certain types of leaders, and not being willing to share power and resources outside of entrenched circles. This does not mean that leaders and seminarians from the majority culture are not needed or that majority-type leadership development and theological training must be discarded, but that they have to be reshaped to include other types of leaders and seminarians, as well as other views of leadership development and theological training.

The necessary change requires a willingness to both be transformed and to relinquish access to power and resources. As I have mentioned, innovation in the same vessel doesn't bring about systemic change. Leadership is about opportunities. Leadership is about observation. Leadership is about listening.

Leadership development will happen when we, as a Church, face the biases and made-up barriers to developing LATINX Episcopal leaders. As I proposed regarding language proficiency, I believe the issue of a pipeline is a made-up barrier. Just because LATINX demographics indicate growth does not mean there will be growth in the Episcopal Church by osmosis. Although the population of the United States has increased in the last two decades, the Church has not grown in raw numbers, much less as a percentage of the population. I believe the reasons behind both statements are similar: an inability to implement structural change and share power and resources, which means a loss in focus as to what the mission of the Church is. Increasing the number of LATINX leaders, and thus LATINX people in seminaries, will require an intentional effort at many levels to promote the Church as a place of fulfilling employment, both lay and ordained. The 1985 progress report indicated:

> There is agreement among us regarding a real need for well-trained clergy: clergy whose seminary training removes the stigma of "second class," and who are free to serve in any community, Hispanic or Anglo, to which they are called.[53]

Congregational Development is not about jobs for clergy. González writes, "In light of the New Testament understanding of the ministry of all Christians, we cannot continue to think of congregational development as a clergy deployment project."[54] Oliver resonates, "What is in fact often taking place when plans are being made for such a Hispanic ministry and congregation is that the needs of the church are made to determine the needs of the people, and the existence of facilities and the need to upkeep them is allowed to determine the nature of the program."[55] As Leonardo Boff coined the term, "congregational development is *ecclesiogenesis*—gestating an assembly or community of worship and witness. This is best done 'from below.'"[56]

## Investment and Opportunity

I've lived a life of educational privilege and I have benefited from the vision of others that have recognized the importance of opportunities alongside investment. I have seen it work. In the summer of 1999, I participated in the Hispanic Summer Program (HSP). That year it was at the Graduate Theological Union in Berkeley, California. I took two classes: one in LATINX church history with Paul Barton, and the other in ethics with Ada María Isasi-Diaz. After the summer program, I immediately went to the summer workshop, in Palo Alto, of the Hispanic Theological Initiative (HTI). Both events were life-changing. By the time I attended HSP, I had completed two years of seminary, had added an MA to my plan of study, and was in the ordination process in Puerto Rico. HSP and HTI have ever since been influential in my life, teaching, and ministry.

There were two revealing experiences on the margins during HSP that are key to present here. First, HSP was held on familiar ground and meals were taken in the CDSP refectory in Parsons Hall. During my time at CDSP, meals were offered in the refectory three times a day, Monday through Friday. I mention this to try to convey, since I lived at CDSP, that I was very familiar with the refectory, and more importantly with the "sound" of the refectory. During meals at HSP the "sound" was different. It was Spanish, English, and much in between. It was louder and livelier. Yet what was most important is that it had a familiarity that you would never recognize unless you had experienced the absence of it for two years. In a way that is the importance of HSP, the ability to bring together LATINX seminarians from across the country so that they can experience that familiarity which is likely absent in their own seminaries. After the two weeks of HSP, I never felt that sound again.

Second, while in line at one of the meals, González introduced himself and had a brief conversation with me. I told him about my intention to pursue doctoral studies and that I was discerning what schools to apply to. I have never forgotten González's advice then—go to the school that values you, wants you, and pays for you: you deserve it. Although my doctoral studies didn't quite take that trajectory, it was that moment of encouragement that I have always remembered. I am privileged that I've many other such insightful brief conversations with González and I know that he has done the same with so many others. That is why his vision and implementation of that vision has been prophetic.

Although always *en conjunto* (together and in collaboration), González has been behind important initiatives that have afforded LATINX people access to theological education and mentorship in ways few have been able to do. González has modeled that leadership for others. Two of those initiatives are the HSP and HTI. Thousands of seminarians have participated in and benefited from HSP for over thirty years. Scores of doctoral students have benefitted from the financial support, mentorship, and collegiality that have been offered through HTI for more than twenty years. Because of HSP and HTI, many LATINX people are exercising leadership across denominations and in academia. What it took was the bold vision of a group of people and the tireless, sustained, consistent, and intentional implementation of that vision.

I presented some of the reasoning behind the need for rigorous and intentional leadership development and access to Anglican/Episcopal theological education. It is important to remember that a prophetic vision for theological education and leadership development must be implemented with the knowledge that the leadership of some of the people we invest on may be manifest outside of the church: that these LATINX leaders are being lifted as a gift for the whole Church, not solely LATINX congregations/communities; that this intentional development and formation is not just for future ordained leaders but also for laypeople called to specific work in the Church. Rev. Juan Francisco Martínez puts this well, "The Latino church is not only producing leaders for its churches. It is also sending leaders to serve in other contexts."[57]

I wrote about the prophetic vision of Bishop Swift in Puerto Rico starting in 1951 and the impact it had even on me even through my ordination in 2002. Here, I present another example—HTI—and their methodical approach to support theological education. When HTI was founded in 1997, there were about fifty LATINX people, of all denominations, in the United States with doctorates in theology and religion, and related fields. Over the past twenty years HTI has helped mint over 120 more LATINX doctors in these fields. This work is as important as that of the doctoral program of the Episcopal Church Foundation or the Fund for Theological Education. There is still work to do, and HTI has continued to reinvent itself while keeping their eye on the fulfillment of their mission. When you think of the whole United States population, the fact that there are around 200 LATINX academics in these fields is still woefully inadequate. Yet the work done by González and HTI is beyond commendable. Sadly, of HTI graduates, there are only two Episcopalians.

González demonstrated that there are LATINX people for the educational pipeline, yet bringing them to theological education is not going to happen by osmosis. The key is not just the theological education but changes in the epistemological content of theological education to move beyond a Western/ white center, and intentionality in mentorship and building community to prevent the inherent isolation given the dearth of LATINX people in seminaries now.

Regardless of emerging and eventually chosen models of theological education and formation, at all levels, they must be as rigorous as ever. Given the thirty-five-year cycle presented above, seminaries must be willing to set a course in which none of the people currently making decisions will be there to reap the benefits—a long view of excellence. Every year that we delay in this it is a year in which the Church is not benefiting in the future. This is because I believe that seminaries are in a unique position to both support the institution (the Church) and speak truth to the Church through its voice and place. Before getting there, though, all seminaries must be willing to be bold and strategic in the structural changes they must make. I honestly believe, and hopefully not solely naively, that one of the key pieces in the prophetic turnaround of the Episcopal Church toward true inclusion and solidarity is found in our theological institutions.

This chapter has been about epistemology, structural changes that lead to power and resource sharing, all aiming to refocus the Church on the fulfillment of its mission—"to restore all people to unity with God and each other in Christ" (#BCP855)—rather than to protect, preserve, and perpetuate the institution as is. In this refocusing, everyone including LATINX people have a role in the fulfillment of this mission. As Mignolo and Walsh argue, the first step is delinking from the rhetoric of modernity and instituting a pluriversality of knowledge:

> Delinking means conceiving of and creating institutional organizations that are at the service of life and do not—as in the current state of affairs—put people at the service of institutions. . . . Putting life at the service of institutions is the basic principle of modernity/coloniality, of Eurocentrism, and of the [colonial matrix of power].[58]

## Notes

1. Walter D. Mignolo and Catherine E. Walsh, *On Decoloniality: Concepts, Analytics, Praxis* (Durham, NC: Duke University Press, 2018), 167.

2. The 2016 prayer book from the Anglican Church of Brazil is clearly a part of the prayer book lineage, and clearly aware of the current vernacular of the church in its own context.

3. Mignolo and Walsh, *On Decoloniality*, 73.

4. Miguel Ángel Asturias, *El Señor Presidente* (Buenos Aires, Argentina: Editorial Losada, 1948); Nobel Prize for Literature in 1967.

5. Luis Rafael Sánchez (b. 1936): *La guaracha del Macho Camacho* (1976), *La guagua aérea* (2000); and Ana Lydia Vega (b. 1946): *Encancaranublado y otros cuentos de naufragio* (1982), *Falsas crónicas del sur* (1991).

6. Mignolo and Walsh, *On Decoloniality*, 136.

7. Mignolo and Walsh, *On Decoloniality*, 125. Mignolo and Walsh are elaborating on the seminal work of Aníbal Quijano, "Colonialidad y modernidad/racionalidad," *Perú Indígena* 13, no. 29 (1992): 11–20.

8. Mignolo and Walsh, *On Decoloniality*, 111.

9. Mignolo and Walsh, *On Decoloniality*, 121.

10. The peer-review process is anonymous. I received notes from the journal editor via e-mail on February 10, 2019. These are taken from reviewer #2.

11. Mignolo and Walsh, *On Decoloniality*, 57.

12. Mignolo and Walsh, *On Decoloniality*, 58.

13. Mignolo and Walsh, *On Decoloniality*, 158.

14. Alberto L. García and John A. Nunes, *Wittenberg Meets the World: Reimagining the Reformation at the Margins* (Grand Rapids, MI: William B. Eerdmans Publishing, 2017), 145.

15. Mignolo and Walsh, *On Decoloniality*, 111.

16. Mignolo and Walsh, *On Decoloniality*, 28.

17. Mignolo and Walsh, *On Decoloniality*, 110.

18. Mary Frances Schjonberg, "Trinity Church Wall Street Acquires Church Divinity School of the Pacific," ENS, March 4, 2019, *https://www.episcopalnewsservice.org/2019/03/04/trinity-church-wall-street-acquires-church-divinity-school-of-the-pacific/*; Kirk Petersen, "Trinity Wall Street Acquires CDSP," March 4, 2019, *https://livingchurch.org/2019/03/04/trinity-wall-street-acquires-cdsp/*; "Trinity Church Wall Street and Church Divinity School of the Pacific Announce Alliance," Church Divinity School of the Pacific, March 2019, *https://cdsp.edu/2019/03/trinity-church-wall-street-and-church-divinity-school-of-the-pacific-announce-alliance/*.

19. Mignolo and Walsh, *On Decoloniality*, 71.

20. For examples see Mignolo and Walsh, *On Decoloniality*, 62, 81.

21. Juan M. C. Oliver, *Ripe Fields: The Promise and Challenge of Latino Ministry* (New York: Church Publishing Incorporated, 2009), 68.

22. Juan Francisco Martínez, *Walking with the People: Latino Ministry in the United States* (Eugene, OR: Wipf & Stock, 2016), 84, 88.

23. Herbert Arrunátegui, "Introduction," in "Ministry in a Culturally Diverse Church: Report of a Hispanic Consultation on Recruitment, Training, and Deployment." (New York: National Hispanic Ministry Office, Episcopal Church Center, 1993).

24. Anselmo Carral, "Statement of Purpose," in "Ministry in a Culturally Diverse Church."

25. Gordon T. Charlton, "Recruitment, Deployment and Training in Hispanic Ministry," in "Ministry in a Culturally Diverse Church,"1–3.

26. William Pregnall, "Preparing for Cross-Cultural Ministry," in "Ministry in a Culturally Diverse Church," 4–6.

27. Durstan McDonald, "Recruitment, Specialization and Missionary Training," in "Ministry in a Culturally Diverse Church," 6–9.

28. James Fenhagen, "Developing a Joint Program," in "Ministry in a Culturally Diverse Church," 9–10.

29. Maria Aris-Paul, "Training Leaders the Jesus Way," in "Ministry in a Culturally Diverse Church," 11–13.

30. Alonzo Pruitt, "Building Supportive Networks," in "Ministry in a Culturally Diverse Church." 14–16.

31. ENS, "Hispanic Vocations to Be Lifted Up," August 28, 1980 [80289].

32. Juan Oliver, *Ripe Fields*, 101, as analyzed in a book review that I wrote in 2011 published in the *Anglican Theological Review* 93, no. 4 (2011): 731–34.

33. Jorge Juan Rivera Torres, *Documentos Históricos de la Iglesia Episcopal Puertorriqueña*, vol. 1, 2nd ed. (Saint Just, PR: Taller Episcográfico, IEP, 2008), 73 (Victor Rivera, Modesto Rivera, Primitivo Maldonado, and Hermenegildo Maldonado).

34. Rivera Torres, *Documentos*, 55.

35. Rivera Torres, *Documentos*, 56.

36. Rivera Torres, *Documentos*, 61.

37. Rivera Torres, *Documentos*, 65. Colmore indicates that some progress was made in terms of equity by 1946. Colmore believed that "clergy that had financial stability would provide greater results in their task and growth of the Church."

38. Rivera Torres, *Documentos*, 61.

39. Rivera Torres, *Documentos*, 77.

40. Rivera Torres, *Documentos*, 77–78.

41. Rivera Torres, *Documentos*, 100.

42. Rivera Torres, *Documentos*, 101.

43. Rivera Torres, *Documentos*, 101.

44. Rivera Torres, *Documentos*, 108. Among the students studying in the United States was Jorge Juan Rivera Torres, editor of the *Documentos Históricos* cited in this section, who graduated from General Theological Seminary in 1962. In May 2019 he received the Distinguished Alumni Award from GTS. Rev. José E. Vilar graduated in 1962 from Berkeley Divinity School.

45. ENS, "Seminary's First Graduation," June 5, 1963 [XI-11].

46. Rt. Rev. Wilfrido Ramos Orench graduated in 1966. Bishop James H. Ottley, of Panamá, graduated in the 1960s.

47. "Evangelical" in Spanish does not have the same connotation as in the United States—it may be best understood as "mainline-Protestant."

48. To my knowledge, the most recent graduates are the now ordained Rev. Bryan A. Vélez (2019) and Karla Sánchez. Sánchez has been delayed in these studies given disruptions caused by the aftermath of hurricanes Irma and María.

49. Comisión para la Educación Teológica para América Latina y el Caribe (CETALC).

50. Arrunátegui, "Recruiting and Training Hispanic Leadership," in "Ministry in a Culturally Diverse Church," 21.

51. A parallel aspect is expressed in Alberto L. García and John A. Nunes, *Wittenberg Meets the World: Reimagining the Reformation at the Margins* (Grand Rapids, MI: William B. Eerdmans, 2017), 109, 144. "Constant vigilance to be sure that no one particular expression becomes a primary unifier, filtering out the fellowship of those who are different." Also regarding contributions by those on the margins see, 68, 101, 133, 139, 143.

52. For our Lenten Program in 2017 we explored spiritual gifts and used as a resource Charles Bryant, *Rediscovering Our Spiritual Gifts: Building Up the Body of Christ Through the Gifts of the Spirit* (Nashville, TN: Upper Room Books, 1998).

53. "The Episcopal Church and the Hispanic Challenge: A Report on the State of Hispanic Ministries," (New York: Office of Hispanic Ministry, Episcopal Church Center, 1985), 22–23.

54. Justo L. González, *The Hispanic Ministry of the Episcopal Church in the Metropolitan Area of New York and Environs* (New York: Grants Board of Trinity Parish, 1985), 10

55. Oliver, *Ripe Fields*, 22.

56. Oliver, *Ripe Fields*, 22.

57. Martínez, *Walking*, 85.

58. Mignolo and Walsh, *On Decoloniality*, 126.

CHAPTER 5

# Building upon
# Anglican Traditions

*Possibilities*

At a Nuevo Amanecer workshop in 2016, we asked participants to introduce themselves by sharing their name and what diocese or congregation they were affiliated with, and to tell us how they came to know the Episcopal Church and what they find compelling in the denomination. A few were lifelong Episcopalians; others had just been with the Episcopal Church a few months. Many shared how they felt welcomed in their congregations, that they valued being known by name, many mentioned coffee hours as a positive, and a number said that they appreciated the democratic nature of the running of the parish and diocese through vestries and the diocesan convention. Often something positive about worship was also mentioned, including its language and music. These comments were not unfamiliar; I've heard them in many other contexts.

It is my firm belief that LATINX people and communities have much to offer to the Episcopal Church, and that the Episcopal Church has much to offer LATINX people and communities. I'm not talking about demographics or survival, but complementary ethos and value systems. Both sides already have resources in their tool kits that are mutually enriching. One of the challenges for the Episcopal Church is to grow into a deeper understanding and recovery of its own history, tradition, and theology—divested of coloniality—while accepting that there is room for much more.

There is no one way to engage in ministry to, with, and among LATINX people and communities, just as there is no one way to do ministry. Nor is there one way of fulfilling the mission of the Church (#BCP855), or one way to be Episcopalian. LATINX people belong to many different communities. This self-reflection, then, is not just a concern for LATINX-defined congregations, although it does mean that LATINX-defined congregations must reflect this complexity and are indeed more than just LATINX; they are already inter/multicultural. In the minoritized context of the United States, LATINX-defined churches have to deal with intercultural dynamics.[1] This will not get any simpler under the current approach. As LATINX communities grow and diversify, there will be no "single type of ministry that will be able to have an impact among all of the Latino diversity."[2] This is a gift—an opportunity—and should liberate the whole Church. This is where discernment of adaptation of Anglicanism to the local context is a place of revelation. If scripture contains all that's necessary for salvation, then our tradition has a robust way to articulate the theology that leads the Church to fulfill its mission. Put differently, our tradition is rich, and we should use it rather than sell ourselves short.

In this chapter I offer my own curiosities around some of positive aspects the Episcopal Church has to offer LATINX people and communities. I hope these are prompts for the reader to explore ways to strengthen our tradition while transforming the institution. After all, there needs to be a willingness to find transformation in the historically silenced or excluded margin of the Church, and welcome our own metanoia as individuals and as a Church. I begin by framing some promising ideas that come from Anglican/Episcopal theologies, such as *both/and*, Article 34 and inculturation, and the prayer book tradition. Although I will present these in very traditional language, the reader should keep in mind the decolonial approach presented in chapter 4. Although these are familiar aspects of Anglican/Episcopal theologies, they must also be epistemically liberated. Thus, I'm not just adding a layer on top; this is the recovery of a foundation, stripped of its U.S.-Euro-centric universalizing assumptions and then creating something fundamentally familiar, but new. In the second part of the chapter I provide some practical thoughts around bilingual and vernacular liturgies. I conclude this chapter by presenting an outline of the contours of elements of a LATINX Anglican/Episcopal theology.

## LATINX Anglican/Episcopal Tradition and Theology

LATINX people often have at least a double cultural experience. The intragroup experience of overall LATINX communities is, from the start, diverse, as is the intergroup experience of LATINX people. Rev. Juan M. C. Oliver states that this makes LATINX people "experts in multicultural ministry."[3] The rest of the Church has much to learn.

> We minister constantly to people of a different culture from ours: cleaning their homes, care for their children, pick their vegetables—some of us even teach their seminarians and grade their term papers. So I suggest that we include the experience of learning to be bicultural as a rich place of revelation where God is present and manifest.

Precisely because we have survived and thrived through a process of learning a second culture, we have discovered that culture and its components— language, manners, rituals, body language—is multiplex.[4]

In a country that is more diverse than ever, LATINX people bring an understanding of how to live in an inter/multicultural context. LATINX people and communities open up *lo cotidiano* to be a "rich place of revelation."[5]

Neither Oliver or I are saying anything new. Rev. Herbert Arrunátegui wrote about this in the 1980s and reiterated it in 1998: the enrichment is mutual, diverse, with value added for both sides.[6] Arrunátegui, in the 1998 report, offered this scheme to summarize the above:

LATINX people/communities offer the Episcopal Church:

- Faith: The possibility of sharing in their daily reliving of the Exodus and the wandering Aramean.
- Experiences: Their joy in times of adversity and thankfulness in the face of extreme necessity.
- Community: A rediscovery of the "base communities"; The spontaneity of their personal warmth, the extended family and the "abrazo" (the hug or embrace).
- Sacraments: A lively liturgy: The celebration of life with color, dance, drama, and fiesta extended beyond the church walls to the streets and the homes.
- Prayers: A profound sense of personal piety and devotions, sacrifice, and the meaning of the Cross.

The Episcopal Church offers LATINX people/communities:

- Faith: Catholic and Protestant: Apostolic teaching (Holy Scriptures) and the universal cross in a framework of reasonableness and dialogue.
- Community: Inclusive, pastoral, and familial: A democratic institution offering multiple opportunities for lay commitment, decision-making, and stewardship at all levels.
- Sacraments: A varied liturgy with apostolic orders: All the sacraments, enhanced by active lay participation and a structure allowing for creative innovations.
- Prayers: Prayer book order and dignity with room for evangelical spontaneity and charismatic spirit: Many and varied opportunities for corporate and personal spiritual growth.[7]

Clearly LATINX people and communities are value added to the Episcopal Church and the Episcopal Church has something to offer LATINX people and communities.

One of the reasons I appreciated participating in the Theologizing *Latinamente* conference in October 2018 is that I saw it as an example of how we are entering a time of renewed Episcopal/Anglican theologizing, including theologizing from a LATINX perspective, and a time to develop more fully LATINX theologies from Anglican/Episcopal perspectives. This has not been engaged fully since the 1980s and is long overdue. Oliver's participation in the conference was one step in the fulfilment of the 2009 vision of developing "our theology as a reflection upon our experience of God from within our own cultural context and within the wider context of an Anglican tradition."[8]

## Both/And

A LATINX Anglican/Episcopal theology should build upon the ideas of both/and (or the *via media*). Holding to inter/multiculturalism and polycentric identities is inherently also about holding in creative tension, the ethos of both/and.

When talking about LATINX people and the Episcopal Church, I have often said that LATINX people and communities in the United States context are already inherently Anglican or Episcopalian because LATINX people know how to live in the "both/and." A trivial example for me is listening to NPR and One Republic, switching to Ricky Martin in English, or listening to Marc Anthony in Spanish. You get the point: many LATINX people do not see contradictions, but enrichment. In the Episcopal Church we have diversity that is mutually enriching.

The idea of both/and can also be seen through the lenses of intersectionality. The Episcopal Church can speak to the polycentric nature of LATINX identities. Both/and can be understood as the third space of creativity described by Homi Bhabha.[9] Both/and alongside diversity/unity can also be understood as a type of "synthesis." One of the definitions of synthesis is as "a complex whole formed by combining"[10]—something we find in the prayer book and our weekly liturgy of invitation to communion, when the longer version is chosen. "The Gifts of God for the People of God. [adding] Take them in remembrance that Christ died for you, and feed on him in your hearts by faith, with thanksgiving."[11] It does not erase the constitutive elements but expands their individual meaning.

Throughout its history, Anglicanism has been very adept at synthesis. In our understanding today, we see synthesis in the both/and of Catholic and Protestant. One of the brilliant aspects of Anglicanism is that seemingly disparate things are held together in tension rather than in opposition. Archbishop Thomas Cranmer often did this in what I call "sandwich form." The additional line to the invitation for communion serves as a prime example. Some

Episcopalians and other outsider sometimes see this as indecisiveness or an unwillingness to take a stand—yet it is about holding together.

The choices that Cranmer made were to hold various theologies together, something that many people fail to understand in the practice of the Church. We function more easily in an either/or paradigm. Being able to hold differing theologies requires a level of discomfort, where the value of common prayer and having communities that function together is put above our ease and individual comfort, or even personal stance. Worshipping in diverse communities is hard; so long as the reign of God that we envision is inclusive and diverse, we must work to make our congregations inclusive and diverse, which requires all aspects of that diversity to be held together in a creative tension, for the sake of the reign.

## Article 34 and Contextuality

It is in human nature to make sense of the world around us by categorizing people and things. That is not inherently a bad thing. It is also, at times, inherent to human nature to create a value system around those categorizations and reify those systems as real. At times these reifications create "isms" and, at other times, create "traditions" that we tend to make not only reified (thingified) but static. Rather than thinking these are local systems of categorization—this generally U.S.-Eurocentric knowledge has been universalized—this is an aspect of coloniality.

The expression of Christianity in England in the sixteenth century was in fact an ordering of worship and theology in a way that made sense in that context. The framers of Anglicanism understood the local nature and concerns of the church in England. Close to a century later, once the Church of England crossed the Atlantic, the expression of Anglicanism in the colonies and later in the United States was a new ordering and contextualization of the English reality. This expectation of adaptation is enshrined in Article 34: "Of the traditions of the church" of the Articles of Religion.

The keynote address of the Theologizing *Latinamente* conference was given by Oliver. Oliver presented on inculturated liturgy. I was one of the responders to Oliver's presentation and asked the audience of seventy-five to one hundred people whether they knew Article 34. Maybe four or five people raised their hands. Although I was not expecting everyone to know the answer to my nerdy church question, I was surprised how few people at a seminary-sponsored conference knew the answer.

> XXXIV. Of the Traditions of the Church. It is not necessary that the Traditions and Ceremonies be in all places one, or utterly like; for at all times they have been divers, and may be changed according to the diversity of countries,

times, and men's manners, so that nothing be ordained against God's Word. Whosoever, through his private judgment, willingly and purposely, doth openly break the Traditions and Ceremonies of the Church, which be not repugnant to the Word of God, and be ordained and approved by common authority, ought to be rebuked openly, (that others may fear to do the like,) as he that offendeth against the common order of the Church, and hurteth the authority of the Magistrate, and woundeth the consciences of the weak brethren.

Every particular or national Church hath authority to ordain, change, and abolish, Ceremonies or Rites of the Church ordained only by man's authority, so that all things be done to edifying.[12]

To point out the obvious, traditions and ceremonies need not be the same everywhere. The Anglican idea of catholicity and being one branch out of many of the Jesus Movement are good examples. We are all reflective of the Church. The individual is not the driver of the tradition, the local community is. There can be an incredible number of expressions that can all be Anglican/Episcopal. The flexibility of our tradition is enshrined in Article 34.

A deeper understanding of what it means to have autochthonous Anglican/Episcopal expressions is an important way to move forward, at all levels—congregations, dioceses, and autonomous churches. This specifically does not mean becoming something else, because we then become independent congregations who do not present a coherent theology, and, perhaps, should be part of a different denominational body. It does mean that there is something specific about the Episcopal Church that we hold on to as a democratic institution; as all clergy declare at their ordination: "I do solemnly engage to conform to the doctrine, discipline, and worship of The Episcopal Church."[13] And "the doctrine, discipline, and worship of The Episcopal Church" is not static and the same everywhere. Part of the problem is treating it as such. Making our tradition look only one way is a way of saying, to join us you must be like us. Article 34 has never been about assimilation. Thus, the idea of tying Protestantism to Americanization is one that only responds to the ugly discourses of the "black legend" as appropriated by white Episcopalians, rather than living into the reality of the Anglican heritage found in Article 34.

## Prayer Book

Although I have repeatedly mentioned that innovation in the same vessel is often stifled, one vessel that has room for and can handle creative changes is our prayer book. We need to have mechanisms for our prayer book to keep up with changes in the "standard" vernacular and also accommodate the more localized vernaculars. The 1979 prayer book reflects a vernacular that is different from the context of today's Church and world. As LATINX communities continue to grow and diversify,[14] alongside the changing demographics of the United States, Episcopal churches need to take seriously new models of worship that are relevantly contextualized.[15] As mentioned earlier, contextualization is part of keeping up with the vernacular of the current time and of a current place. How can we have a nonstatic liturgy when the process of prayer book revision or introducing new liturgical resources takes a long time? The first step is to understand the flexibility and creativity already allowed by the current prayer book and other approved liturgical resources.

The Book of Common Prayer is a fundamental piece of Anglican history, theology, and practice. Throughout the world, the various prayer books, whether the 1662 Church of England version or local prayer books, have a common ancestry dating back to the 1549 and 1552 versions. The prayer book tradition is part of what binds us as a Communion; one may say that it is indispensable. There are aspects of Cranmer's prayer books that have never been replicated because the prayer book that emerged in England was in its origin inherently contextual and unifying. The fact that the prayer book was in English was a significant change from the Roman liturgy (in Latin) and a fundamental call to worship in the language of the people. To be able to worship in your own language—in the vernacular—is powerful. The vernacular includes all expressions of the community gathered.

It is not an either/or proposition. I would add that for me as a bilingual and bicultural person, "in my own language" means in the style and language that is most comforting, meaningful, and familiar. In my case that can be hymn texts and tunes from *The Hymnal 1982*, LEVAS II, WLP, or various Spanish-language hymn books. The fact that I identify as LATINX, and am a Spanish speaker, does not mean that I cannot feel at home in an English-language vernacular.

Imagine for a moment what it would mean to listen to liturgy in your vernacular for the first time, including hearing or reading scripture in language that is intelligible to you. In the sixteenth century, liturgy and scripture became accessible for laypeople (most of the Church) in a way it had never been before. In the 1549 preface Cranmer wrote about the liturgy in English:

> And moreover, whereas s. Paule would have suche language spoken to the people in the churche, as they mighte understande and have profite by hearyng the same; the service in this Churche of England (these many yeares) hath been read in Latin to the people, whiche they understoode not; so that they have heard with theyr eares onely; and their hartes, spirite, and minde, have not been edified thereby.[16]

This vernacular contextuality supports another important quality of prayer book theology: its ability to hold together different theological stances. The only non-negotiable aspect of the various books of common prayer is the very ability of a myriad of people and communities gathered to pray together. If we can pray together, much else will follow. The ability of Anglicanism to hold seemingly disparate things in positive tension is a multifaceted dexterity (adroitness). Seeking uniformity, Cranmer notes in the 1549 preface:

> And where heretofore, there hath been great diversitie in saying and synging in churches within this realme: some folowyng Salsbury use, some Herford use, same the use of Bangor, some of Yorke, and some of Lincolne: Now from hencefurth, all the whole realme shall have but one use. And if any would judge this waye more painfull. . . . they will not refuse the payn, in consideracion of the greate profite that shall ensue therof.
>
> And farsomuche as nothyng can, almoste, be so plainly set furth, but daubtes maie rise in the use and practisyng of the same: to appease all suche diversitie (if any arise), and for the resolucion of all doubtes, concernyng the maner how to understande, do, and execute the thynges conteygned in this booke: the parties that so doubt, or diversly take any thyng, shall alwaye resorte to the Bishop of the Diocese, who by his discrecion shall take ordre for the quietyng and appeasyng of the same: so that the same ordre be not contrary to any thyng conteigned in this boke.[17]

The uniformity is not for conformity or assimilation but for establishing common prayer and the interrelatedness of the congregations in the realm. Furthermore, the value of common prayer is put above comfort. In fact, Cranmer maintains the intentional flexibility of the prayer book; something gives for the greater good.

As I read the words written by Cranmer, I am transported to another vernacular, even as an English speaker. No one would say that we need to use the English from Cranmer's time. If I had to read out loud the preface of the 1549, I would have a great and amusing difficulty. I still remember the first time I participated in a Rite I service and how foreign it felt. It was 1997, my first week of seminary, when I still attended worship every chance I had. I made it through communion unscathed, then kneeling, next to my classmate Aron, we began to say together the prayer for after communion that begins:

> Almighty and everliving God, we most heartily thank thee for that thou dost feed us, in these holy mysteries, with the spiritual food of the most precious Body and Blood of thy Son our Savior Jesus Christ; and dost assure us thereby of thy favor and goodness towards us.[18]

I began fumbling through the words and got the giggles. It was a tongue twister and my contained laughter was my realization that I had no idea what I was saying. The giggles were contagious, but we made it through and soon we were dismissed from worship. Rev. William Countryman, professor of New Testament, turned around and commented, "Not the usual reaction to Rite I." More than a decade later, I supplied at a midday worship service at Church of the Incarnation in Manhattan at the invitation of Rev. Amanda Kucik-Robertson. The service was Rite I and it still felt as foreign as that time at CDSP; my worry then was fumbling through the words of the Eucharistic Prayer. No matter how beautiful folks find Rite I, its vernacular is too foreign for it ever to be accessible for me.

The question becomes how to develop prayer books and liturgical resources that value both contextualization and the breadth of expressions and also remain true to the tradition and theology? This is a question for Oliver and others; we must listen to those experiencing the prayer book and understand how to reflect their and many vernaculars in the common books of the Church. This is not yet the reality around the Communion. Not all prayer books are contextualized. In some locations the prayer book from England is still in use; in other regions translations of the English or Episcopal Church prayer books prevail. Context is difficult to translate. Context is also ever-changing, thus leading to the need for new prayer books. The Book of Common Prayer has been translated into at least two hundred languages.[19] There has been a Spanish language translation of the prayer book since 1623 (English prayer book) and 1789 (Episcopal Church's prayer book).

The first serious attempt at more than a translation of the English-language prayer book into Spanish occurred in Spain in 1881, combining an "Anglican structure with an indigenous prayer tradition."[20] Around the same time in México, the Iglesia de Jesús, as it worked to strengthen its ties with the Episcopal Church in the United States, attempted to get their support to adapt Mozarabic liturgies as the basis for their liturgies in México, this time in relation to the "American" prayer book—something that the Episcopal Church initially did not accept.

In 1875 Bishop Alfred Lee, of Delaware, and a member of the Episcopal Church's Mexican Commission, advocated for contextualization,

> not, in the judgment of the writer, by imposing our formularies, or by proposing hasty emendations. The liturgy must be formed by the deliberate and mature action of the Church which is to use it, a Church, be it remembered, whose members are of Spanish, not Anglo-Saxon race and education.

Precious materials may be drawn from the ancient Mozarabic Liturgies. Time, learning, study, and experience must all combine to perfect so important a work as the permanent cultus of this Church.[21]

The realization of a more contextualized prayer book with Mozarabic influences in México did not occur until 1894.[22] Other attempts at translations of the Episcopal Church's prayer book occurred in the 1860s. These translations were literal and made little inroads in Spanish-speaking missionary dioceses. The 1892 and 1928 prayer books were also translated into Spanish.

Other serious attempts to more contextualized prayer books in Spanish had to wait until after 1958 and the intentional opening of Latin America to Anglicanism. Unfortunately, local Latin American interests didn't always win when North Americans made the decisions.[23] Some examples of more recent contextual prayer books are Chile (1973), Puerto Rico (1983), New Zealand (1989), and Brazil (2015). Living into the spirit of contextualization called for in Lambeth 1958, the preface of the 1973 prayer book of Chile captures the continual process of creating an autochthonous Anglican liturgy:

> Forms and expressions have been adapted to the needs of our cultural situation, although time may demonstrate that more need for this still exists. Therefore, it should not be imagined that this is the last word in liturgy, but, yes, the latest liturgical expression for the current time in the Church. It is expected that in using these liturgies, the Church will appreciate more deeply the place of liturgy in worship; thus, if in the future there is a need of a more adequate material, those who are called to revise it will have a text in Spanish and a liturgical structure as a base sufficiently clear and doctrinally sound for such revisions.[24]

In 1978, the Diocese of Puerto Rico became extraprovincial to Canterbury. This was done in preparation for joining with other extraprovincial churches in an Anglican Caribbean province. The province never materialized, but in 1983 the Diocese of Puerto Rico issued a prayer book of authorized rites.[25] It did not include a preface that expressed the intention behind this prayer book. The use of this prayer book eventually waned in favor of the 1982 translation of the Episcopal Church's 1979 prayer book.

Initially there were competing translations of the 1979 prayer book. But indicative of a lack of interest in changing structures of power and authority, the least autochthonous one won the day since it was attached to the larger power structure and had the resources for distribution. In fairness, bishops Anselmo Carral, Sergio Carranza Gómez, and Onell Soto were involved in the translation. The other version had been published by Province IX of the

Episcopal Church. This translation and rejection were described as "much more felicitous, especially in the Eucharist, but these better translations were not adopted in the official publication of 1982, the Custodian of the Standard Book of Common Prayer having determined that the translation had to be literal." The history of Spanish-language translations was described as "more or less slavish translations of English originals."[26]

In 1971 the liturgical scholar Rev. Louis Weil, then ministering in Puerto Rico, said in an address to a Eucharistic Congress, "The translation into Spanish that I must use week to week is very badly done; it is not idiomatic, and employs a vocabulary unknown to the people." Translation, Weil noted, is only a transitional phase in the process of liturgical adaptation. No translated liturgy can become the authentic liturgy of a culture. "The times require that each part of the world enjoy the freedom to experiment with all the available forms— language, gesture, music—in which they respond to God."[27] Acknowledging the multicultural and polycentric nature of LATINX communities (and, in reality, all communities), prayer books may be able to "keep an Anglican structure and ethos, but are nevertheless real expressions of the soul of the people, so that they may be edified—as Cranmer himself hoped."[28]

The preface to the 1989 New Zealand Prayer Book expresses well the tradition and new contextualization:

> Though new in language and content, *A New Zealand Prayer Book, He Karakia Mihinare o Aotearoa* preserves the ethos of Anglican spirituality and incorporates the best liturgical insights modern scholarship provides. It is also more faithful to the earliest liturgical traditions of the Church and allows more flexibility than the book of 1662.
>
> More importantly, *A New Zealand Prayer Book* has been created in our own Pacific cultural setting, and shaped by our own scholarship. It belongs to our environment and our people.[29]

To my knowledge the most recent contextualized prayer book is that of the *Igreja Episcopal Anglicana do Brasil* (Anglican Episcopal Church of Brazil) ratified in 2015. This prayer book includes the 1549 preface and a new preface for the 2015 local edition. The 2015 preface places liturgy as a central mark in the life of the Church. While respecting the Anglican heritage, the revisions and purpose are described as follows in the new preface:

> Knowing the value of the forms and rites contained in this book, which point to the identity of our faith and the strengthening of our spirituality, we sought to offer a more contemporary way to relate to this faith by the actualization

and use of inclusive language, which advances us in the context of worship, transforming men and women into integral parts of the act of celebrating life and life in abundance. In the same way, attention was given to contemplating the different contexts and cultures existing in the specific context of the Brazilian Church, offering a deeply rooted liturgy.

This edition of the Prayer Book brings back and strengthens the dimension of devotion to our daily lives from the Daily Offices of the Word, especially in the Daily Prayers for Individual or Family use. We hope this Book will be used beyond the time of Church worship, *Lex orandi, Lex credendi*. The Book gives us a form and structure of worship, but it does not work automatically. The liturgy will become true worship when each person uses it as daily devotion, and thus the Holy Spirit of God rekindles their flame in each life to the Glory of God.[30]

There is great intentionality in inclusive language and social justice. The marriage rite is not gender specific—referring to people, both those getting married, but also the congregation gathered.[31] Understanding that there are still limitations in inclusive language when these break other rules, including theological ones, there are still places that are not specifically inclusive; yet the reality is that the inclusion of more expressions in itself show a broader understanding of the reign of God and its people. They allude to this in the explication of the psalm translations that are faithful to the Hebrew and to liturgical conventions. "In agreement with the inclusive language, changes were made in the translation always respecting the original meaning of the text."[32] Earlier I mentioned, agreeing with Oliver, that for LATINX people *lo cotidiano*—the quotidian—is a rich place of revelation. One aspect of this is expressed in the Brazilian preface: moving worship and prayer to everyday life.

For the Episcopal church, over decades and centuries, prayer book revision has not always been straightforward or swift. The revision process of the Book of Common Prayer used in the Episcopal Church maintains the vision expressed in the preface of 1789.

> The same Church hath not only in her Preface, but likewise in her Articles and Homilies, declared the necessity and expediency of occasional alterations and amendments in her Forms of Public Worship; and we find accordingly, that, seeking to keep the happy mean between too much stiffness in refusing, and too much easiness in admitting variations in things once advisedly established, she hath, in the reign of several Princes, since the first compiling of her Liturgy in the time of Edward the Sixth, upon just and weighty considerations her thereunto moving, yielded to make such alterations in some particulars, as in

their respective times were thought convenient; yet so as that the main body and essential parts of the same (as well in the chiefest materials, as in the frame and order thereof) have still been continued firm and unshaken.

Her general aim in these different reviews and alterations hath been, as she further declares in her said Preface, to do that which, according to her best understanding, might most tend to the preservation of peace and unity in the Church; the procuring of reverence, and the exciting of piety and devotion in the worship of God; and, finally, the cutting off occasion, from them that seek occasion, of cavil or quarrel against her Liturgy.[33]

Even for prayer books that are contextualized, how do the structures of the Church keep up with the changing contexts? The most current effort at revision and translation was mandated from the 2018 General Convention. There are aspects regarding current efforts at revision that relate to ministry to, with, and among LATINX people and communities.

The 79th General Convention of the Episcopal Church in Austin, Texas, called for the revision of the prayer book in resolutions A068 and A070. A Task Force on Liturgical and Prayer Book Revision (TFLPBR) is to report and make recommendations to the 80th General Convention in 2021. Some of the fundamental tenets of revision for our time include: contextualization (Article 34), inclusive and nonbinary language, more expansive theologizing (more expansive input), an intention regarding the care of creation (A016, A068.11), as well as creative ways of dissemination beyond the printed book (A068.12).

Comparable to my take on the budgets of the Church, in addition to issues in prayer book revision, it is important to make note of the process and presentation of the resolutions as they come through in the General Convention website. It is illustrative of the way in which English is normative in the Church and everything else is hyphenated. This concerns us because of the legislative process that establishes the process of revision. It is organized is a way that privileges whiteness/English-language and maintains anything else as "additional" or "other." It is an epistemological choice. Just as language matters, so do the structures we establish as a Church.

In the virtual binder of the 79th General Convention there are 517 resolutions listed in alpha-numeric order.[34] One can search through the resolutions by number, committee, proposer, or topic. Under "Book of Common Prayer" one can find the resolution on prayer book revision (A068). The resolution offers no room in the revision process for linguistic reciprocity and mutual enrichment in the liturgical life of the Church. This means that the Church can only envision English revisions and then Spanish, French, and Haitian Creole translations. Liturgies not originally in English cannot make it into the English-language prayer book. The next prayer book will not reflect the diversity of the church.

13. Resolved, That the SCLM create a professional dynamic equivalence translation of The Book of Common Prayer 1979 and the Enriching Our Worship Series in Spanish, French, and Haitian Creole; and that the SCLM diversify the publication formats of new resources, liturgies and rites to include online publishing; and be it further

14. Resolved, That this church ensure that, at each step of the revision process, all materials be professionally translated into English, Spanish, French, and Haitian Creole, following the principles of dynamic equivalence and that no new rites or liturgical resources be approved by this church until such translations are secured.[35]

The changes in Spanish-, French-, and Haitian Creole-language prayer books are found under the topic "Language Translation" (A070). This is significant because the structure tells the Church that the main task is the revision of the Book of Common Prayer, which the vast majority of Episcopalians will think of as the revision of the red prayer book; then comes the work of the translation of those "other" books used by those "other" groups of people. These other revisions do not carry the same weight.

Similar to what I expressed in chapter 3, when I began looking at the budget and accounting codes for the congregation I serve, I was disheartened at the structure of the budget. For example, the budget had lines for evangelism and "Hispanic" evangelism; clergy and "Hispanic" clergy. Based on the arguments presented in this book, it should be self-evident that if the binary is clergy and Hispanic clergy, then clergy is normative (white) and Hispanic clergy is not (other), thus perpetuating the idea that LATINX ministry is a project of the Church or of a congregation, not the reality of the Church itself. One immediate change we made was to make the budget inclusive. This inclusivity meant that the entire congregation was responsible for the bills and contributed toward the maintenance of the church, rather than part of the congregation being treated as a program with an assigned chaplain. There was one line item, the Hispanic Commission grant, we could not change because it was the name of a grant offered by the Diocese of New York. This exemplifies the "project" quality of LATINX ministry in the Episcopal Church as expressed in a particular diocese. Prayer book revision that does not take Article 34 fully into consideration will not be successful.

## Bilingual and Vernacular Liturgy, and Worship[36]

For those that have been waiting on some very practical and tangible aspects that have to do with ministry to, with, and among LATINX people and communities, I now share my observations about liturgy over the past two decades in a monolingual and bilingual community. I cannot say that I am a perfect, or even great, worship leader—congregations can be very forgiving—but these observations may prompt in those that have particular gifts in these areas to provide the means through which to adapt, expand, and implement them. These are observations that should encourage reflection beyond LATINX-defined congregations. I believe that contextualized worship combined with base communities will be key in our ministry with and among LATINX people and communities.

Oliver's academic field is liturgy. Oliver has a keen sense of humor and manner to explain the difference between the liturgies we do in our various communities and how they differ from the liturgy that we would want for ourselves if we didn't have anyone else to take into consideration. As worship leaders, it is ultimately not about us, but about the community gathered. Worship is a space where we can achieve so much; worship is also difficult, especially when we think of worship as a personal experience, not as a communal one. Worship in the Episcopal Church with its foundation in the prayer book must be community centered. This reminds us to always ask: where is the locus of worship? Sandra Van Opstal describes this tension: "God invites to come to [the] table in unity. That has always and will continue to cause tension, given the diverse nature of [God's] people. This is particularly pronounced in worship, where people desire authentic spaces to express themselves."[37] This is a challenge since, often, we go for ourselves, but it is ultimately not about us. As presented before, this is a move away from a self-serving *diakonia* to an everyday life (cotidiano) *diakonia* for the sake of our life together in Christ, *koinōnia*.[38]

Rev. Juan Francisco Martínez proposes the following characteristics of LATINX Protestant worship: "participatory, passionate, and multicultural, a fiesta where people celebrate God."[39] Oliver tries to show the places of disconnection and connection between LATINX and Anglo worship and asks, "What is the essence of Anglican worship? How can we incarnate Anglican liturgy in our Latin culture? Can we create a truly Latino worship and remain Anglican?"[40] The 1985 published report of a 1984 consultation provides an answer in the agreed statement:

> "Anglo and Hispanic cultural heritages are not incompatible; they are indeed complementary." The Episcopal Church has "The apostolic teaching, we articulate it in a language, at once Catholic and evangelical, and we know ourselves

to be obligated to reasonable dialogue. We are also a fellowship or community; our Anglican ethos is democratic and open to lay participation in decision making at all levels. We are at home with all the Sacraments of the Church celebrated with liturgies that are at once faithful to primitive models and open to varied adaptation. And we are a praying Church: our hallmark is the Book of Common Prayer which has always nourished our piety and served us well with Catholic order, evangelical witness or occasionally charismatic renewal."

For their part, the Hispanics come to us now with the additional theme of the faith nurtured in the Exodus, the Wandering in the Desert, the entrance into the Land of Promise and the assurance of divine Providence in the face of extreme perils. Hispanic Christians have grown up in the Faith, which they recognize in our midst. They have developed forms of community, including most recently the "base communities" that enrich and extend the life of parishes, and they have expressed in the "abrazo" (embrace) their spontaneous affirmation of the extended family. They are acquainted with the Sacraments, which they celebrate with color, dance, drama, and fiesta uniting the sacred and secular in a living wholeness. And they are a praying people, bringing with them a natural sense of the sacred, a profound piety, and a theology of the Cross with long and honorable antecedents.[41]

Similar to the 1985 report, Oliver provides the following lists in *Ripe Fields*. These lists are ultimately about epistemological priorities by the majority institutional Church, and what is considered *other*.

### Latinx Worship

- Time is flexible, elastic.
- Participate through things: flowers, candles, and offerings.
- Visual images are important.
- Emotional preaching.
- The sermon is extemporaneous.
- Chant or popular music.
- Engages the physical.
- Sense of being at a fiesta or a fair.

### Anglo Worship

- Time is evenly measured.
- Participate through listening, singing, and offering money.
- Visual images are secondary.
- Intellectual preaching.

- The sermon is read from a text.
- "Classical" hymnody or folk music.
- Engages idea.
- Sense of being in a lecture hall.

Anglican liturgy "cannot merely be English liturgy colonizing the whole world." It needs to "welcome a whole array of different styles of worship arising from a worldwide array of cultures," all the while honoring from Anglican liturgy the fact that it is vernacular, biblical, incarnational, syncretic, trinitarian (diversity in unity), and communicates verbally, visually, audibly, and kinetically.[42]

## The Eye Is Not Bilingual

In the Episcopal Church, the principal act we do together is to gather and worship God on Sunday mornings, while being nourished by word and sacraments.[43] This allows us to fulfill one of our promises in the Baptismal Covenant: to participate in "the apostles' teaching and fellowship, in the breaking of the bread, and in the prayers."[44] The concern of this section is corporate and public worship, not individual practices or private prayer. I offer here a compilation of experiences from the congregation I serve and bilingual worship. Again these are prompts to help practitioners think through their own particular context and needs.

As Christians, our witness in the world emanates from Sunday's public worship, variously called a service, the mass, or liturgy. We gather to worship God, to be fed by word, bread, and community, and strengthened to be sent into the world to share the Good News of God in Christ—a sentiment echoed in the prayers for after communion. This is our regular oscillation between discipleship and apostleship, both rooted in the gospel, and thus evangelism.[45]

With the 1979 Book of Common Prayer, there was a shift in emphasis and understanding on the role of the congregation in worship and in the sacramental life of the Church. Everyone participates in worship; everyone works in worship. The word "liturgy," which we publicly enact on Sunday morning, means "the work of the people."[46] Public worship is not solely the work of the clergy. The entire community participates according to their order: laity, bishops, priests, and deacons. Worship is most inclusive and beautiful when it represents the entire community. The laity actively participates, whether in the congregation or serving at the altar. This was a very specific and profound change in the ecclesiology and theology of the 1979 revision.[47]

There are two reasons to speak of liturgy or public worship. One has to do with the idea of worship being public; the other is the exploration of who participates in worship. In my over fifteen years at the Church of Saint Matthew and Saint Timothy, I have only done one baptism outside of the context of a Sunday or Easter Vigil service. The reasons were extraordinary. After the date was settled, one of the most important tasks was to make the baptism as open to the public as possible, telling people in the congregation to attend and letting others know about the additional service.

In baptism, godparents and parents or guardians make promises, but the congregation gathered as witnesses promise to support these people in their life in Christ. This is followed by the renewal of the Baptismal Covenant.[48] The congregation similarly assents and participates in ordinations, weddings, and confirmations. The fact that these celebrations are public reminds us of our responsibility for one another as Christians.

Notwithstanding the expected full participation of the community gathered, for many congregations, including Latinx congregations, there is great deference to the clergy as leaders of worship. There is a differentiation of roles, but deference to the clergy does not mean absolution from active participation, nor that worship, in all cases, requires clergy. Similarly, clergy should not behave as if they are the only ones participating in liturgy or are indispensable for all worship. It is a dance: a dialogue in community. The deference to the clergy for some is based on a history of the separation of clergy and laity in our tradition. This is also, on occasion, gendered, meaning there is greater deference to male clergy and male participation in worship, even though many of our congregations are attended primarily by women.[49]

Deference to the clergy limits evangelism, church planting, and leadership development. I am not a huge fan of "Ashes to Go," yet I love that it does not require clergy. The liturgy is most effective and meaningful when there is full participation from all orders, and everyone works or does their part. The work occurs both at the altar and in the pew, therefore it should take into consideration not only those serving at the altar, but also those attending the service.

You may have noticed that I have not specified the type of Sunday worship or public worship at other times during the week. There are two reasons. First, although the principal type of worship on a Sunday morning is the celebration of the Holy Eucharist, that is not the only type of liturgy that can be done on a Sunday morning. Liturgy reflects the community gathered, which is different in every context, with the underlying foundation of our local and church-wide traditions and history, including the Book of Common Prayer. Not every congregation or gathering is the same. Many clergy are taught in seminary that when preparing a sermon to always keep in mind who the community gathered is and the purpose for the gathering. We probably should think about this more often when developing Sunday worship. Ultimately, liturgy is about interconnectedness.

When deciding new projects for a church, education, ministry, or outreach, I like to encourage congregations, vestries, committees, and clergy to think about matching the needs and wants with the talent and resources. We can waste resources or create frustrations by embarking on projects that are not needed, or have garnered no interest, or have no people or resources to carry them through, as opposed to projects that are autochthonous or organic to the congregation and context. I am reminded of this every time I think I have a great idea that doesn't work when I, in my brilliance, implement it alone.

Having great worship requires a similar discernment. No two congregations are alike. Therefore, what are the various ways that each congregation is interconnected? By blood, language, age, profession, ethnic background, place of birth, education, sexuality or gender identity, economic background, values, or traditions. Many more "identity markers" could be added to the list, especially for the composition of people gathered in a specific congregation. When as many factors are taken into consideration, a sense emerges of a particular "sweet spot"—a reflection of the identity of the congregation. As counterintuitive as it might sound, this "sweet spot" is one in which everyone loses. I say that because the sweet spot is the point where the value of being congregation together is held up above any other individual want.

The Church of Saint Matthew and Saint Timothy is a bilingual (Spanish and English) congregation, which has offered worship in Spanish since the 1950s and traces its roots to the late eighteenth century. When I got there in 2004, I noticed how some referred to the group who attended the 9 a.m. service regularly as the "Spanish congregation," and those who attended the 11 a.m. service as the "English congregation." Some who attend the 9 a.m. service were English speakers and vice versa for the 11 a.m. service. St. Matthew and St. Timothy's has one vestry, so, technically speaking, it cannot be more than one congregation. Thus, I prefer to indicate that we are "*one* congregation that worships God in *two* languages."

As one congregation, we offer one bilingual Sunday service on a regular basis. There are many reasons, including at times convenience, that dictate when it happens. Yet having bilingual services emanates from a shared congregational identity that values being together in worship, and values common worship above any extra comfort experienced in the more familiar monolingual services. One thing we have not been able to manage fully is the decision of what time to have the service. For years the default has been 11 a.m.; as of the summer of 2019, it is now 10 a.m. in order to accommodate the whole congregation.

Our liturgical tradition as seen in the prayer book is flexible and provides for many vehicles of inclusion. We are called to remember that throughout the centuries the requirement that brings us together in the worship of God is NOT a shared/equal view of the world or of the Church, but our ability to gather for common prayer, despite our differences.

## Designing Bi(multi)lingual and Inclusive Worship

Designing bi(multi)lingual and inclusive worship goes beyond offering parts of the liturgy in one language and others in another. Designing bi(multi)lingual worship requires a knowledge of what kind of congregation you are. The English-language prayer book has only one requirement for the inclusion of a separate language in the liturgy: "When a portion of the congregation is composed of people whose native tongue is other than English, a reader appointed by the celebrant may read the Gospel in the language of the people, either in place of, or in addition to, the Gospel in English."[50] It is important to remember that this is a minimum requirement, or a starting place; it is not sufficient. Thought needs to be given to the various levels of literacy in the languages of the community in terms of speaking, writing, and reading different languages. There may be differences even within the same family or age group depending on a variety of factors.

Liturgy design requires intentionality around the mechanics of liturgy in all aspects: music, ornamentation, space. There are so many questions we need to ask about liturgy: Is the liturgy intercultural or multicultural? Is the liturgy reaching across groups? Are there various races and ethnicities in the congregation? How are they welcomed to participate? How are they represented? Accounting for the various groups is often reflected in music, language, and art. Does the liturgy account for intracultural groups? What are some subgroups that need to be identified and considered? How is worship inclusive of multiple generations? How does it include people of different ages and abilities in the liturgy? How does it include people of different generations within the same families or extended families, while still welcoming everyone else? What are the generational dynamics?

Rev. Albert R. Rodríguez from Texas has written on transgenerational LATINX congregations. Rodríguez uses transgenerational to describe congregations that reach immigrants who differ in immigration status, age at immigration, or generations since the original immigration, if immigrants at all. There are several challenges when it comes to congregations with immigrants. First, the Episcopal Church tends to minister to recent immigrants or first-generation immigrants and does so in terms of language and not culture, not even a vernacular expression. Second, outside of multigenerational families, many of our congregations are not transgenerational. Third, the younger generations that are predominantly English speaking are alienated in our Spanish-only liturgies, but would also be alienated in English-language worship that is not in a familiar vernacular/expression.[51] This is impacted by language proficiency (both written and oral), levels of acculturation and assimilation, and relationship to the "dominant" culture.

This is not unique to LATINX congregations. Most congregational leaders have an intuitive sense of the various constituencies and needs that should be considered in any given parish. Following are just some reminders of how varied the aspects are. What are the identities present in the community (polycentric, intersectional, multi(bi)intercultural)? Are there particular constituencies that need to be intentionally included? Such as LGBTQ+ communities, women, adults with families, single people, the differently abled, people with dietary needs/restrictions or who are in recovery (bread and wine).

## Thinking Practically about more Inclusive Liturgy

Liturgy is about building relationships. Being an inclusive congregation can be daunting, often because we create obstacles that do not exist. For example, a church might have a great food pantry attended mostly by Spanish-speaking or LATINX people, or by a group different than the worshipping community. The food pantry guests may resemble the community surrounding the church more than the congregation does. The number of people welcomed at the food pantry may even be greater than the number of people who attend that church on a regular basis. The instinct of many is to offer worship in Spanish so that "those people" whom we "feel good" by serving can fill our pews. And, often, this fails. The failure is multifaceted.

There is a difference between ministry to, ministry with, and ministry among. If you are ministering to someone, you cannot expect the result to be worshipping together, especially if you do not get to know them beyond a transactional relationship. We feed someone because that is Jesus's imperative to us as Christians. Rather than beginning a new service, take an inventory of how welcoming and inclusive our existing programs are of Spanish-speaking and LATINX people. Elsewhere I have written about starting ministries with and among LATINX and Spanish-speaking people; here my emphasis is in some inclusive strategies for what already exists. As a reminder, please know that these things apply to a multiplicity of scenarios.

## Thinking about Music

I am probably the last person to talk about music. I am tone deaf. Yet there are considerations we can contemplate. In English, the Episcopal Church has three commonly used music resources: *The Hymnal 1982, Lift Every Voice and Sing II* (1993), and *Wonder, Love, and Praise* (1997).[52] In Spanish, there is *El Himnario* (1998). It seems that the 1990s were a fruitful decade for hymnals. *El Himnario* includes many hymn texts that were translated from English with their accompanying hymn tunes, some bilingual hymns, and some hymns which were written in Spanish. In the church that I serve, as in many other Episcopal churches which offer music in Spanish, the hymnal of choice is *Flor y Canto* published by Oregon Catholic Press.[53] The Episcopal Church also has many diverse musical traditions and expressions in worship.

It is generally assumed that the use of *El Himnario* has been limited, in part, because it does not reflect the musical traditions, tastes, backgrounds of LAT-INX or Spanish-speaking people new to the Episcopal Church. I say new to the Church because, although the practice of translating hymn texts is a colonial one, for many who have a long-standing relationship with the Episcopal Church these hymns hold a dear and familiar place for them. This is true of the use of the organ as well. Furthermore, there are many gaps in musical traditions, tastes, and backgrounds of music in the three English-language hymnals mentioned above.

Some of the music challenges go beyond the availability of resources in our tradition to the cumbersome processes and limited ways by which new music can be introduced to broader audiences in the Episcopal Church. I have spent some time in England and the change in perspective gave me some insight on this. In seminary I learned that liking or not liking a hymn tune or text often has little to do with the tune or words, but with the context in which they were experienced or our familiarity with them. I have found this to be true. On any given Sunday, whether at a bilingual, Spanish, or English language service, you may hear me humming along with a tune. I am transported, and the familiarity gives me comfort and grounds me in the moment. I am often worried that I may have left my microphone on and I am subjecting the congregation to my off-key sounds. I know that the most familiar hymn tunes are those that I heard when I was younger. That does not mean that they speak similarly to others.

We have a composer-in-residence, Ms. Elaine Romanelli, who has composed a gospel-style mass setting in English, with a bilingual variation. I have a great attachment to it. I know the composer; it fits our context. I have filed it in my timeless music box.[54] This long introduction illustrates the idea that the success of music in a congregation is not just about its language. There are many factors.

In the summer of 2017, we experimented with having a combined bilingual service all summer for a couple of reasons. First, as a congregation we felt that we did bilingual worship well. Also, we don't have a choir at the 11 a.m. service from Trinity Sunday until after Labor Day and the attendance is small. We thought combining the services would make the service feel fuller. We learned a lot that summer.

We learned we do bilingual worship well, but we do it better when it is a special occasion and we have a choir. I underestimated how much the choir led the congregation in singing. Until we got a cantor at the end of July, we had a lot of instrumental offerings for the service; the congregation did not sing many of the hymns. Regular bilingual bulletins were much more difficult to develop and use than we thought. Our regular practice with bilingual worship was to have an all-inclusive booklet with the liturgy, music, and readings. But to save paper and time, I thought it would be better to have a bilingual bulletin with all the portions of the service that don't change week to week, and only hand out an order of worship with the specific readings, music, announcements, and prayers for the week. To add other challenges, I was away for four Sundays that summer, and it was difficult to find a bilingual and culturally competent person to cover for me. The last two Sundays we were left with bilingual Morning Prayer. Weekly bilingual worship was not as easy as opening the prayer book and doing the service in two languages.

In 2003, the Convocation of Episcopal Churches in Europe published an abridged prayer book with English and Spanish on facing pages. In 2005, we purchased a hundred copies for our parish. It fully included all Rite II Eucharistic Prayers. Our thought was that we would use the books when we had a bilingual service. It did not work. We use them once or twice a year for very small services. The principal reason is the layout of the page numbers. On the top margin on both sides it has the English-language prayer book page number. Since it is abridged, there are sequential sections missing, and since the page numbers in English and in Spanish do not match, the English-language prayer book number on the Spanish side has no meaning for those accustomed to the prayer book in Spanish.[55] There are also sequential page numbers on the bottom of the page, which makes it difficult to announce a page number without creating confusion. In our summer bilingual experiment, I created a similar confusion. In having both a generic bulletin and a specific weekly bulletin, I created confusion as to which bulletin we were using.

We have now had three summers of bilingual worship and it is becoming easier. For a regular bilingual service, we print everything needed in one booklet. English and Spanish are on facing pages, and there is a particular rhythm to what is in English, in Spanish, or said bilingually congregationally. Here are some considerations that go into the production of the bulletin and the execution of the liturgy.

In the execution of the liturgy, we try to balance the participation of the congregation based on the service each person typically attends. We draw liturgical assistants, readers, and ushers from both services. The first reading is in Spanish, the second in English, and the Gospel is in both. When we have the choir, the psalm is chanted in English with a refrain sung in Spanish. It is an adventure. We have tried alternating English and Spanish, but it doesn't work because the congregation is more accustomed to alternating between reader and congregation. We have better results with doing half in one language and changing languages for the second half. Different sections of the eucharistic prayer are said in one language or the other: the bread in one, the wine in the other. For the portions of the service that are said in unison, we have found that if people say them softly that there is less stumbling and confusion. We have a balance between English, Spanish, and bilingual hymn texts; the service music is bilingual.

For bilingual worship the hymn texts and hymn music are printed in the bulletin in multiple ways. Typically, on the right side is the tune and text as one would normally see in *The Hymnal 1982*. On the left side, the hymn text is printed. On the left side, there is also a brief contextual translation of the hymn text, perhaps a verse or the refrain, to give a monolingual person a hint as to the content of the hymn in the language other than their own. In our specific context, people who are accustomed to *The Hymnal 1982* do not mind the music staff format, even if they do not read music. Most of our *Flor y Canto* hymnals are words only, which is the preference at the monolingual Spanish-language service. Please note that this is not a Spanish/English difference, but a "what you are accustomed to" difference. In many places English-language hymnals are words only or formatted with just a hymn tune line on top and the words beneath. For hymn texts that are bilingual and have a familiar tune, people can sing in their own language in unison, or language can be alternated by verse. Foundationally, all other factors that go into choosing music are still valid: placement within the service, themes in the readings, liturgical season, or occasion.

Another way to create more inclusion in a bilingual service is by expanding the instruments used. We use the organ and piano regularly. On occasion we have a trio: piano, trumpet, and bongos; our current music director also plays saxophone. In addition to familiar types of tunes, rhythms, and texts, music done well can be appreciated as offered in any language. Another challenge is to determine how to introduce and teach new music. We have found that this is possible in a bilingual liturgy with the support of the choir.

## Thinking about Words We Hear, Words We See, Words We Speak, and Words We Read

The Episcopal Church has a tradition that is heavily dependent on books and reading. As a result, we must find ways to understand how the ear and the eye experience liturgy differently. Furthermore, we must have a conversation that includes different kinds of literacy as part of ideas of inclusion.

I had most of my primary and secondary education in Spanish and most of my postsecondary education has been in English. I studied in Spanish in a Spanish-language context with English as a second language. All my postsecondary education has been in predominantly English-language contexts. Given the context I serve as a priest, I write and speak in both English and Spanish on a regular basis. My context in New York City also provides for many bilingual opportunities. I have family members that only speak English, others that only speak Spanish, and many who are bilingual with different levels of "ear" and "eye" comprehension.

I am, however, terrible at learning to speak other languages and have failed in both French and Arabic, to my dismay. In any language, exposure to vocabulary is crucial in many of these literacy components: reading and reading and reading are key to create a greater proficiency in any language. I mention all of this because every single person that walks through our church doors has a different relationship to language, whether written, read, spoken, or heard. Although the ear may be bilingual, the eye is not always bilingual. People who speak more than one language may not necessarily read them all.

The congregation I serve is a congregation primarily of grandmothers. The reasons for this have much to do with the cost of housing in our neighborhood. Many LATINX grandparents remain because they can afford the rents since they have been in the neighborhood for decades. Their children had to move away, but their grandchildren may live with them to take advantage of better schools or for childcare; some even have great-grandchildren. Many of these families have members of four generations attending worship together. The LATINX grandmothers are typically monolingual Spanish speakers. Those in the next generation are Spanish speakers and can also read in Spanish, depending on the language they studied in. Generally, those in the next generation can understand Spanish, speak some, but do not read in Spanish, and function primarily in an English-speaking context, although some have made it a point to study Spanish as a second language in school. All of them may be in the same Spanish-speaking service on Sunday morning. They all attend a Spanish-language service because of the familiarity of the music or the cadence of the liturgy. How are these various language needs within the same family honored and dealt with? This is where the Anglican tradition and value of the both/and shines in our liturgies.

When congregations are not multigenerational, the focus has often been on recent immigrants and the differences in Spanish-language literacy are not as immediate. Yet soon school-age children in these communities begin to learn primarily in English, and Spanish becomes the language of private life, including family and church. This tends to be addressed first in Sunday school rather than in worship. Some strategies we have used are a bilingual sermon and a concordance in the bulletin connected to pages in the English-language prayer book. We also think about how to include children that are not of reading age or school age. None of these concerns are unique to LATINX-defined congregations.

When thinking about worship, we think about those who have diminished eyesight or hearing. A simple strategy is to print readings and other parts of the liturgy in a larger font and make sure that the ear is taken care of with amplification or enhanced sound, assisted listening devices, or sign-language interpretation. Speakers and amplification may be challenging for those with sensitive hearing aids. For those diminished in hearing, the eye may become primary.

At our church, we have many people with diminished hearing. Some wear hearing aids, others are content with not hearing and just being in worship, trusting in the familiarity of the liturgy. Others can be disruptive, as they fill in the gaps, at times, inappropriately. One of the people who can hear very little of the liturgy even while sitting next to the speaker system is in fact a person who is engaged with everything that is happening in the congregation; the parishioner reads the bulletin announcements and calendar.

Music done well can be appreciated in any language and style by anyone who does not speak that language or is not familiar with a particular style of music. At the same time, familiar styles of music for represented communities are also a tool of inclusion for groups historically excluded.

Liturgy, whether bilingual or multilingual or more inclusive, need not be longer in length. Not everything needs to be repeated in all the languages. If done with intentionality, any time spent in worship will not be resented. Everyone needs to trust that they are familiar with the contours of the liturgy even if parts of the service are in a language with which they are not familiar. This is more difficult for people new to the congregation or who are visiting for the first time and find themselves in a bilingual service.

The assumption is that everything that is done to facilitate bilingual worship will reach the broadest number of people attending the service. Unfortunately, it is not possible to reach everyone. I am amazed by how much people do or do not do in worship. There are those who are content being in the space, even if they do not hear or see much. There are people for whom the bilingual worship is very difficult. For many different reasons both bilingual and monolingual people can come to dislike it. But many who do not like it put up with it because they value being together as a congregation.

There are some we cannot reach unless we can come up with additional strategies of and resources for inclusion. I have a monolingual parishioner who is now legally blind. Our assumption is that if you are monolingual and something is being read in the opposite language that you can follow along in the bulletin. She cannot follow along in the bulletin. In an ideal world I would want someone to be able to read to her in her language when needed. Some dedicated technology needs to be purchased and a volunteer to use it needs to be identified. The preceding sections on liturgical consideration are meant to offer a series of questions or areas of concern for how to make our worship more accessible and inclusive, and better reflect the local vernacular. Finally, after this more utilitarian section, I move to the last task in this chapter, provide some starting points for a Latinx Anglican Theology

## Initial Contours of a LATINX Anglican Theology

One of the goals of this book is to encourage the development of LATINX theologies from an Anglican/Episcopal perspective and Anglican/Episcopal theologies from a LATINX perspective. This book is also part of the process of theologizing from a LATINX Episcopal perspective because that is what I bring to the endeavor. I am keenly aware of the challenges of this overall proposition. First of all, and not possible here, to do the task justice there would have to be an extensive presentation and analysis of the contemporary state of LATINX theologies in the United States. Second, as alluded earlier, from the LATINX Episcopal side there are many sources to build upon, but few are familiar, thus this institutional history being one aspect of recovery of the LATINX Episcopal theologizing that already exists and build upon it. Who will be those that step up to this task? I can imagine a formative gathering of LATINX Episcopal/ Anglican scholars to work *en conjunto* for the theology needed for the Church today. And, to be clear, this work *en conjunto* must also include the wisdom of those at the margins and grassroots of the Episcopal Church. I also believe that if this is about the Church and not just the programs of the Church or the commodified few, that one aspect of this work must be done *en conjunto* with all the communities that have been marginalized, silenced, and excluded from the theologizing by the majority-culture Church. Having said all of this, the reality also is that throughout the pages of this book are found many varied pieces of what a Latinx Episcopal theology would look like. Here I try to summarize these, and, as usual, add my commentary to it.

So far, I have expressed some thoughts as to where we have some existing Episcopal/Anglican and Latinx foundations to build upon: a discovery of Latinx and Episcopal mutuality and complementarity; an exploration of our Anglican tradition through the ideas of the both/and, contextuality, and common prayer. One of the areas that I am most excited about is how ecclesial base communities, following an adapted and intentional Latin American liberation theologies model, can be a gift Latinx people and communities bring to the Episcopal Church; and one that can lead us to a greater understanding of our responsibility today at the southern U.S. border. I think that parallel to a profound investment in theological education and leadership development, we should invest in supporting the sustainable and sustained development of base communities, and not just for Latinx people and communities. As we have seen, this is not new; this is the basis of much of Arrunátegui and Rev. Justo L. González's writings, among others, as presented earlier. Ecclesial base communities are a model that should be explored further.

Although I include them here, a starting point for a Latinx Anglican theology does not start with "models of ministry." These approaches are neither theology nor ministry in themselves. This is because these models of ministry are ways in which these ministries remain a program of the Church and function within existing structures. Only a model that breaks from what has been normative will begin to change the institution. The following summary should show that my assertion is accurate.

At the turn of the twenty-first century, seven models of congregational ministry with Latinx constituencies exist in the Episcopal Church.[56] These may seem familiar to most readers. The first is the "traditional"—although becoming less so—Episcopal Church model with a full-time priest, a building, and a vestry; this model is not normative for congregations where most of the congregation are Latinx people. A second model is two congregations (one of them generally of the majority culture) sharing the same building, whether the Latinx congregation rents or is nested. Another model is that of starting a Latinx congregation in its own building, either an unused church or a storefront, which depends on the diocese or a sponsoring organization.

A fourth "more promising" model adapts the liberation theology aspect of base communities of five or six families with strong lay leadership. We have to value this lay leadership. Clusters of base communities may gather together on Sundays for the Holy Eucharist/worship or outside of Sundays seek clergy for sacramental needs. A caveat must be that these communities do not function as chaplaincies, but are outwardly focused in evangelism and liberation. Similar to the base-community model is the house church, which begins meeting in a home and has clergy leadership from the beginning. A sixth model is that of an afflu-ent parish sponsoring a LATINX congregation within itself, funding the full-time clergy. The final model is dependent on using a specific model for the commu-nity that is being reached; the model chosen depends on the long-term strategy and is under the supervision of a diocesan staff person: a program of the diocese.

Any ministry in the Episcopal Church reflects its polity and mission and should have "ecclesiological and missiological implications."[57] Any model should be decolonial and delinked from the epistemology of modernity that is hindering these ministries, thus disassociating itself from the current power and resource structures. If we are to be reconcilers, we need to have churches that enact rec-onciliation by being multicultural churches and "churches with interdependent relationships."[58] The Episcopal Church is uniquely qualified to do this.

Membership in the Episcopal Church today is significantly different than it was in 1965. We can no longer presuppose that we are a church of "cradle Episcopalians" or that the average person sitting in our churches knows about our history, theology, and ecclesiology. I'm not saying that people know less today than they did in the past, but that people's relationship to those aspects is different. According to Rev. Harold T. Lewis, theological changes since the 1960s have had the effect "that many of the church's ordained leaders today are those who have had virtually no experience in the rank and file of church life."[59] Parallel to this are the curious ways the Episcopal Church has worked over the decades, especially in terms of its polity. From its beginnings it has been char-acterized by a democratic decision-making process at all levels, congregations, dioceses, and as a denomination. This is precisely one of the strengths of the Episcopal Church, and one of its gravest weaknesses.

Let me explain. In Lewis's analysis of whether anything characterizes Anglican theology as distinctive, Lewis contends that "this is both the bane and blessing, the flaw and the genius, of Anglicanism."[60] One of the ways that the both/and tension plays out in the polity of the Episcopal Church is the ten-sion between dioceses and their respective bishops and the Episcopal Church Center and its staff. This is like the tension between being part of the Anglican Communion but not having anything imposed. It leaves gaps in accountability.

The way the structure has functioned is inefficient. Inevitably, the work of the governing bodies of the Episcopal Church has been primarily for its function-ing as an institution, rather than for the fulfilling of is mission to restore all peo-ple to unity with God and each other in Christ.[61] Among the signs that indicate that this is true is the way the Church manages its resources and the way donors and dioceses can withhold funds from the denomination if it is doing work with which they do not agree. Another sign is the difficulty we have as a Church in sharing power. All of this was seen in the GCSP and in the current insistence on hyphenated-ministry or ethnic ministries that are projects of the Church.

All this is to say something about what autonomy means, especially when belonging to larger corporate bodies. From congregations to dioceses to provinces to the Anglican Communion: what keeps it all together? We know it is certainly not total agreement. One of the ways it stays together is because Anglicans and Episcopalians deep down understand that our communion, in its best expression, is a place we all can belong. Base communities are about belonging. When we have a sense of belonging, we have a stake in each other's lives, and if we care for one another we show and proclaim the Good News. Yet before we can belong, we need to move beyond "welcome and inclusion." The ideas of welcome and inclusion are still a "ministry to" model. We have to radically change the questions and add to the sources of knowledge and see the problems from a different angle—this is the decoloniality of which I wrote before. One thing about decoloniality that is very important to understand is that in the commodification and exploitation of some there are real bodies that are threatened in the communities we serve. In other words, when asking whether or not we are working for the institution and not for the mission of the Church, we can ask—in our actions which bodies are being made vulnerable by our actions?

Ecclesial base communities (CEBs) are an opportunity for the Episcopal Church to strengthen its ministry and accomplish its mission, including ministry among LATINX people and communities. The Episcopal Church has an opportunity to become a place of belonging from which the Good News of God in Christ is brought to the world to bring about reconciliation, healing, and liberation.

Of all of the models presented, which are by no means ideal, we should explore having base communities as the foundation to these ministries. Base communities are small groups that are sacramental (internal) and evangelistic (external). These small groups are eucharistically centered and strengthened to go out into the world. They are places of agency and liberation that promote justice and peace. Base communities are places of solidarity, education/formation, and deepening of relationships; a place to find liberation and work toward the liberation of all those who are marginalized or oppressed. Yet these small groups are deeply connected to the broader church—part of a tradition—not in isolation.

In the introduction I defined ministry as all the ways laypeople, deacons, priests, and bishops help to carry out the mission of the Church "to restore all people to unity with God and each other in Christ."[62] Gustavo Gutierrez writes that being in communion with God and one another is the "fullness of liberation."[63] I believe that base communities are a way to do this in the Episcopal Church.

LATINX theology in the United States is an adaptation of Latin-American liberation theologies. Although informed in part by Latin American liberation theologies, it is its own contextualization in the different United States majority/ minority matrix than in Latin American countries.

> Latinos in the United States, unlike our counterparts in Latin America, have another experience, which to my knowledge has not yet been named as a place of divine revelation: our experience of learning another culture—Anglo culture.[64]

LATINX theologies or Anglican theologies from a LATINX perspective cannot come solely from academia or the institution. The theology also needs to come from below and account for *lo cotidiano*—the stuff of daily life. Yet for it to come from below, laity and clergy must be deeply rooted in our histories and traditions, as well as our Christian faith.

> Latino clergy must take responsibility, as teachers and pastors in the congregation, to form their members in Anglican ways of governance at all levels, from local to national, as well as in Anglican views of leadership and ministry, stewardship and authority.[65]

A LATINX Anglican theology will be polycentric, community-centered, sacramental, and emanate from groups of base communities that gather for worship on a regular basis. A LATINX Anglican theology will be done *en conjunto* and will have a variety of expressions and vernaculars that account for the breadth of expression of those created in the image of God and those reflecting the reign of God in our communities and the new creation in Christ. A LATINX theology will be joyful even as a community suffers on the margins. A LATINX theology will be enacted in worship that is a *fiesta*, lively, with the participation of extended family, blood and chosen family. A LATINX theology will be expressive of a variety of languages and mixes of languages. Above all, a LATINX theology will intentionally search and search again for wisdom in places where God will guide us.

• • •

What does a LATINX Episcopal/Anglican theology look like to you?

# Notes

1. Juan Francisco Martínez, *Walking with the People: Latino Ministry in the United States* (Eugene, OR: Wipf & Stock, 2016), 32; Juan Francisco Martínez, *Walk with the People: Latino Ministry in the United States* (Nashville, TN: Abingdon Press, 2008), 47.

2. Martínez, *Walking*, 52.

3. Juan M. C. Oliver, *Ripe Fields: The Promise and Challenge of Latino Ministry* (New York: Church Publishing, 2009),14.

4. Oliver, *Ripe Fields*, 14.

5. *Lo cotidiano* means "the quotidian."

6. Herbert Arrunátegui, "Evaluation of the Development and Implementation of Hispanic Ministries Programs in the Episcopal Church and the Role of the National Hispanic Officer" (DMin. Thesis, Drew University, 1985), 33–34, 65.

7. "Hispanic Ministry: Opportunity for Mission" (New York: Office of Hispanic Ministry, Episcopal Church Center, 1998), 23–24.

8. Oliver, *Ripe Fields*, 12.

9. Homi K. Bhabha, *Location of Culture* (New York: Routledge, 1993).

10. Dictionary.com, s.v. "synthesis," accessed October 11, 2018. *https://www.dictionary.com/browse/synthesis*.

11. BCP, 364–65.

12. BCP, 874.

13. BCP, 513, 526, 538.

14. Juan Francisco Martínez, *The Story of Latino Protestants in the United States* (Grand Rapids, MI: William B. Eerdmans, 2018), 196; *Walking*, xii, xiii, 49,52, 94, 110.

15. See Martínez, *Walking*, 53.

16. The Book of Common Prayer—1549, accessed July 20, 2018, *http://justus.anglican.org/resources/bcp/1549/front_matter_1549.htm#Preface*.

17. *http://justus.anglican.org/resources/bcp/1549/front_matter_1549.htm#Preface*.

18. BCP, 339.

19. "The Book of Common Prayer in Other Languages," accessed July 20, 2018, *http://justus.anglican.org/resources/bcp/languages.htm*l.

20. Juan M. C. Oliver, "The Book of Common Prayer in Spanish," in *The Oxford Guide to the Book of Common Prayer: A Worldwide Survey*, edited by Charles Hefling and Cynthia L. Shattuck (Oxford: Oxford University Press, 2006), 384.

21. John L. Kater, "Through A Glass Darkly: The Episcopal Church's Responses to the Mexican *Iglesia De Jesús* 1864–1904," *Anglican and Episcopal History* 85, no. 2 (June 2016): 208–9.

22. Oliver, "BCP in Spanish," 384.

23. Oliver, "BCP in Spanish," 385–86.

24. "Libro de Oración Común," July 20, 2018, *http://justus.anglican.org/resources/bcp/Chile/intro.html*: "Formas y expresiones han sido adaptadas a las necesidades de nuestra situación cultural, aunque el tiempo puede demostrar que aún existe una mayor necesidad de ésto. Por lo tanto no se ha de imaginar que ésta es la última palabra en liturgia, pero sí es la última expresión litúrgica para el momento actual de la Iglesia. Se espera que al usar estos cultos, la Iglesia llegará a apreciar más profundamente el lugar de la liturgia en la adoración, y que si en el futuro hay necesidad de un material más adecuado, aquellos que sean llamados a revisarlo tendrán un texto en Castellano y una estructura litúrgica como una base suficientemente clara y doctrinalmente sana para tales revisiones."

25. *Comisión Litúrgica de la Diócesis de Puerto Rico, Ritos Autorizados para la Iglesia Episcopal Puertorriqueña con el Rito aprobado para la Celebración de la Santa Eucaristía y las formas de la Oración Matutina y Vespertina junto con los Ritos de Iniciación Cristiana, las Oraciones Propias (Colectas) y el Salterio* (printed in the Dominican Republic: Iglesia Episcopal Puertorriqueña, 1983).

26. Oliver, "BCP in Spanish," 386.

27. Oliver, "BCP in Spanish," 386. Rev. Louis Weil, PhD, was also teaching at the Episcopal Seminary of the Caribbean at that time.

28. Oliver, "BCP in Spanish," 387.

29. *A New Zealand Prayer Book, He Karakia Mihinare o Aotearoa*, ix, accessed June 15, 2018. *http:// anglicanprayerbook.nz/ix.html*.

30. Livro de Oração Comum. *Administração dos Sacramentos e Outros Ritos e Cerimônias conforme o uso da Igreja Episcopal Anglicana do Brasil com o Saltério e Seleção de Salmos Litúrgicos* (Porto Alegre, Brasil: Igreja Episcopal Anglicana do Brasil, 2015), 19–20. A good article on the Brasilian prayer book is Luiz Coelho, "IEAB's 2015 Book of Common Prayer: The Latest Chapter in the Evolution of the Book of Common Prayer in Brazil," in *Studia Liturgica* 49 no. 1: 26–42.

31. Livro de *Oração Comum*, 597–612.

32. Livro de *Oração Comum*, 763.

33. BCP, 9–10.

34. Virtual Binder, House of Deputies, accessed March 15, 2019, *https://www.vbinder.net/menu? house=hd&lang=en*.

35. Virtual Binder, House of Deputies, accessed March 15, 2019, *https://www.vbinder.net/menu? house=hd&lang=en*.

36. I have shared versions of this section at various workshops over the last five years.

37. Sandra Maria Van Opstal, *The Next Worship: Glorifying God in a Diverse World* (Downers Grove, IL: InterVarsity Press, 2016), 23.

38. See my discussion on this—borrowing from García and Nunes, *Wittenberg*—in pages 97–98 of chapter 3 above.

39. Martínez, *Walking*, 42.

40. Oliver, *Ripe Fields*, 5.

41. "The Episcopal Church and the Hispanic Challenge: A Report on the State of Hispanic Ministries," (New York: Office of Hispanic Ministry, Episcopal Chruch Center, 1985), 7–8.

42. Oliver, *Ripe Fields*, 48–56.

43. See BCP, 13. *Concerning the Service of the Church*, "The Holy Eucharist, the principal act of Christian worship on the Lord's Day and other major Feasts, and Daily Morning and Evening Prayer, as set forth in this Book, are the regular services appointed for public worship in the Church."

44. See BCP, 304.

45. Disciples are vessels that are filled and nourished. Apostles are disciples sent out.

46. See BCP, 13. Etymology of Liturgy: C16: via Medieval Latin, from Greek *leitourgia*, from *leitourgos* minister, from *leit*- people + *ergon* work; 1550s, "the service of the Holy Eucharist," from Middle French *liturgie* or directly from Late Latin/Medieval Latin *liturgia* "public service, public worship," from Greek *leitourgia* "a liturgy; public duty, ministration, ministry," from *leitourgos* "one who performs a public ceremony or service, public servant," from *leito-* "public" (from *laos* "people"; cf. *leiton* "public hall," *leite* "priestess"; see lay (adj.)) + *-ergos* "that works," from *ergon* "work" (see urge (v.)). Meaning "collective formulas for the conduct of divine service in Christian churches" is from 1590s. liturgy. Dictionary.com. *Online Etymology Dictionary*. Douglas Harper, Historian. Accessed November 12, 2015. *http://dictionary.reference.com/browse/liturgy*.

47. A reminder that the current prayer book in Spanish is a translation of the 1979 BCP. It is not a full translation; therefore, it does not have the equivalent sections to Rite I.

48. BCP, 304–5.

49. For example, abuelas matriarcas.

50. BCP, 406.

51. Albert R. Rodríguez, "Mega-Trends in Latino Ministry," Seminary of the Southwest, June 14, 2016, *https://ssw.edu/blog/mega-trends-in-latino-ministry/*.

52. Yes, there are many other resources; these are just the most commonly used.

53. John J. Limb, *Flor y canto* (Portland, OR: OCP [Oregon Catholic Press], 2011).

54. See *www.elaineromanelli.com*.

55. The LOC does not have the equivalent to Rite I; therefore, the offices, Eucharist, and burial rites are only in the corresponding Rite II language. By the time you reach the psalms, the LOC is about 100 pages shorter than the BCP. In other words, whereas the Holy Eucharist Rite II begin on page 355 of the BCP, it begins on page 277 of the LOC.

56. These models are summarized in *Hispanic Ministry: Opportunity for Mission*, 3rd ed. (New York: Office of Hispanic Ministry, Episcopal Church Center, 2001), 8–12.

57. Martínez, *Walking*, 63.

58. Martínez, *Walking*, 75.

59. Harold T. Lewis, "By Schisms Rent Asunder? American Anglicanism on the Eve of the Millennium," in *A New Conversation: Essays on the Future of Theology and the Episcopal Church,* ed. Robert Boak Slocum (New York: Church Publishing, 1999), 9.

60. Lewis, "By Schisms Rent Asunder?," 4.

61. BCP, 855.

62. BCP, 855.

63. Gustavo Gutiérrez, *Teología de la liberación: Perspectivas. Con una nueva introducción, "Mirar Lejos"* (Lima, Perú: Centro de Estudios y Publicaciones, 1991), 113. "La plenitud de la liberación-don gratuito de Cristo-es la comunión con Dios y con los demás." See also p. 114 and note 114.c.

64. Oliver, *Ripe Fields*, 13.

65. Oliver, *Ripe Fields*, 69.

# Conclusion

n my review of Rev. Juan M. C. Oliver's book *Ripe Fields* in 2011, I called for someone (else) to write more on the ministry to, with, and among LATINX people and communities. God, with God's divine sense of humor, chose me to write this book, which has stretched me in ways that I would not have necessarily chosen, such as God did with putting me in parish ministry and LATINX ministry; I don't necessarily have a call to either. If I could spend my time reading, writing, teaching, and mentoring, while remaining connected to an altar, I would be quite happy.

I set out to unmask LATINX Ministries in the Episcopal Church. This meant (re)framing the history of the Episcopal Church as it pertains to ministry to, with, and among LATINX people and communities, and showing the institutionalization and commodification of LATINX communities as a program of the Church that treats LATINX people as hyphenated-Episcopalians, especially by controlling and containing them. This history goes back to the sixteenth century and the historical and discursive animosity between England and Spain, and how these get replicated in the United States by creating an *us/them* dynamic between white Episcopalians and LATINX people and communities. I proposed that the Episcopal Church, as a colonial and imperial church, uses Anglicanism and its English roots in a way that is consonant with the discourses of the "black legend."

I presented a brief history of the missionary forays by the Episcopal Church and other Anglican Churches before the middle of the twentieth century and looked at Latin America after the 1958 Lambeth resolution that opened this region to evangelization. This was followed by the history of the institutionalization of LATINX Ministries, which I argue has as an immediate precursor in the General Convention Special Program (1967) and subsequent creation of Ethnic Ministries in 1973—a history of the last fifty years. One aspect of this institutional history that will be very useful is the compilation of a substantial record of reports over the last fifty years, as well as an extensive chronology of important events. These are two areas that will be ready for expansion as more information and different types of sources become more readily available and known to me. And it would be my hope that there are those who will take on this task; let's see who steps up to the challenge. As mentioned earlier, it would be ideal to publish a critical edition of primary texts accompanied by a corresponding analysis. As part of the institutional history it became evident that the demise of the Special Program and the handling of issues related to the FALN continue to inform how LATINX people and communities, and anti-racism initiatives, are approached by the Episcopal Church to this day: as programs of the Church. Programs do not liberate.

I also aimed to (re)focus the Church toward ministry, given that LATINX Ministry is nothing other than ministry, and to call the Church to have a renewed and unequivocal focus on fulfilling its mission (#BCP855) and stop concentrating power and resources for the sole maintenance of the institution. As a program of the Church, LATINX ministry is dissociated from the most basic understanding of ministry. My use of the phrase "ministry to, with, and among LATINX people and communities" is intentional in putting ministry first.

The institutionalization of ministry to, with, and among LATINX people and communities roughly coincides with the development of Latin American liberation theologies. In the late 1970s and into the middle of the 1980s, elements of Latin American liberation theologies entered reports about LATINX ministries in the Episcopal Church. Given the migratory patterns at the time, and the crisis at the southern border of the United States nowadays, it was clearly a missed opportunity for the Episcopal Church not to build upon liberation theologies. In fact, as Rev. Justo L. González wrote in 1985, the challenge for the Episcopal Church had two foci: the *challenge of numbers* and the *challenge of the poor*. The Church chose the challenge of numbers over the challenge of the poor. Becoming more and more remote from answering the *challenge of the poor*, the Church has almost obsessively focused on numbers—a "Demographic Panic" has been a driver for the Church for the better part of the last quarter century. This also has meant that daily life (*lo cotidiano*), suffering, poverty, oppression have not been sources of revelation for the Episcopal Church. Or, as the 1988 manifesto expressed, "an occasion for rejoicing while allowing the poor and destitute of this country to evangelize us."[1]

A third task has been to remind the Episcopal Church of the strengths of its theology and tradition, and how these can speak to LATINX experiences and how LATINX experiences speak to Anglicanism. This led to some thoughts on directions the Episcopal Church could take to move forward with respect to ministry with and among LATINX people and communities, and the respective needed parallel theologizing. This theologizing includes elements of both/and, contextualization, autonomous and interrelated Churches, inculturated prayer books, and ecclesial base communities. This is the development of LATINX liberative theologies from Anglican perspectives and Anglican liberative theologies from LATINX perspectives. The contextualization of Anglicanism will not be a task solely for churches outside of the United States; the Episcopal Church needs to develop an ever evolving and growing sense of contemporary contextualization today—the new and evolving local vernaculars. In other words, what could a contextual Anglicanism and Anglican identity bring to the needs and hopes of Episcopalians in the United States, including Latinx people and communities?

Since I call for the dismantling of racialized discourses, I tried to show how these function in the Episcopal Church. Some of the discourses are about demographics, the Spanish language, immigration status, education and poverty, Roman Catholic background, or the "deficiency" of these communities. I wove these elements into opening our understanding of what the vernacular means in the Church and for efforts of contextualization, and what it would mean to have ministry among communities, rather than to the *other*. It became quite evident that arguments about theological education and leadership development also need to be debunked, and I called for the intentional, appropriate, and sustained investment in theological education. Yet this investment or the dismantling of any of the above will have no effect—in the Episcopal Church or for Latinx people and communities—if a decolonial epistemology is not pursued. In short, we must change the structures of the Church fundamentally by changing the way the Church thinks, otherwise any innovation will not lead to a new emphasis on the mission of the Church but will continue to benefit current power and resource structures. For example, some clear examples were included in my analysis of various Church budgets.

There are serious challenges faced by the Episcopal Church in order to have a chance at changing the way it treats Latinx people and communities. This requires dismantling the institutional structures that are hindering the Episcopal Church in the fulfillment of its mission, including delinking from *othering* and colonial discourses that hinder ministry to, with, and among Latinx people and communities. Then the Episcopal Church must have the humility to trace a prophetic path that will veer from its focus on control of power and resources and the preservation of the institution.

The changing of discourses and development of a vision for a different future will not be enough unless the Church and all its constitutive elements make a bold choice to "double-down" on a decolonial epistemology, formation, and education that includes an epistemic pluriversality. This change in epistemological points of view will challenge the long-standing racism and misogyny of the Church. Given the long-term effects of decisions made or not made today, there is no time for the Church to wait. The Church at the turn of the twenty-second century depends on the decisions made today regarding epistemology, theological education, and Christian formation. Changing epistemologies also require "correcting" our standard histories of the Episcopal Church and changing the current points of view and epistemologies that are privileged over others. There is room for histories of the Episcopal Church to add LAT-INX narratives, and for histories of LATINX protestants to include Episcopal narratives. In undoing coloniality, the Episcopal Church needs new ways of thinking, knowing, being, and doing.

From the work I have been able to do with LGBTQ+ people in the Episcopal Church and in other faith communities, I know that change can happen. I also know that this change will not fundamentally transform the Church if corresponding structures are not equally challenged. I am putting great hope in the prophetic space of base communities and seminaries.

I want to close this book with another area that I believe is of utmost importance. I want to belong to a Church in which others have a great sense of belonging, so that we all get to the work of living into our baptism and work toward the fulfilling of the mission of the Church—reconciliation with God and one another (#BCP855).

## Unmasking "The Episcopal Church Welcomes You": Moving toward Belonging

What does the phrase "diversity and inclusion" mean? Beyond the fact that it is not decolonial, it cannot capture the work that the Church is called to accomplish. Furthermore, in our own church language welcome should be reconsidered. We must go beyond welcome and inclusion, beyond diversity to polycentric congregations, and move to solidarity and belonging. Solidarity is sacramental—the outward and visible sign of inclusion. There must be a place at the table for LAT-INX people and communities, which involves participating in the power structures of the Church and benefiting from all its resources in an equitable manner.

In January 2019, I led a workshop at the Forma Conference, titled "From Welcome to Belonging: Inclusion of and Solidarity with LATINX and LGBTQ+ Communities." Early in the presentation I asked whether anyone knew or remembered when the slogan "The Episcopal Church Welcomes You" came into use. In my perception, people responded based on their own generational experience, meaning that it came into being in their lifetimes. "The Episcopal Church Welcomes You" signs have been a part of the Episcopal Church since their approval in October 1950.[2] I remember the slogan being around in the 1990s. For me, it was a very meaningful statement—then. I was proud to be an Episcopalian and I was proud of the stances the Episcopal Church had taken, especially with regards to women's ordination and lesbian and gay people. Yet, after thirty years, the question is, why are we still at welcome?

As has been evident in this book, my optimism about the Episcopal Church has frustratingly waned since the late 1990s because of the inability of the Church to have a robust and dignified ministry among LATINX people and communities. If you asked, generally, whether society was more welcoming of LGBTQ+ or LATINX people and communities, what would you, the reader, answer? My answer is that the Episcopal Church has made greater and clearer inroads into LGBTQ+ rights and welcome, specifically lesbian and gay, because there have always been white gay men in the Church.

Yet notwithstanding the solidarity with LGBTQ+ communities, in the last few years my frustration has increased with my disappointment in the Episcopal Church's understanding of interculturality and true solidarity with LGBTQ+ people of color. Again, all this is to say that welcome is not enough. The real question is, when are we going to stop being content with guests in our churches? Rev. Tara K. Soughers, in the book *Beyond a Binary God: A Theology of Trans\* Allies* writes:

> DURABLE UNLESS SHOT AT
>
> A model of the proposed Episcopal Church welcome sign was set up in the Council's meeting room. It consisted of a standard with a base, and an arm from which the sign hangs. Mr. Jordan explained that the sign was (1) a road sign, to be placed at the entrance of a town; (2) a street sign, to be put in the immediate neighborhood of the church; and (3) a church sign, to be placed on or very near the church.
>
> The model was finished with aluminum paint, the lettering on the sign being distinct. The only colors were the red cross of the Church seal, below the words: "The Episcopal Church Welcomes You," and the blue field below the seal, for the name of the particular church or churches. Mr. Jordan said the sign, with standard, would last ten years, unless shot at or hit with a rock. The cost would be about $28, without shipping expense.
>
> The Council members were interested in the sign; but several expressed a fear that boys would use it for a target. One member suggested that it be given a cement base, in order that it might not be carried away, on Halloween, or at any other time. The Council then voted approval of the sign.

Many churches are becoming much more welcoming for members of the trans\* community, and God knows we need to be more welcoming. It is not enough simply to welcome. To welcome them into our congregations is to imply somehow that this is our church: we are the hosts and they are guests. To place them in the role of guests is to require them to behave in socially acceptable ways and to follow the rules of the house they are visiting. To welcome them as guests is to imply that we have the right to invite them or not invite them. To welcome them as guests is to proclaim that they are not really a part of the family. To welcome them as guests is to keep them separate and contained. To welcome them as guests is to state, although perhaps more nicely than we do many other times, that they are not related to us. If we really believe, however, that they, like all of us, are made in the image and likeness of God, then they are not our guests, and we are not their hosts. God is the host, and all of us are God's family, gathered around the dinner table. There are always people we are less comfortable with at large family gatherings. There are the people who don't dress properly, who don't use appropriate table manners, or who tell off-color jokes at family holidays. If they are family, however, we keep eating with them and celebrating together. We manage to put up with their flaws and faults, as they graciously put up with ours.[3]

A tiny part of the answer is found in the concept and work of inclusion, where people can be incorporated into the life of congregations, leadership, and the work of the broader church. Inclusion, though good for the ASA (Average Sunday Attendance) of congregations, and thus feeling good about diversity, is not good enough. What is the prophetic witness of inclusion?

In 2016, when I was a finalist for diocesan bishop of Puerto Rico, the question of inclusion came about in all the walkabouts; it was "code" for issues of sexuality. My answer at the time was, "Our work of inclusion is trying to catch up to the radical inclusion that Jesus showed millennia ago." It is the most radical way of living into our baptismal promises. It is hard work; it is well worth it. Yet inclusion solely to get people in pews but not help them belong is not enough. "The outward and visible sign of inclusion" is solidarity—when others different from the included stand in witness against the injustices suffered and get some skin in the game. In the last few years, there are glimpses of the Episcopal Church learning anew and again to walk in solidarity with marginalized communities that are already represented in their congregations. This is an important step.

In my work with the Center for LGBTQ and Gender Studies in Religion (CLGS), we have come to recognize that the majority of people in our congregations are people of goodwill who want not only to welcome and include, but also want to affirm the dignity of every human being. It is often to these people of goodwill that we are speaking when we say not to be complacent, not to stay at welcome, not to stay at inclusion, not to even stay at solidarity. This can be exhausting.

Language changes are happening more and more rapidly. In the last fifty years we have moved from referring to people of "Spanish origin" as Hispanics, to Latinos, to Latinos/as, and now to LATINX or even Latine. It may seem to many that just as they are getting accustomed to a new term that they have been left behind for the next one. The same is true for LGB to LGBT to LGBTQ to LGBTQIA+. The expansive language asks us to bring the Good News of God in Christ to the world by including more and more of God's children and witnessing to the suffering of the world. This is done so that through the ministry of all members we many continue to fulfill the mission of the Church "to restore all people to unity with God and each other in Christ" through prayer, worship, the proclamation of the Gospel and promoting justice, peace, and love (#BCP855). We need to welcome, understand, include, affirm—all before we get to a sense of belonging. Then, with belonging, we can invite one another to proclaim and share the Good News. We should strive for ministry that is welcoming, inclusive, solidarious, and that creates a sense of belonging for LATINX people and communities. Yes, we are called to alleviate the needs and sufferings of our neighbors. Yes, we are called to build the beloved community.

I would say the Church is beginning to understand the role of ministry to and is engaging more in ministry among LATINX people. As characterized by Rev. Juan Francisco Martínez, this means that "Latinos can take a certain level of responsibility for the project,"[4] although, I fundamentally believe that it is not a project. It is the beginning of agency, and with agency, the claiming of an identity, and with an identity, belonging. According to Martínez, when LATINX people become agents of ministry, "they will take full responsibility for the leadership, vision, administration, and finances of the church."[5] Are you ready, Episcopal Church?

Martínez and I mostly coincide in our understandings of "to," "with," and "among." I must also add that although Martínez' book is about LATINX ministries, the ultimate vision is one of a multicultural reflection of the reign of God (Rev. 7). So in understanding the fact that to, with, and among are coexisting, we also lift the understanding that LATINX people can also evangelize and have a missional expression. This evangelism and missional expression come precisely and are enriched by the fact that LATINX communities are pluricultural and polycentric and can model this for the broader Church.

We must ultimately ask, "What does ministry that empowers LATINX people in the Episcopal Church at all levels, denominationally, diocesan, parochial, programmatic, in all types of congregations, urban, rural, suburban, rich, poor look like?" It looks the same as it has for white men; the difference is found in the narrow epistemological foundations that must be delinked from the institution and expanded with many other epistemic points of view.

Saying that we are the Episcopal branch of the Jesus Movement means that we recognize that we are not THE Jesus Movement itself. Therefore, we acknowledge that our Anglican/Episcopalian expression of catholic

Christianity—or catholicity—is one among many, and, although rooted in Anglicanism, it is contextualized to the particular expression in the United States and even (re)contextualized in its related churches in other countries (such as those in Province IX, the Caribbean, and the Convocation of Episcopal Churches in Europe). The branch of the Jesus Movement or of the vine cannot function or exist by itself; we are first Christians and then idiosyncratically Episcopalian.

Saying that we are part of the Jesus Movement also requires our willingness to build the reign of God. This willingness is an expression of our vows made at baptism. I understand the reign of God to be pluricultural, which means it includes people of all sorts of polycentric identities. We all (should) know that living into the way of Jesus is not easy. Loving neighbor is not easy; loving stranger is not easy; loving our enemies is not easy. Yet Jesus invites us to all these loves. Above, I spoke of unmasking comfort, as an invitation to a motto of being "Uncomfortable for Christ." This constant uncomfortableness will lead to freedom, justice, and peace.

The Jesus Movement, which Presiding Bishop Curry envisions as the Way of Love, is not about the world "out there" with its problems, it is about the Church. We will not change the world without changing ourselves. As Rev. Martin Luther King Jr. expressed, that requires those in power to recognize and relinquish that power, as well as let go of fear and bitterness; and those who have been powerless and oppressed to not live into the bitterness and look for retaliation.

> There is a danger that those of us who have lived so long under the yoke of oppression, those of us who have been exploited and trampled over, those of us who have had to stand amid the tragic midnight of injustice and indignities will enter the new age with hate and bitterness. But if we retaliate with hate and bitterness, the new age will be nothing but a duplication of the old age. We must blot out the hate and injustice of the old age with the love and justice of the new.[6]

The 242nd Diocesan Convention of the Diocese of New York in November 2018 had the theme "Building the Beloved Community." The Rt. Rev. Andrew M. L. Dietsche borrowed the image from the writing of Dr. King. Dietsche saw the building of community as an imperative during the time we are living in the United States, where there is incredible tension and polarization. Dietsche understands, as do I, the allure of living in our own "silos," and the prophetic call to reaching across the breach and understanding that we are all children of God. Will we dare to live into this community?

## God Is in Charge

This may sound weird, but I'm always amazed at the dynamism of my ever-evolving relationships with God and God's Church. Early in my discernment process, I was often asked why I stayed in the Episcopal Church and why I did not go somewhere else that was more welcoming. Thirty years ago, I answered that I believed in our tradition and the possibility of changing it from within. In all my discernment, ministry experience, and academic studies, I have explored my faith, and chosen again and again to stay in the Episcopal Church. Since 1997, I have experienced much frustration with the institutional church, again and again; naively, I am never quite prepared to be disappointed. There is a part of me that is always hopeful, but it is in constant struggle because we "fall short" time after time, even though we should know better and we should do better and we can do better and God is asking us to be better.

Researching for and writing this book has not done much to ameliorate the disappointment and frustration with the institution's dismal history of ministry to, with, and among LATINX people and communities. I find it astonishing that we are where we are as an institution given how great our tradition is and all the resources we have and all the gifts LATINX people and communities bring to the table. Thus, I have been challenged to present open-ended areas of reflection and promise that could lead us to a better place in terms of this opportunity for the Church. What I am left with, though, is hope, and gratitude that if we listen, if we are not fearful, and if we allow ourselves to be faithful, that God is indeed in charge.

Epistemologies, belonging, welcome, solidarity, dignity are some of the ideas included in this book, yet I must remind the reader and myself that this is not without its Jesus-centered foundations. This has not been a mere academic exercise and is not about everyone else; it is as much about me as it is about the Church and God's Reign. We must move beyond welcome to create a sense of belonging and this is about our baptism. In the baptismal rite, after the water has been poured, we pray for God to "sustain them, O Lord, in your Holy Spirit. Give them an inquiring and discerning heart, the courage to will and to persevere, a spirit to know and to love you, and the gift of joy and wonder in all your works."[7]

Every time I say this prayer I imagine a person or family leaving their home knowing that they are sustained by the Holy Spirit, their eyes are wide open, and thus can be inquisitive about the world about them, fearless in encountering life, have a willingness to deepen their relationship with God and thus one another, while in awe of the ever-revealed abundance and beauty of God's creation. I imagine that people who can live this way are bringing to fulfillment the reign of God by living their Baptismal Covenant. I also imagine that people that can live this way have a deep sense of belonging in a community of the faithful. A community from which they are renewed and strengthened to do the work that God has called them to do.

From the moment we are knitted in the womb, we are a child of God in the image of God. Our life is a journey of discovery of whom God already knows us to be in our wholeness, plenitude, and fullest potential. In our baptism we are strengthened in this understanding. I believe in the vision of Revelation 7 of that diverse and polycentric expression of the breadth of the image of God.

> After this I looked, and there was a great multitude that no one could count, from every nation, from all tribes and peoples and languages, standing before the throne and before the Lamb, robed in white, with palm branches in their hands. They cried out in a loud voice, saying, "Salvation belongs to our God who is seated on the throne, and to the Lamb!" And all the angels stood around the throne and around the elders and the four living creatures, and they fell on their faces before the throne and worshiped God, singing, "Amen! Blessing and glory and wisdom and thanksgiving and honor and power and might be to our God forever and ever! Amen." (Rev. 7:9–12)

The reign of God is like an ever perfecting Trinitarian community; like sitting with interesting people for long hours having meaningful conversations while eating Puerto Rican food. The reign of God is a world in which everyone can participate in the joy and wonder of all of God's works. The reign of God that we are trying to build is one in which all that we do "promotes justice, peace, and love." A glimpse of the reign of God is when all are sustained by the Holy Spirit, can look at the world with an inquiring and discerning heart, can have the courage to will and to persevere, and all have the spirit to know and love God. If we created such a world, we would be realizing the reign of God.

The last time I walked the Camino in Spain, in 2012, I walked through many vineyards in La Rioja. That memory brings to life the image of God as the vine and God's humanity as the branches. The intricacies of that image are rich, as rich as the wine. The other image is that of the body of Christ—both powerful invitations to community. Our polycentric and interconnected lives require a care and concern for one another that reflects God's care and concern for each of us, whom God knows by name.

> I am the vine, you are the branches. Those who abide in me and I in them bear much fruit, because apart from me you can do nothing. (John 15:5)

For just as the body is one and has many members, and all the members of the body, though many, are one body, so it is with Christ. For in the one Spirit we were all baptized into one body—Jews or Greeks, slaves or free—and we were all made to drink of one Spirit. Indeed, the body does not consist of one member but of many. (1 Cor. 12:12–14)

# CODA

Some of the most important things about the Hispanic Summer Program (HSP) and the Hispanic Theological Initiative (HTI) have been the community and mentorship that have endured for two decades, and the critical mass of LATINX students and scholars studying and working together—*en conjunto*. LATINX seminarians, and even sometimes LATINX seminary faculty, are often isolated in their respective seminary communities. Seminary is hard and it should be a time of deep learning and discernment, yet seminary should build up rather than break down. What can be avoided is the way certain students have a normative experience— seminary functions around their experiences and knowledge base—and others tend to feel isolated, exceptionalized, and tokenized, or even erased.

I came to know the Church Divinity School of the Pacific through the Rt. Rev. Jennifer Baskerville-Burrows, who also attended the Episcopal Church at Cornell. As Baskerville-Burrows researched and visited Episcopal seminaries throughout the country, she shared with me many brochures and other information. I wanted to attend an Episcopal seminary, but my options were limited in terms of which seminaries would be welcoming of lesbian and gay students. At that point queer students at the seminary in Virginia had to sign a celibacy clause—something I was not willing to do—just as I had not been willing to officially enroll in ROTC (Reserve Officer Training Corps) in 1993 (something I wanted to do), given that being gay or lesbian was against the Uniform Code of Military Justice and could lead to a dishonorable discharge.[8] Many changes occurred in those years in terms of civil rights for LGB people, though not always in time for me to benefit from them.

In 1997, my summer before seminary was full of joy and nervous expectation. I travelled a lot that August, meeting my then months-old cousins Peter and Andrew in Toledo, Ohio; it turned out to be my last visit with Grandpa Rudy too. I visited college friends in New York and Philadelphia, and family in Texas. My dad helped me choose my first car and I drove from the Texas panhandle to Berkeley, California. I went to a WNBA game in Phoenix, Arizona, and visited my cousin Carlos who lived in San Diego. I was thrilled to be going to seminary. In late-August 1997 I began my seminary training.

From the time of my acceptance at CDSP in 1994 to attending, three years had passed. During that time even CDSP had become a more welcoming place for queer students, in part because of the retirement of Charles A. Perry, dean and president, and the election of Donn F. Morgan as successor. Having lived in Ithaca, New York, and then in Berkeley, California, I have lived in many progressive bubbles. Up to that point I had never thought of myself as LATINX in church.

My memories of growing up in the Episcopal Church in Puerto Rico were not tied to my Puerto Rican identity, which makes sense because the environment was Puerto Rico. Neither was my participation at St. Peter's in Amarillo, Texas, as a preteen. I moved to Ithaca, New York, for college in 1989 and attended ECC, where the chaplain was Rev. Gurdon Brewster, and the *Protestant Cooperative Ministry,* whose chaplain was Rev. Barbara Heck. In neither of these chaplaincies was I welcomed particularly because I was Puerto Rican, although I do know I stayed because they included me and were queer friendly. Therefore, because of my background and experiences, I had never felt *outside* of the purview of the Episcopal Church, or *other*. As an activist at Cornell, I was prepared for homophobia, but not for LATINX tokenism. Therefore, as a cradle Episcopalian who knew the Church since my childhood in Puerto Rico, I continue to be confounded by the inability of the Episcopal Church to welcome LATINX people and communities.

Although the Church has yet to grapple fully with the issues of gender and sexuality, and these continue to express themselves in disappointing ways, my most time-consuming struggle over these decades has been over ethnicity and race and the way the Episcopal Church fails in respecting the dignity of LATINX people and communities. This is always curious to me since I am a person who easily passes as "white" given my white skin color, but who has still been tokenized and marginalized. I have white-skin privilege and I have had the privilege of access to higher education and as such have the responsibility to speak truth to the institutions especially over its continued marginalization of LATINX people and communities. If my story was isolated, I wouldn't be as frustrated, but sadly it is not.

In the history of blacks in the Episcopal Church, this racist/ethnocentric feeling of tokenism also exists. In 1998, Rev. Harold T. Lewis, a cradle Episcopalian, expressed this feeling from a few decades earlier.

> I was not prepared, therefore, for the question posed to me by a professor who interviewed me at Berkeley Divinity School: "Mr. Lewis, did it ever occur to you that the Episcopal Church doesn't particularly like you?" I did not understand the comments of my colleagues at Yale Divinity School who wondered

why I was in a "white church. . . . [Yet], I have remained ever firm in my resolve to work from within the church that I love to improve it, believing that although attitudes, policies and behavior have attempted, and in some cases succeeded in marginalizing, disenfranchising and ostracizing us, such actions have been attributed to the shortcomings of their perpetrators, and not to the intrinsic nature of the church, which is one, holy, catholic, and apostolic.[9]

Even in conversations in 2019, there are LATINX and African-American clergy who continue to experience alienation in the Episcopal Church, yet continue to stay within its ranks committed to the possibilities and the hope of being agents of liberation in our Church and for the people and communities we serve.

At CDSP, if I remember correctly, fifty-four students started at the same time in various degree programs; some were full-time, others part-time, and some commuters. As a group we gelled—we joked that we were legion. My seminary experience was very good. Yet something continues to tug at me and has tugged at me for over twenty years. What brought me to LATINX Ministry? And how is this related to writing this book? Yes, God has had a hand in my ministerial path; the Church has had a hand in me being tokenized.

I don't remember exactly, but CDSP did not have many LATINX students. Over my four years there, maybe there were a handful. I might have been the only one in the legion that started in 1997. With a lack of representation, at CDSP is where I first began to be tokenized in the Episcopal Church. CDSP had various faculty members with a deep and prophetic commitment to LATINX communities in the United States and Latin America, both of whom I consider friends and mentors, Rev. John L. Kater and Rev. Don Compier.

In December of my first year I was invited to participate in the celebration at the chapel of CDSP of the Feast of Guadalupe. I will admit that I asked, "Guadalupe who?" You see, growing up Guadalupe was not a pan-LATINX expression of the Virgin, and was not a familiar apparition of the Virgin in Puerto Rico. Ours is *la Virgen de la Providencia*. But being on the West Coast and closer to Mexican and Mexican American communities, it made sense for CDSP to celebrate this feast. I bring this up, though, for two reasons. First, not all LATINX people or communities celebrate the same things, and, second, this marked the beginning of my understanding that I was *other*. My thought was that, if anything, the challenge in seminary was going to be over LGBTQ+ issues. I did not expect to feel my *latinidad* so acutely. Thus, this began my journey of advocacy for this community, specifically, in the Episcopal Church. I could not understand how backwards the Episcopal Church was when it came to LATINX people and communities.

Another thing that brought me to this ministry is the fact that I knew Spanish. Curiously enough, SMST got to know me as I supplied for their English-language service. Ancillary to that they knew I was fluent in Spanish. So God put me there when there was a need. Yet would I have been thought of as qualified if I wasn't LATINX?

In the fall of 1997, I took my first "History and Theology" course at the Church Divinity School of the Pacific. My professor was Rev. J. Rebecca Lyman. Having focused on science and math for most of my education since high school, I was enthralled by this new (to me) subject. I ended up getting a master of arts and PhD in various aspects of church history. I love church history. My academic foci have been Augustine of Hippo, medieval and early modern Iberia, and sixteenth-century New Spain. These fields inform some of the aspects of chapter 1 in this book. My fields are decidedly not the history of the Episcopal Church, let alone the history of the institutionalization of LAT-INX ministries. I come to these subjects in my person, and as a minister in a context considered part of LATINX ministries. I am an advocate for LATINX people and communities, and LGBTQ+ people in the Episcopal Church. I have written this church history because it does not exist, and it is needed for this advocacy work. My hope is that twenty years from now no seminarian or scholar will find themselves in the same conundrum.

## Notes

1. "Un Manifesto Hispano," in *Reflexiones Teológicas: Modelos de Ministerios, Revista Teológica de la Comisión Hispana de la Diócesis de Nueva York* 2 no. 2 (Jan.–Jun. 1989), 37.

2. "Durable Unless Shot At," *The Living Church* 121, no. 18 (October 29, 1950): 7. It is surprising to me that there isn't a history of this phrase. Thanks to the help of Caitlin Stamm, reference librarian at GTS, we found this early reference in *The Living Church*.

3. Tara K. Saughers, *Beyond a Binary God: A Theology of Trans\* Allies* (New York: Church Publishing, 2018), 111.

4. Juan Francisco Martínez, *The Story of Latino Protestants in the United States* (Grand Rapids, MI: William B. Eerdmans, 2018), 24.

5. Martínez, *Story*, 24.

6. Martin Luther King Jr., "Facing the Challenge of a New Age," in *A Testament of Love: The Essential Writings of Martin Luther King, Jr.*, ed. James Melvin Washington (New York: Harper & Row, 1986), 139.

7. BCP, 308.

8. This would "end" with the legislative compromise of "Don't Ask, Don't Tell" during the Clinton Administration

9. Harold T. Lewis, "Racial Concerns in the Episcopal Church Since 1973," Pittsburgh Conference Papers: Papers "Mine Eyes Have Seen the Glory": Anglican Visions of Apocalypse and Hope, June 1997, *Anglican and Episcopal History* 67, no. 4 (December 1998): 478.

# Bibliography

**Reports** (in chronological order)

1966. SPCK, *The Anglican Communion and Latin America: The Report of a Consultation at Sao Paulo, Brazil, 24–28 January 1966* (London, England: SPCK, 1966).

1968. Resolution 64 from "Lambeth Conference Resolutions Archive 1968."

1980. "The Report of the Special Task Force of the National Commission on Hispanic Ministries: 'The Hispanic Challenge to the Episcopal Church: Opportunity for Mission in the 80's.'"

1981. "Report on the 1981 Hispanic Theological Consultation."

1983. Report of the conference "Latin America in the 80s: A Challenge to Theology."

1985. "The Episcopal Church and the Hispanic Challenge: A Report on the State of Hispanic Ministries."

1985. *The Hispanic Ministry of the Episcopal Church in the Metropolitan Area of New York and Environs.*

1985. "A Time for Understanding: A Colloquium on Central America."

1988. "Now Is the Time: Report of the National Hispanic Strategy Conference."

1988. "A Celebration of Diversity: Hispanic Ministry in the Episcopal Church. An Evaluation of the Current State of Hispanic Ministries in the Episcopal Church."

1988. "Hispanic Ministries: Recruitment, Training and Deployment."

1988. "The Hispanic Challenge to the Diocese of New York," A Working Paper Prepared by The Committee on Mission and Strategy of the Hispanic Commission of the Diocese of New York.

1989. "Reflexiones Teológicas: Modelos de Ministerio," *Revista Teológica de la Comisión Hispana de la Diócesis de Nueva York.* (Includes the first Hispanic Manifesto.)

1989. "Our Hispanic Ministry I: Essays on Emerging Latin American Membership in the Episcopal Church."

1990. "Theological Education and Preparation for Hispanic Ministry: A Survey of Accredited Episcopal Seminaries in the United States."

1991. "Our Hispanic Ministry II: How We Claim Ethnic Membership in the Episcopal Church." Also titled, "Our Hispanic Ministry II: How Latin Americans Consolidate their Growth in the Episcopal Church."

1993. "Ministry in a Culturally Diverse Church: Report of a Hispanic Consultation on Recruitment, Training, and Deployment."

1998. "Strategies for Renewal in the Episcopal Church: Recruitment, Training, and Deployment for Effective Ministry in the Hispanic Communities."

1998. "Hispanic Ministry: Opportunity for Mission." Reissued in 2001.

2001. "Atlanta Manifesto: The Wake-Up Call to Action."

2002. "The Atlanta Manifesto with 'Addendum' and a Pastoral Letter."

2005. "The Hispanic Ministry: A Challenging Future."

2009. "The Episcopal Church: Creating a Welcoming Presence: Inviting Latinos/Hispanics to Worship. (Planning Document)"

2009. "The Episcopal Church's Strategic Vision for Reaching Latinos/Hispanics."

2018. "The Task Force for Latino/Hispanic Congregational Development and Sustainability."

**Episcopal New Service** (The following articles are in the digital archives of the Episcopal Church and are indexed by the bracketed number. *www.episcopalarchives.org* Here they are in chronological order.)

"Seminary's First Graduation," June 5, 1963 [XI-11].

"Episcopal Church Approves Funds for Ghetto Organizations, Businesses," June 5, 1968 [66-1].

"Special Program Grants Approved," June 5, 1968 [66-2].

"Bishop of Kentucky Defends Crisis Program," June 5, 1968 [66-14].

"$675,000 Deposited in Ghetto Banks," July 15, 1968 [67-2].

"Executive Council Awards Grants in Response to Race and Poverty Crisis," September 27, 1968 [69-13].

"Grants Awarded to Community Action Organizations," December 16, 1968 [72-7].

"Council Awards and Declines Special Program Grants," February 13, 1969 [74-9].

"Black Manifesto Demands $500.000,000 in Reparations," May 1, 1969 [77-4].

"Council Rejects Black Manifesto," May 23, 1969 [77-12].

"General Convention Special Program Reports to Executive Council," May 26, 1969 [77-14].

"Churches Respond to Black Manifesto," August 8, 1969 [78-4].

"General Convention Special Program Receives Praise," May 21, 1970 [87-8].

"Protestant Episcopal Church in the USA National Commission on Hispanic Affairs," February 23, 1972 [72023].

"Executive Council Summary of Action," February 24, 1972 [72026].

"Changes in Hispanic Commission Staff Announced," August 8, 1973 [73192].

"Modeste to Produce Permanent Report on GCSP," December 13, 1973 [73266].

"Executive Council Meets—A Summary," December 13, 1973 [73265].

"Mr. Nelson Canals Appointed Associate Hispanic Officer," September 13, 1974 [74231].

"Grant Made to Assist Diocese of Puerto Rico in Mining Concerns," September 25, 1974 [74249].

"Hispanic Ministry Consultation Held," April 23, 1975 [75143].

"National Consultation on Hispanic Ministries Held," September 15, 1975 [75314].

"Meetings on Hispanic Ministries Held," October 31, 1975 [75382].

"Bishops Attend Hispanic Meeting in Houston," February 11, 1976 [76054].

"Hispanic Task Force Meets in Puerto Rico," March 23, 1976 [76105].

"Caribbean Seminary to Close," June 8, 1976 [76190].

"Fr. Arrunátegui to Be Hispanic Officer," January 6, 1977 [77007].

"Church Center Cooperates in Bombing Investigation," February 17, 1977 [item 77058].

"Hispanic Commission Plans for Mission," March 14, 1977 [77086].

"Bishop Allin Puts Two Staff on Leave of Absence," March 14, 1977 [77094].

"Chicago Puerto Rican School Investigated," May 12, 1977 [77154].

"Hispanic Conference to Be Held in Miami in September," May 19, 1977 [77170].

"Hispanic Projects Receive Funding," July 14, 1977 [77241].

"Three Brothers Jailed in F.A.L.N. Inquiry," August 31, 1977 [77283].

"Council Deplores Misuse of Grand Jury System," September 18, 1977 [77306].

"Hispanic Delegates Set Directions," October 7, 1977 [77318].

"Liturgical Commission Issues 'First Communion' Statement," November 9, 1977 [77368].

"Bishop Allin Praises Order Freeing Two," January 27, 1978 [78020].

"Province VIII Panel Begins Hispanic Work," April 26, 1978 [78124].

"Council Accepts Report on Two Former Staff," May 18, 1978 [78146].

"Provincial Hispanic Ministry Expanded," June 29, 1978 [78183].

"Bishops Allin, Primo Engineer Accord," July 27, 1978 [78207].

"Hispanic Consultation Examines Future Mission," October 19, 1978 [78292].

"Prayer Book Translation Is Well Advanced," November 9, 1978 [78317].

"Hispanic Ministries Grants Given to 18 Groups," February 8, 1979 [79037].

"Hispanic Consultation Sets Education Goals," August 2, 1979 [79246].

"Photo Caption: Book of Common Prayer Translated into Spanish," November 1, 1979 [79322].

"Hispanics Envision Churchwide Report," January 31, 1980 [80032].

"Hispanic Vocations to Be Lifted Up," August 28, 1980 [80289].

"Provisional Hymnal Published in Spanish," November 6, 1980 [80393].

"Conference Asserts Racism Is Relevant Issue," February 11, 1982 [82028].

"Conference Lays Ground for Hispanic Ministry," October 12, 1983 [83188].

"Consultation Views Hispanic Ministry," February 7, 1985 [85027].

"Aris-Paul to Head Instituto Pastoral," January 30, 1986 [86018].

"Allen Symposium Challenges Church," May 30, 1986 [86094].

"Maria Cueto Comes Home," June 5, 1986 [86125].

"Hispanic Bishops' Advisory Group Meets," October 30, 1986 [86237].

"'Encuentro' Gathering Examines Hispanic Ministry," March 19, 1987 [87063].

"National Conference Reviews Problems and Solutions to Racial Polarization in America," December 12, 1990 [90322].

"Black Episcopalians to Attend General Convention," February 14, 1991. [91042E].

"Healing the Sin of Racism Requires Repentance and Hard Work, Say New York Episcopalians," April 4, 1991 [91090].

"'Clear Pattern of Institutional Racism' Emerges from Convention Audit," July 25, 1991 [91150].

"Report on Racism Audit Predicts Continuing Resistance to Change," June 26, 1992 [92145].

"Bishops Release Letter on Sin of Racism, Urge Reading in Parishes on May 15," April 21, 1994 [94080].

"House of Bishops Pastoral Letter on Sin of Racism, March 1994," April 21, 1994. [94090].

"Once More, with Feeling: Will Racism Get Our Attention?" June 15, 1994 [94123].

"People of Color Harmonize on Issue of Ordination," May 9, 1997 [97-1760].

"The Future of Hispanic Ministry," March 19, 1998 [98-2119].

"Mexican Meeting Offers Episcopal Bishops and Staff a Hispanic Experience," March 19, 1998 [98-2118].

"Scholars Explore Hispanic Influences on Theological Education," April 11, 2001 [2001-77].

"Council Told Staff Changes Will Enhance 20/20 Movement," March 1, 2002 [2002-051].

"Episcopales Latinos Se Reúnen en Los Ángeles por un 'Nuevo Amanecer,'" May 21, 2002 [2002-128E].

"Hispanic Episcopalians Gather for 'New Dawn' in Los Angeles," [2002-128].

"Carey Dedicates Hispanic Mission in Diocese of Chicago," November 6, 2002 [2002-256].

"Spanish-Language Sermons in Focus with College of Preachers: To Note: Brief Items of Interest in the News," July 13, 2004 [071304-1-A].

"Learning Spanish, Latino Ministry: Courses Set in Mississippi, Texas," January 18, 2005 [011805-1-A].

"Hispanic Missioner to Retire from Church Center Staff," June 9, 2005 [060905-1-A].

"Latino/Hispanic Missioner Appointed," September 20, 2005 [092005-1].

"CREDO Adds Program in Spanish, Repeat Sessions," February 27, 2006 [022706-2-A].

"The Sin of Racism: A Call to Covenant," March 22, 2006 [032206-3-A].

"Connecticut Latino Leader Appointed Bishop of Central Ecuador," March 22, 2006 [032206-4-A].

## Episcopal News Service (in chronological order; articles at www.episcopalnews service.org)

"Uganda: Orombi Says He Will Not Sit with Jefferts-Schori at Primates Meeting," December 15, 2006.

"Same-Sex Spouses Not Invited to Next Year's Lambeth Conference of bishops: Archbishop of Canterbury Bases Decision on 20-Year-Old Resolution from Previous Gathering," February 18, 2019.

"Diocese of New York Bishops and Spouses Will Be at Lambeth 2020 Despite Same-Sex Spouse Exclusion," March 1, 2019.

"Welby's Lambeth Invite Apology Smooths Way for Anglican Consultative Council to Walk Together: Weeklong Effort by Oklahoma Bishop to Have ACC Speak on LGBTQ People Ends in Negotiated Measure," March 4, 2019.

Mary Frances Schjonberg, "Trinity Church Wall Street Acquires Church Divinity School of the Pacific," March 4, 2019.

David Paulsen, "House of Bishops Opens Fall Meeting with Discussions of Same-Sex Spouse Exclusion from Lambeth 2020," September 17, 2019.

## Episcopal Church Reports (in chronological order)

1967. "A Declaration by Priests Who Are Negroes," The Church Awakens: African Americans and the Struggle for Justice.

1968. "Report to the Church on the GCSP," The Church Awakens: African Americans and the Struggle for Justice.

1976. General Convention Journal (Minneapolis).

1977, September 16–18. Executive Council Minutes, "Concern for the Imprisonment of Maria Cueto and Raisa Nemiken" [EXC091977.37].

1994, March. "Pastoral Letter Issued in 1994," The Church Awakens: African Americans and the Struggle for Justice.

2006. General Convention Journal (Indianapolis, IN).

2009. General Convention Journal (Anaheim, CA).

2009, July 15. Adopted Budget: 2010–2012: Report of The Joint Standing Committee on Program, Budget and Finance.

2012. Episcopal Church Domestic Fast Facts: 2007–2011.

2012, July 10. Adopted Budget: 2013–2015: The Episcopal Church, Report of The Joint Standing Committee on Program, Budget and Finance.

2014. Episcopal congregations overview.

2015, June 20. Adopted Budget: 2016–2018: The Episcopal Church, Report of The Joint Standing Committee on Program, Budget and Finance.

2017. Episcopal Church Domestic Facts: 2016: Based on the Parochial Report Data.

2018. Episcopal Domestic Fast Facts Trends: 2013–2017.

2018. Episcopal Church Domestic Facts: 2017: Based on Parochial Report Data.

2018. vbinder for GC79

2018, July 12. Adopted Budget: 2019–2021: The Episcopal Church, Report of The Joint Standing Committee on Program, Budget and Finance.2019, September 12. Baptized members by province and diocese, 2008–2018.

2019, September 12. Average Sunday Attendance by Province and Diocese, 2008–2018.

2019, September 12. Episcopal Church Domestic Facts: 2018.

## Pew Forum (pewforum.org)/ Pew Research Center (in chronological order)

2014. Religious Landscape Study.

2014, May 7. "The Shifting Religious Identity of Latinos in the United States: Nearly One-in-Four Latinos Are Former Roman Catholics."

2014, November 13. "Religion in Latin America: Widespread Change in a Historically Catholic Region."

2015, May 12. "America's Changing Religious Landscape."

2017, October 31. Jens Manuel Krogstad and Mark Hugo López, "Use of Spanish Declines among Latinos in Major U.S. Metros."

## Newspaper/Magazine/Blog Articles (in chronological order)

"A Spanish Episcopal Church Has Been Formed in New York City," The Pacific Churchman, October 17, 1867, 146.

"The Church of Santiago," The Church Journal, March 30, 1870 (reprint from The New York Times.)

"Death of the Rev. Joaquin de Palma." The New York Times, July 14, 1884.

"Durable Unless Shot At." The Living Church 121, no. 18 (October 29, 1950): 7.

"Rev. James A. Gusweller." WNYC Public Radio interview. December 28, 1958. Audio courtesy of the NYC Municipal Archives (LT8289); WNYC Collection (72125). *https://www.wnyc.org/story/rev-james-a-gusweller/.*

Robert Rice, "Church-I," The New Yorker Magazine 40, no. 24 (August 1, 1964): 41–60.

Robert Rice, "Church-II," The New Yorker Magazine 40, no. 25 (August 8, 1964): 37–73.

Philip McCandlish. "A 'Trouble' Block Feeds on Misery. Drunkenness, Joblessness and Addiction Thrive on West 84th Street. 'Ghetto of Sociopaths.' Minister Blames Bias and 'Criminal Landlords'—Urges City to Act." The New York Times, July 7, 1961, 27.

Stephen F. Bayne Jr. "Latin American Mission." The Living Church 146, no. 18 (February 24, 1963): 18–19.

Arnold H. Lubasch. "Two Episcopal Aides Are Ordered to Testify in a Terrorism Case." *The New York Times*, February 6, 1977.

William Claiborne. "Puerto Rican Group Claims Responsibility for N.Y. Blasts." *The Washington Post*, March 22, 1977.

"Hispanic Commission Approves Grants." *The Living Church* 175, no. 8 (August 21, 1977): 5.

"Former Consultant Jailed for Refusing to Testify," *The Living Church* 175, no. 13 (September 25, 1977): 5.

Frank del Olmo. "Commentary: Latino 'Decade' Moves Into '90s." *Los Angeles Times*, December 14, 1989.

Victor Ruiz. "Opportunity Knocks." *Episcopal Life* 14, no. 2 (February 2003): 1, 6–9.

Alice June Lindsay (Tucson, AZ). Letter to the editor. *Episcopal Life* 14, no. 6 (June 2003): 29.

Evelyn Morales. "Immigrant Success Story: Church Biggest Influence in Family's Acculturation." *Episcopal Life* 14, no. 8 (November 2003): 28.

"Global South Primates Meeting—Kigali Communique," *Anglican News Service*, September 22, 2006.

"1968: The Year That Changed History." *The Guardian,* January 17, 2008, *https://www.theguardian. com/observer/gallery/2008/jan/17/1.*

Albert R. Rodríguez, "Mega-Trends in Latino Ministry," Seminary of the Southwest, June 14, 2016, *https://ssw.edu/blog/mega-trends-in-latino-ministry/.*

Ana Marie Cox. "Trevor Noah Wasn't Expecting Liberal Hatred." *New York Times Magazine*, November 2, 2016.

Kirk Petersen. "Hispanic Growth = Episcopal Growth?" *The Living Church*, November 29, 2017. *https://livingchurch.org/2017/11/29/hispanic-growth-episcopal-growth/.*

Yuichiro Kakutani and Meredith Liu, "Cornell to Establish LGBTQ Program House 25 Years After Initial Proposal," *Cornell Daily Sun* March 1, 2018. *https://cornellsun.com/2018/03/01/ cornell-to-establish-lgbtq-program-house-25-years-after-initial-proposal/.*

Paul Elie. "The Martyr and the Pope." *The Atlantic*, November 2018, 62–68.

Joan C. Williams. "The Democrats' White-People Problem: Donald Trump Likes to Pit Elite and Non-Elite White People against Each Other. Why Do White Liberals Play into His Trap?" Politics Section, *The Atlantic,* December 2018.

Woody Register. "'The Real Issue': A Reconsideration of the Turbulent Desegregation of Sewanee's School of Theology, 1952–1953, Part I." *Meridiana: The Blog for the Sewanee Project on Slavery, Race, and Reconciliation*, December 11, 2018. *http://meridiana.sewanee.edu/2018/12/11/ the-real-issue-a-reconsideration-of-the-turbulent-desegregation-of-sewanees-school-of-theology-1952-1953-part-i/.*

Kirk Petersen, "Trinity Wall Street Acquires CDSP," March 4, 2019, *https://livingchurch. org/2019/03/04/trinity-wall-street-acquires-cdsp/.*

"Trinity Church Wall Street and Church Divinity School of the Pacific Announce Alliance," Church Divinity School of the Pacific, March 2019, *https://cdsp.edu/2019/03/ trinity-church-wall-street-and-church-divinity-school-of-the-pacific-announce-alliance/.*

Angela Li, "Loving House Grand Opening 'A Victory,' But 'Not the End of the Story," *Cornell Daily Sun* September 15, 2019 *https://cornellsun.com/2019/09/15/loving-house-grand-opening-a-victory-but-not-the-end-of-the-story/.*

## Other Sources Cited

Armentrout, Donald S. "A Documentary History of the Integration Crisis at The School of Theology of The University of the South, 1951–1953." *Sewanee Theological Review* 46, no. 2 (Easter 2003): 172–212.

Armentrout, Donald S., and Robert Boak Slocum. *Documents of Witness: A History of the Episcopal Church, 1782–1985.* New York: Church Publishing, 2000.

Arrunátegui, Herbert. "Evaluation of the Development and Implementation of Hispanic Ministries Programs in the Episcopal Church and the Role of the National Hispanic Officer." Thesis (D.Min.), Drew University, 1985.

Asturias, Miguel Ángel. *El Señor Presidente.* Buenos Aires, Argentina: Editorial Losada, 1948.

Baskerville-Burrows, Jennifer. "Feast of St. Paul's Conversion." Sermon. 2019 Forma Conference, Indianapolis, IN, January 25, 2019

Bhabha, Homi K. *Location of Culture*. New York: Routledge, 1993.

Boff, Leonardo, and Clodovis Boff. *Introducing Liberation Theology*. Translated by Paul Burns. Maryknoll, NY: Orbis Books, 1996. Originally published as *Como fazer teologia da libertação* (1986). (Spanish) *Como hacer teología de la liberación*. Bogotá, Colombia: Ediciones Paulinas, 1986.

*Book of Common Prayer and Administration of the Sacraments and Other Rites and Ceremonies of the Church: According to the Use of the Protestant Episcopal Church in the United States of America: Together with the Psalter, or, Psalms of David*. New York: Seabury Press, 1979.

Booty, John. *The Episcopal Church in Crisis*. Cambridge, MA: Cowley Publications, 1988.

Bornstein, Kate. *Gender Outlaw: On Men, Women, and the Rest of Us*. New York: Routledge, 1994.

Branson, Mark Lau, and Juan Francisco Martínez. *Churches, Cultures and Leadership: A Practical Theology of Congregations and Ethnicities*. Downers Grove, IL: InterVarsity Press, 2011.

Brewster, Gurdon. *No Turning Back: My Summer with Daddy King*. New York: Orbis, 2011.

Brooks, Ashton Jacinto, ed. *Eclesiología: presencia anglicana en la Región Central de América*. San José, Costa Rica: Departamento Ecuménico de Investigaciones (DEI), 1990.

Bryant, Charles. *Rediscovering Our Spiritual Gifts: Building Up the Body of Christ Through the Gifts of the Spirit*. Nashville, TN: Upper Room Books, 1998.

Coelho, Luiz. "IEAB's 2015 Book of Common Prayer: The Latest Chapter in the Evolution of the Book of Common Prayer in Brazil." *Studia Liturgica* 49 no. 1: 26–42.

Consejo Episcopal Latinoamericano (CELAM), *La iglesia en la actual transformación de América Latina a la luz del Concilio II*. 3rd Edition. Santafé de Bogotá, Colombia: Secretariado General del CELAM, 1969.

DeGuzmán, María. *Spain's Long Shadow: The Black Legend, Off-Whiteness, and Anglo-American Empire*. Minneapolis: University of Minnesota, 2005.

Diocese of New York. *The Centennial History of the Protestant Episcopal Church in the Diocese of New York, 1785–1885*. New York: Committee on Historical Publications D. Appleton, 1886.

Dubois, W. E. B. *The Negro Church: A Social Study*. Atlanta, GA: Atlanta University Press, 1903.

Fuchs, Barbara. *Exotic Nation: Maurophilia and the Construction of Early Modern Spain*. Philadelphia: University of Pennsylvania Press, 2009.

Goetz, Rebecca Anne. *The Baptism of Early Virginia: How Christianity Created Race*. Baltimore, MD: Johns Hopkins University Press, 2012.

González, Justo L. *The Hispanic Ministry of the Episcopal Church in the Metropolitan Area of New York and Environs*. New York: Grants Board of Trinity Parish, 1985.

_____. *The Story of Christianity, Volume II: The Reformation to the Present Day*. Rev. ed. New York: Harper Collins, 2010.

González, Justo L, and Ondina E. González, eds. *Nuestra Fe: A Latin American Church History Sourcebook*. Nashville, TN: Abingdon Press, 2014.

Goodpasture, H. McKennie, ed. *Cross and Sword: An Eyewitness History of Christianity in Latin America*. Maryknoll, NY: Orbis Books, 1989.

Gordon, Milton, *Assimilation in American Life: The Role of Race, Religion, and National Origins*. New York: Oxford University Press, 1964.

Greer, Margaret R., Walter D. Mignolo, and Maureen Quilligan, eds., *Rereading the Black Legend: The Discourses of Religious and Racial Difference in the Renaissance Empires*. Chicago: University of Chicago Press, 2007.

Gutiérrez, Gustavo. *Teología de la liberación: Perspectivas. Con una nueva introducción, "Mirar Lejos."* Lima, Perú: Centro de Estudios y Publicaciones, 1991.

Holmes, David L. *A Brief History of the Episcopal Church*. Valley Forge, PA: Trinity Press International, 1993.

_____. "Presiding Bishop John E. Hines and the General Convention Special Program," *Anglican and Episcopal History* 61, no. 4 (December 1992): 393–417.

Hood, Robert E. *Social Teachings in the Episcopal Church*. Harrisburg, PA: Morehouse Publishing, 1990.

Irizarry, José Enrique, ed. "The Hispanic Challenge to the Diocese of New York," A Working Paper Prepared by The Committee on Mission and Strategy of the Hispanic Commission of the Diocese of New York, 1988.

Irizarry, José Enrique. "El Reto Hispano a la Diócesis de Nueva York." In *Reflexiones Teológicas: Modelos de Ministerios, Revista Teológica de la Comisión Hispana de la Diócesis de Nueva York: Publicación Cuatrimestral.* Year 2, Vol 2 (Jan.–Jun. 1989), 11–23.

Isasí-Díaz, Ada María. *En la Lucha/In the Struggle: Elaborating a Mujerista Theology.* 2nd ed. Philadelphia: Fortress Press, 2003.

_____. *La Lucha Continues: Mujerista Theology.* Maryknoll, NY: Orbis Books, 2004.

_____. *Mujerista Theology: A Theology for the 21st Century.* Maryknoll, NY: Orbis Books, 1996.

Jones, Sharon Lynette. *Critical Companion to Zora Neale Hurston: A Literary Reference to her Life and Work.* New York: Facts on File, c2009.

Kater, John L., Jr., ed., "At Home in Latin America: Anglicanism in a New Context." *Anglican and Episcopal History* 57, no. 1 (1988): 4–37.

_____. "Experiment in Freedom: The Episcopal Church and the Black Power Movement." *Historical Magazine of the Protestant Episcopal Church*, Historical Prolegomenon to the Renewal of Mission: The Context of the Episcopal Church's Efforts at Outreach 1945–1975 48, no. 1 (March 1979): 67–82.

_____. "Latin American Anglicanism in the Twentieth Century." In *The Oxford History of Anglicanism, Volume V: Global Anglicanism, c. 1910–2000*, edited by William L. Sachs, 98–123. Oxford: Oxford University Press, 2018.

_____. *Somos Anglicanos: Ensayos sobre el anglicanismo latinoamericano.* Panamá: Iglesia Episcopal, Diócesis de Panamá, 1987.

_____. "Through a Glass Darkly: The Episcopal Church's Responses to the *Mexican Iglesia De Jesús* 1864–1904." *Anglican and Episcopal History* 85, no. 2 (June 2016): 197.

_____. *We Are Anglicans: Essays on Latin American Anglicanism.* Panamá: Iglesia Episcopal, Diócesis de Panamá, 1989.

Kesselus, Kenneth. *John E. Hines: Granite on Fire.* Austin, TX: Episcopal Theological Seminary of the Southwest, 1995.

Kinder, A. Gordon. "Creation of the Black Legend: Literary Contributions of Spanish Protestant Exiles." *Mediterranean Studies* 6 (1996): 67–78.

King, Martin Luther, Jr. "Facing the Challenge of a New Age." In *A Testament of Love: The Essential Writings of Martin Luther King, Jr.,* edited by James Melvin Washington, 135–44. New York: Harper & Row, Publishers, Inc., 1986.

Lewis, Harold T. "By Schisms Rent Asunder? American Anglicanism on the Eve of the Millennium." In *A New Conversation: Essays on the Future of Theology and the Episcopal Church*, edited by Robert Boak Slocum, 467–79. New York: Church Publishing, 1999.

_____. "Racial Concerns in the Episcopal Church Since 1973." *Anglican and Episcopal History* (Pittsburgh Conference Papers "Mine Eyes Have Seen The Glory": Anglican Visions of Apocalypse and Hope, June 1997) 67, no. 4 (December 1998).

_____. *Yet With A Steady Beat: The African American Struggle for Recognition in the Episcopal Church.* Valley Forge, PA: Trinity Press International, 1996.

Limb, John J. *Flor y canto.* Portland, OR: Oregon Catholic Press, 2011.

Livermore, Abiel Abbot. *The War with Mexico Reviewed.* Boston, MA: American Peace Society, 1850.

*Livro de Oração Comum. Administração dos Sacramentos e Outros Ritos e Cerimônias conforme o uso da Igreja Episcopal Anglicana do Brasil com o Saltério e Seleção de Salmos Litúrgicos.* Porto Alegre, Brasil: Igreja Episcopal Anglicana do Brasil, 2015.

Magliula, Robert J. "Absalom Jones: A Biographical Study." MDiv thesis, Union Theological Seminary, 1982.

Maiztegui, Humberto. "Homosexuality and the Bible in the Anglican Church of the Southern Cone of America." In *Other Voices, Other Worlds: The Global Church Speaks Out on Homosexuality*, edited by Terry Brown, 236–248. London: Darton, Longman and Todd, 2006.

Maltby, William S. *The Black Legend in England: The Development of Anti-Spanish Sentiment, 1558–1660.* Durham, NC: Duke University Press, 1971.